How to create your own
POWERFUL
Ads & Promo Pieces

By Larry Mersereau

How to create your own POWERFUL Ads and Promo Pieces

By Larry Mersereau, CTC

©Copyright, 2003, Larry Mersereau, All rights reserved

Published by PromoPower Publishing

ISBN 0-9742286-0-5

Contents

Introduction 7

An article to start things off 15

Keys to Marketing Success 21

The Magic Formula for Persuasion 37
        Attention 40
        Promise 45
        Proof 48
        Proposition 55
        Action 62

Directors and Distractors 65

Layout 75
        Eye Patterns 75
        The relationship between designer and copy writer 81

Photographs 87

The "Art" of Typography 95
        Type Faces, Type Styles 103

Layouts that look like C.R.A.P. 115

How to write killer copy 131

One-step vs Two-step proposition 141

How to Write Breakthrough Headlines 151
        Headline Hooks 157

Where to Advertise 167

Brochures 179

Email and Ezines 193

Flyers, Fax Blasts and Inserts 205

On-Hold and Voice Mail Messages 211

Trade Show Exhibits & Point-of-Purchase Displays 219

Classifieds & Small Space Ads 227

Web Pages 239
        Promoting Your Web Site 240

Yellow Pages Advertising 253

Direct Mail 101 265

Testing 271
        Testing by the book 278

The Last Word 299

Appendices 309
    EMOTIONAL APPEALS 311
    WORDS THAT <u>SELL</u> 311
    The Phrase That Pays 313
    The Marketing Master's Complete Library 315

Introduction

I believe in *Truth In Advertising*.

And the truth is: Most advertising doesn't work.

Maybe you've experimented with print advertising, and got nothing to show for it. It's a common experience.

Most business owners and professionals are do-it-yourselfers.

Of course, they discourage that behavior from their customers/clients/patients …

A dentist would certainly reprimand any patient who tried to fill a cavity on their own. A travel agent would cringe at the thought of her clients looking online for vacation arrangements. And heaven forbid that you teach yourself the game of golf.

But these same business people think they can put together a brochure, advertisement or web site for themselves. Well, the good news is: you can. The bad news is: you can't just depend on your own creativity to do it well. In fact, your creativity can kill you!

I know, I promised to share the "secrets of top advertising creatives" here, and I will. But the secrets won't be much about creativity. They'll be about structure, design and language that anybody can put together to create promotional communications that grab the prospects' attention, walks them step by step through a methodical sequence, and culminate in the prospect responding.

This manual is for you, the do-it-yourselfer.

I'm not here to send you running to an advertising agency. I'm here to help you compete effectively with the businesses who did. You don't have to spend mega-bucks on ads and promo pieces to make them work. You have to design and write them properly, then place them where your prime prospects ... your *clearly defined target customers* will see them ... without paying for a lot of non-prospects to see them.

> **IMPORTANT LESSON:** *It all starts with a clearly defined target customer.*

You'll see the term *clearly defined target customer* in numerous places throughout this manual. I refer to it often, because it's key to effective advertising and promotion. You have to know who you're talking to before you can open your metaphorical mouth.

Before you ever sit down to design and write a piece, you have to have a clear picture of who you are selling to. How old are they? What gender? How do they live? Do they have kids? Are they active people? What kind of income do they earn? The more clearly you define them, the more effective you'll be in tailoring your message to them.

The broader your definition of a *clearly defined target customer*, the more general your message has to be. As it gets diluted to talk to more people, it eventually talks to nobody!

And that's the mistake too many organizations make. They try to talk to everybody. But not you.

You're going to know your customer like they're your best friend. You know all about their interests and their lives. When you write copy, you know exactly what about your product or service will appeal to them and why. And you'll remind them with every line that your product or service was designed specifically for them ... not for the masses.

So, know them intimately.

Know who you're selling to and what it is about your product or service that will make their lives more fulfilling, their business more profitable … whatever it is you do for them. And get used to presenting that information in their terms. You can only do that if you know exactly who you're talking to. So, know them intimately.

The professional help you need is right here in this manual.

You don't need no stinking advertising agency!

You'll learn step by step how to structure your message in the proper selling sequence. Your prospect has to receive your information in a specific sequence, or they get lost in your verbiage.

But it's not enough just to write your message in the proper sequence. You have to present it graphically so the reader will receive it in the order in which you intended. If they skip around, they get lost.

You have to use graphic design and typography to draw the reader's eye to the beginning of the message, then take them by the hand and walk them through every line in the proper sequence.

If you don't do this right, all the work you put into writing great copy is wasted.

And speaking of writing great copy: I'm going to tell you exactly how it's done. And it's not difficult. Anyone with a mastery of seventh-grade-level grammar can do it. In fact, the PHD's have a hard time doing it, because they want to show everyone how eloquent they can be. They want to roll out their flowery vocabulary and impressive knowledge.

Fact is, nobody will be impressed by your knowledge or vocabulary.

The only thing that will impress you *clearly defined target customer* is how your product or service will make their life better, in language they understand.

This Ain't No Charm School, Baby!

It's not about "proper" grammar or form - Strunck and White would roll over in their graves if they read some of this stuff.

This is about how to create marketing communications that really work.

From creating graphic design that pulls the reader in and guides them through your message, to writing engaging copy that motivates your prospect to respond, you're getting the hard, cold truth in this one.

So, don't highlight my misspellings and grammatical errors and send me emails complaining about the sloppy editing. I'm not losing sleep over them and you shouldn't be either! Pay attention to what I'm saying, and use the information and ideas to grow your business.

Your business is what matters here, not a few typos or grammatical faux pas.

Looking to win awards with your ads? Look somewhere else!

You probably won't win any Addy's using my advice. In case you don't know what an "Addy" is: it's the Advertising Federation's answer to the Grammy, or the Emmy. Cute, huh? Grammy, Emmy, Addy? See, "creative" is in the eye of the reader.

The top advertising minds in the country came up with "Addy" for the name of their award. If that's the best name the top advertising agency minds in the country can come up with for their own premier award, you should be able to create circles around your local ad agency!

In other words: Don't be intimidated by advertising agencies. Yes, they have some capabilities you don't. Yes, they can design Hollywood-class promo pieces.

But they're motivated by their own income, not yours. They charge the client for all that Hollywood stuff, then collect a commission from the media they choose to place your ads in. Whether it's print or broadcast, the agency gets a commission based on how much you spend for space or time. Obviously, the more space or time you buy, the more the advertising agency makes.

And, whether you're interested in Addys or not, it's top of mind for your advertising agency. In fact, if you've got the budget for it, they'll go all out to create something that will make all the other advertising agencies say; "WOW!" Then, they'll get the Addy and you'll have an outrageously expensive ad that sells squat, because it wasn't designed to sell … it was designed to impress other advertising people and thereby win an award. So, they make money, they get an award, and you get a big bill.

It's a free world, and I have no problem with advertising agencies making money. But their income is determined by the "media buy." (Of course, they make money when they charge you for the production, too.) How much YOU make …or lose … as a result of the campaign has no bearing on the agency's income.

What's wrong with this picture?

What you want is a graphic designer that can help you put your words into an attractive design. I pay my designer by the hour.(Don't tell her, but she doesn't charge nearly what she's worth!) I give her a script. Each line is numbered. I want the readers eye drawn to see item number "1" first. Then I want them led visually to item number "2."

You'll learn all about the sequence when you read about my *Magic Formula* for compelling communications.

You'll learn what makes for good graphic design in another chapter. You'll learn what words to use, what typefaces. It's all here.

Is your advertising and promotion working for you …

Or, is it actually working *against* you?

You've probably already asked yourself at least the first half of that question, or you wouldn't have bought this manual!

Odds are, yours is among the majority – yes, I'm so bold as to say majority – of businesses and professional practices who burn thousands of dollars every year on ineffective and inefficient marketing communications.

After you've spent some time reading and working with the ideas in this manual, you'll quickly see that most advertising does nothing to encourage people to buy. In fact, most so-called "marketing communications" do nothing to invite the prospective buyer to even pay attention, let alone respond.

Soon, you'll find advertising to be the most entertaining part of your time spent watching television and reading newspapers and magazines. When you know what makes an ad work for the organization, you'll notice hundreds of ads every day that ignore reality.

IMPORTANT LESSON: *Your prospective buyer is bombarded*

with over 500 commercial messages every day. Most of them were a total waste of the advertiser's money!

If you are going to stand out among the 500+ commercial messages your prospect is exposed to every day, you have to talk to them about their favorite topic: <u>Themselves</u>.

Start paying attention to the commercial messages all around you. Who do they talk about? Most talk about how long they've been in business, the quality ingredients they use, the family that founded the business, their terrific staff … don't they know that nobody ~~gives a rat's~~ cares?

The only thing your prospective buyers care about, is what will be better about their world after they've put your product or service to work for them. It's the only thing that matters to them, so you'd better make it the most important thing to you.

Think about it now: Can you articulate how your buyers' lives will be improved after they do business with you?

You'll learn the difference between "features" and "benefits" in these pages. And, you'll learn how to present your organization, product or service in terms of benefit to the prospective buyer.

In other words, you'll answer the question that's on their mind; "What's in it for me?"

Think you've heard it all?

Is this "features vs benefits" business old hat to you? That's OK.

Odds, are, you will read some things you already knew somewhere in this manual. Consider it "confirmation." Maybe it will be a reminder of something you already knew, but don't use as well as you could.

Read with an open mind.

Just because your grand-daddy's picture has been the visual focal point of every ad and brochure your organization has put out for the past 40 years doesn't mean it's a good idea.

Don't let your ego dictate what you say in your marketing communications, as it does for so many misguided business owners and professionals. People want to know that you're qualified to do the things you promise you can do for them, but that's about as much as they want to know about you.

They don't want to see your family photo or the car that you drive. They don't care much what you look like. They don't care what your building looks like, or how many trucks you have in your fleet.

They care about themselves, and nothing else …

And, most of those 500+ commercial messages they're bombarded with every day don't talk about that. They're ego-driven diatribes about what a wonderful organization the advertiser is.

And that's why most of those 500+ messages are a waste of money for the advertiser … other than the stroking they give their own ego.

Demand results …

One last point: You should demand a measurable return on your investment in advertising and promotion.

If you hired a sales person, and sent them out on the street for six months, you'd expect them to deliver some business. You'd expect them to hand you orders that they alone were responsible for. You'd expect their efforts to provide real fruit. And, if they didn't, you'd fire them!

Too many business owners and professionals have fired their advertising.

"They tried it and it didn't work." I hear it all the time from consulting clients.

What happened was, they put together some schlock advertisement, placed it in a publication where their real prospects would never see it, and can't understand why it didn't make the phone ring!

That made them decide that advertising is a waste of money. Heck, it didn't do anything for them, so why do it again? Maybe it's happened to you – no matter how much you spent, no matter how often you advertised – nothing happened.

After you put the ideas in this manual to work, you'll be able to design and write ads that grab your prospective buyers' attention and demand response. You'll know how to "test" your advertising. You'll fine-tune your pieces so that each one draws more response than the last. You'll learn how to start with a small budget, then escalate your investment in promotion when it starts working.

Once you arrive at a format and message that makes the phone ring, you can use it in bigger(more expensive) publications confidently.

You won't just throw money and advertising messages around hoping something will stick.

You'll demand … and get … RESULTS.

That's what this manual is all about. Enjoy.

Chapter 1

An article to start things off ...

I thought it might be nice to give you some easy reading that puts my feeling about advertising design and copy writing into a nutshell.

This article was written for one of the Business Journals. Most major cities have one – it's the newspaper for local business. They have articles(such as this one), plus all of the news about changes at local businesses. Moves, new openings, promotions – if you want to know what's going on in your business community, you have to subscribe.

And, if you want your advertising to reach local business leaders, it's the place to advertise and to send your press releases.

This article described a makeover I did for a professional ad. It kind of summarizes what's contained in greater detail in this manual. In fact, you'll see these ads again later on, and learn more about how I dissected and rebuilt the original.

 The same principles in the article ... and throughout this manual ... apply to your advertising. Hope you enjoy it!

Advertising Alchemy
by Larry Mersereau, CTC

STOP and See Us!

GRAND OPENING

Eye Clinic · Eye Surgery · Glasses · Contacts

Ahad Mahootchi, MD, PA
Board Certified Ophthalmologist-Vanderbilt Trained
813 - 779 - 3338

6739 GALL BLVD - ZEPHYRHILLS, FL - 33541

Accepting Medicare & most insurance plans

Look Good See Great

- Complete Eye Clinic
- Fashion Glasses
- Color & Plain Contacts
- Eye Surgery & Lasic

Grand Opening specials save you 20%
Stop in or call before May 15, for details

Medicare, most major Insurance plans accepted

Ahad Mahootchi, MD, PA
Board certified ophthalmologist - Vanderbilt trained
(813) 779-3338
6739 Gall Blvd - Zephyrhills

Which of these two ads looks better to you?

Small changes in ad design and copy can make a huge difference in the effectiveness of the ad. Taken individually, the changes I made in the original ad were minor. But

I think you'll agree that the result is a much cleaner, easier-to-read ad.

Sequence

Selling is a sequential process. Your prospect must receive your information in the proper order, or you lose their attention and any chance of making a sale.

The first step in the sequence is getting the prospect's attention. They're looking through the paper for articles of interest to them. Most people won't admit it, but their eyes also scan the ads, even if only peripherally.

So, the reader's eye is scanning the page for items of interest to themselves.

Photos Draw The Eye

Nothing draws the reader's eye away from everything else on the page like a good photograph. What makes a good photograph? People are drawn to photos of people just like themselves. That means your models should be normal people, similar to your target prospect in as many ways as possible. Age, gender, dress, physical fitness, you get the picture.

And a good photograph shows the model enjoying or demonstrating the benefit you are promising in your ad. This ad promises that you will look good and see great after you visit Dr. Mahootchi. This model is also looking you in the eye. That eye contact makes an instant emotional connection with the reader.

Visual Focal Points

Since selling is a sequential process, it's important that we not only present our case in order, but make sure that the reader's eye is drawn through the message in sequence. In the original ad, you have a hard time deciding where to look first. You can't afford to let your prospect enter your message just anywhere.

In the madeover version, the photo is the first visual focal point. The eye contact draws you to the upper, left-hand corner of the ad. That's where I wanted you to start. Then, you're drawn into the headline; "Look Good, See Great." Don't the bullet points pull you straight down from there? Then, you see the Grand Opening Specials.

The last piece of information you need is where to buy.

The Mistake Most Advertisers Make

Most advertisers make their organization's name the dominant graphic focal point. In the original ad, the doctor's name and photo are two of four visual focal points competing for the reader's attention. In the early stages of the selling sequence, the prospect isn't interested in who you are or what you look like. They care how their life is going to be better if they buy from you. Only after they are convinced that their life will be improved do they want to know where to buy.

The biggest single difference between the original ad and my madeover version, is that my ad pulls the reader's eye to the beginning of the message, then takes them by the hand and walks them through the message in sequence.

Left to their own devices, readers will jump around willy nilly, grabbing bits and pieces of your message in random order. When they do that, they don't understand what you're about, and they don't see the benefit of owning your product or taking advantage of your service.

The Sequence

The sequence buyers must go through is simple. I call it the *Magic Formula for Persuasion*;

1.) Attention
2.) Promise
3.) Proof
4.) Proposition
5.) Action

The <u>attention</u> step is what we saw in the photograph. The best ads make some kind of an emotional connection with the reader. If you don't use a photo, then your headline has to grab them.

Now, <u>promise</u> a benefit. A benefit is something that will be better about their life, their world, or their business after they buy from you.

Then, the <u>proof</u> step. The public is jaded – substantiate your promise.

The <u>proposition</u> is the difference between getting response from your ad and just hoping someone noticed it. A proposition rewards the reader for responding immediately. It must be valuable enough to motivate them, and have a short enough deadline to add urgency.

The <u>action</u> step is where they find out what they have to do to own this thing you've got them salivating for. It has to be easy, fast, and free.

Present your message in the proper sequence. Make it about them and the benefit they'll enjoy when they own your product or use your service. Lay your ad out graphically to draw the reader's eye to the beginning, then walk them through your message in the order you intended. Make propositions that motivate your prospects to respond in stead of turning the page, and you'll easily justify the extra help you need to field the calls.

Chapter 2

Keys to Marketing Success

Consider this chapter a kind of "Marketing 101."

It's pretty basic, but I want you to have this information in mind as you read the rest of the manual. How you plan and execute your marketing and promotions is as important as how you design your marketing communications.

You can use all of the tools in this manual to design dynamite marketing pieces ... and, you will ... but if nobody sees them, it's all wasted effort and expense. More specifically; if the RIGHT PEOPLE don't see them, it's all wasted effort and expense.

Unless your product is toilet paper, you have to accept that not everyone on the planet needs it. In fact, there are places on the planet where there's not even a market for toilet paper!

So, your first job, before you ever spend a dime on advertising, web site development, or printing, is to identify who you are best suited to do business with.

IMPORTANT LESSON: *You must pinpoint a **Clearly Defined***

Target Customer before you ever spend time or money on your marketing communications.

This may sound basic … because, it is. But it's one of the first thing I ask new consulting clients, and very few are able to articulate who they're built to do business with.

Why does it matter?

Well, a couple of things;

1.) People choose suppliers of products and services based on a number of criteria. One of them(a big one) is whether the vendor has experience with people like themselves.

I don't want to trust my business travel arrangements to a travel agent who specializes in cruise travel. Conversely, I wouldn't book a cruise through the travel agent that specializes in business travel. Yet, open the yellow pages, and look under "travel agencies & bureaus." You'll see that most travel agents try to do a little bit of everything for just about everyone.

And, I don't mean to pick on travel agents. There's a lot of this disease going around.

Look under "roofing." Does everyone do both "commercial" and "residential?" How about new construction and repairs?

Look under "computers." My phone book has one listing that says "we specialize in," followed by a list of fifteen disciplines. Fifteen!

The point is; People prefer to do business with people who specialize in customers/clients/patients like themselves.

Everything about your business of practice should address a certain kind of person. You can define them by age, gender, income, hobbies, special interests, where they live, what they do for a living …

But do something to narrow down the field of prospects from "everyone on the planet," to … well, that's up to you.

2.) You can't afford to reach everyone on the planet.

Even if you advertise during the Super Bowl, you won't reach everyone. But that's the mistake a lot of advertisers make. They invest a huge chunk of their advertising budget into one big splash, hoping enough people see it … and respond to it … to make the gamble pay off.

That's the word for "big splash" advertising: gamble. Buying one big ad and hoping for a payoff is only slightly worse than buying lottery tickets. The odds are heavily against you.

3.) People have to see you half a dozen times or so before they even start to recognize you.

Even if you could cough up the $2,000,000.00+ for a :30 second spot on the Super Bowl, that would only get you one exposure to this huge number of people. Unless you already have significant name recognition established, that one exposure is like spitting in the wind. It may get noticed, but it will soon evaporate from the viewers' memories.

Here's the first key:

The great balancing act; Reach vs Repetition

Now you know, people have to see you half a dozen times before they start to recognize you.

And, their memories are short. If they don't see you at least half a dozen times a year, you're easily forgotten.

> **IMPORTANT LESSON:** *The Rule Of Seven says a prospect has to see you seven times in eighteen months before they start to recognize you.*

Most of my clients aren't willing to wait eighteen months to build recognition!

I recommend you put yourself where prospects can see you weekly, if possible. They may not see it every time, but if you're not out there, you don't have a chance.

At the very least, your mission(should you decide to accept it), is to get yourself in front of your prospects at least once every other month. And that, by the way, is the bare minimum for them to remember who you are. If you want to actually sell them something, you'd better be doing more than that.

That's the repetition you need.

Let's look at the life of one of your typical prospects;

We'll assume that you are a dentist who specializes in treating children for the moment.

You have to get your name in front of parents(the decision makers) of that specific group half a dozen times within a year.

> **IMPORTANT LESSON:** *Your "customer(decision maker)" may not be the same person you provide products or services for. The end user may not be the person you have to reach with your marketing and promotion.*

There are millions of parents in the United States. Is your dental practice accessible to all of them? Of course not.

You wouldn't advertise in a national parenting magazine, because that's more *reach* than you need(or can afford).

Your **clearly defined target customer** is probably parents of children under 12 years old who live in your area. Your geographic area could be as small as a neighborhood in a large city, or as large as several counties if you're in a small town. It has to be reasonable for everyone in the geographic area you reach to physically visit you.

And, you have to be at least as convenient as the equivalent alternative they have to choose from. If there are twenty "family dentistry" specialists in your three-county area, you're probably going to have to tighten your geographic reach.

You have to be realistic about how far people will come to do business with you.

And don't tell me you're well worth going out of their way for! I'm not saying you're not ... you may well be. But you have to make that case with your *target customers*. They have to believe you're worth the drive. In today's time-crunched world, you may have a tough time selling that.

OK, back to the topic!

Part of your definition of a target customer will be geographic reach. The point is, you don't advertise in national publications if your customers are all local. That's a pretty simple concept.

But look at the advertising in your metropolitan newspaper. Really, pull it out and look. Count the number of display ads in your paper. As you count them, keep a tally of which you could potentially do business with yourself, and which have no chance of ever seeing any of your hard-earned dollars.

This time around, just base your "way" or "no-way" decision on location. Would you drive clear across town to buy groceries when there is a similar competing supermarket right in your neighborhood? Probably not.

But the grocery store across town paid to reach you with their ad. They wasted that money, didn't they?

They had to pay to reach all of the subscribers to your local paper, whether all of them are realistic prospects or not. Sure, everyone in town buys groceries. But, most of us buy from a nearby supermarket. Even their discounts and coupons aren't enough to draw most people clear across town.

The money spent to reach non-prospects is "Overflow."

Overflow advertising expense is wasted money. The metropolitan newspaper is a perfect example, and an easy one to relate to.

But, where else are you burning cash on overflow?

If you do direct mail advertising, is absolutely every name on your list a realistic prospect? Or, are you spending printing and postage dollars trying to talk to people who will never buy from you? It's scary enough that most of the realistic prospects on your mailing list toss your expensive piece in the trash. Add to that the pure "overflow" in your list, and you know you're putting a match to some serious cash every time you send out a mailing.

Do you do outdoor(billboard) advertising? You pay by the number of vehicles that pass by the sign every day. How many of them are realistic prospects for your product or service? You're paying to talk to all of them, whether they're all prospects or not.

To some degree, you can't escape overflow. But, you should do your best to minimize it by knowing exactly who your prime prospect is, and selecting media whose readership/viewers/listeners predominantly fit that profile.

So, back to our young-people's dentist. She needs to reach parents of children under twelve who live within a reasonable driving distance of the practice. The local newspaper's reach is probably much larger than that. 80+% of their readers are either not parents of young children, or don't live within a reasonable distance … or neither. That means 80+% of the dollars they spend in the newspaper are overflow; WASTED REACH.

So, where should they advertise?

Do the nearby schools have newsletters that sell advertising? How about the Parent/Teachers Association? They may be able to rent a well-qualified mailing list. Are there neighborhood associations? Can they do something with pee-wee football or little league baseball?

> *The point is, you want to eliminate "overflow" (minimize **reach**) as much as possible, so you can maximize **repetition**.*

If you spend all of your money on reach, you won't be able to afford the repetition you need to establish your name in your prospects' minds. Advertising in the local newspaper is probably the easiest route – heck, they'll even help you design and ad. They'll put it in as often as you want, and just send you a bill. Simple, right? Expensive, too!

I wish I had a dollar for every time a business owner or professional said to me; "I've tried advertising, and it was a waste of money." One(or both) of two things probably happened; Either A.) Their ad was not well-conceived, or/and B.) they spent a lot of overflow dollars, and ran out of money before they established enough repetition with the small portion of the readership that might actually buy some day.

> **IMPORTANT LESSON:** *Advertising only works if it repeatedly seen by your realistic prospects. You are much better off reaching a smaller number of people frequently than you are reaching a large number of people occasionally to rarely.*

If you've tried newspaper, and didn't get the kind of return you wanted on the investment, either or both of the above reasons could be to blame.

Don't get me wrong: I am not against newspaper advertising. For some products and services, it can be ideal. But for many, it's flushing money down the toilet.

Focus

I'm talking about getting focused. Identify a *clearly defined target customer* (the more clearly, the better), find advertising media whose readers predominantly fit that profile, and be there frequently enough that you are making yourself unforgettable.

If the publication/list/media is too expensive to utilize frequently, it's not appropriate for you. Maybe you can negotiate a lower rate based on the percentage of their base that may realistically do business with you. Maybe you can advertise in a localize edition, or rent a portion of the list.

But if you can't afford to be in regularly, find another place for your promotional dollars.

> **IMPORTANT LESSON:** *Don't assume that being in one publication, or mailing to one list every other month will give you the half-dozen exposures you need in a year. People don't read every issue or tune in every day, so they may miss some of your spots. They may be on vacation, or someone else may open the mail at times. For many reasons, you can't count on any one individual seeing every one of your "exposures." You have to put out many to get the half-dozen.*

No matter what media you choose, the tools you need to create effective promotional messages are contained in this manual.

> **IMPORTANT LESSON:** *A great message delivered to the wrong audience ... or not delivered frequently enough to make an impression ... is still going to be a waste of effort and money.*

Differentiation

What makes you a better choice than the other alternatives your prospect has to choose from?

What makes you different ... in terms of benefit to the buyer?

Unless you have invented a revolutionary new widget, that nobody else comes close to matching, you have competitors who offer similar to identical products and services. If your prospect is going to choose you over one of those competitors, you have to articulate a material difference that is <u>of value to the buyer</u>.

It doesn't matter that it's of value to YOU. It matters that is's of value to the BUYER.

"Seventy-two years in business" may sound important to you. "Seventy-two years managed by the same family"(yours) may sound even more important ... to YOU. But they don't amount to a hill of beans to your prospect.

That experience is valuable, if it means your prospect can count on a better outcome than they'll get from the competitor who's only been doing what you do for a few years. If it doesn't, it's not a useful area of differentiation. In fact, what sounds more enticing to you "old," or "new"? This ain't your father's Oldsmobile® ...

What matters to the prospect?

The prospect wants to know what will be better about their life after they've done business with you.

And it had better be something more important than what your competitor said makes them different.

Here's the good news; <u>Most of your competitors haven't a clue</u> that the prospect wants to know what makes them different, and why it's a benefit to the buyer.

Most of your competitors didn't buy this book.(Although, I'm working on it - you'd better get started on this stuff before they do!)

Take some time to read your competitors' marketing communications. Would you want to buy from them if you were one of your *clearly defined target customers*? Do they speak directly to that kind of person, and tell them that their kids will have fewer cavities, whiter teeth, less gum disease and lower dental bills in the long run after your revolutionary treatment?

What if they do? Well, then you have to either do something different, or take it to a higher level.

If you and a competitor offer virtually the same product or service, and promise the same benefit, then you're going to provide an in-depth explanation of why it's so. You'll write a special report, complete with photos and graphs, explaining the process you use. Each step of the way, you'll tell them why it's done this way and what it means to the patient.

You will differentiate yourself by educating your prospect.

And, since you're the one that educated them, they will assume that you do more or know more about it than your competitor. Only the competitor that does this first in the market place will be believed. Copy-cat education later will look just like that.

Differentiation doesn't have to be in terms of benefit to the buyer to be effective, although that's what I recommend. For some businesses, just looking different is enough to get noticed and remembered. I'm a professional speaker, so I notice what other speakers do to promote themselves. One guy in our association wears red sneakers with a suit. It's different. It gets noticed(hey, I noticed it!). He's a humorist, so it shows he has a sense of humor, I guess. I have a sense of humor, but I don't wear goofy outfits to demonstrate it! It doesn't demonstrate a benefit. It has no value. It's just different. For some people, different is enough.

Your "Personality"

Every business or professional practice has a personality.

You may not realize it, but the people who do business with you do.

You may be cheery, dull, anal-retentive, focused, flexible, loud, rude …

But here's the deal; Most organizations leave their personality to happenstance. Worse yet, they let their employees create their personality.

> **IMPORTANT LESSON:** *Smart organizations decide what their personality is going to be, and train their staff - decorate their facilities - paint their vehicles - write their phone scripts - mold everything about the organization to reflect that personality.*

Just your personality can be a differentiation point. If you're fun to deal with, and your competitor is boring, I'd rather buy from you … unless you're a funeral home. You still don't have to be boring, but you ought to at least be serious.

Figure out what your personality is, and make sure everything about you reflects it. (I guess the guy with the red sneakers and the suit is at least doing that!)

Continuity

You know that it takes half a dozen exposures for people to remember you.

What I didn't mention(yet) was that you must look the same every time they see you, or they don't make the connection that you're the same organization.

IMPORTANT LESSON: *If you don't look the same every time people see you, the necessary repetitions don't accrue.*

So, if you are running print advertising, for example. Every ad you place must look the same. Same border, same shape, same typefaces, same organization of information, same colors.

That means that creativity can be hazardous to your health!

Entrepreneurs are risk takers. They thrive on change, and on coming up with new ideas and solutions.

So, it's not unusual for a business owner to get bored with their advertising and make frequent, major changes.

Don't fall into this dangerous trap!

You see your ad every time it comes out. Your prospects don't. You get bored with it. Your prospects don't.

Remember, it takes that half a dozen repetitions just to get recognized. But, if you look different every time, or even half the time, you fragment the exposures. People don't realize you're the same guy that ran the different-shaped ad last week. Last week's ad made 1/6th of an impression, and this week's new ad made 1/6th of a totally different impression.

Pick an ad format and stick to it. There's a chapter later in the manual on testing. You'll notice that it doesn't suggest you test layouts, colors, typefaces ... cosmetics should stay the same. You'll be testing much more important components to try to make your ads more effective.

It's not just ads ...

And this doesn't just apply to advertising. Your company brochure, your letterhead, your business card, your signage ... all should share a common identity that makes them easy to associate with one another. Then, each of those items adds to the repetitions when people see them.

They drive by and see your sign. They get a letter in the mail. You hand them a business card at the Chamber of Commerce meeting. They see your ad, your billboard, your fax blast, your web page … that's your half dozen exposures right there IF it's obvious that they're all from the same organization.

Continuity is key to building those repetitions.

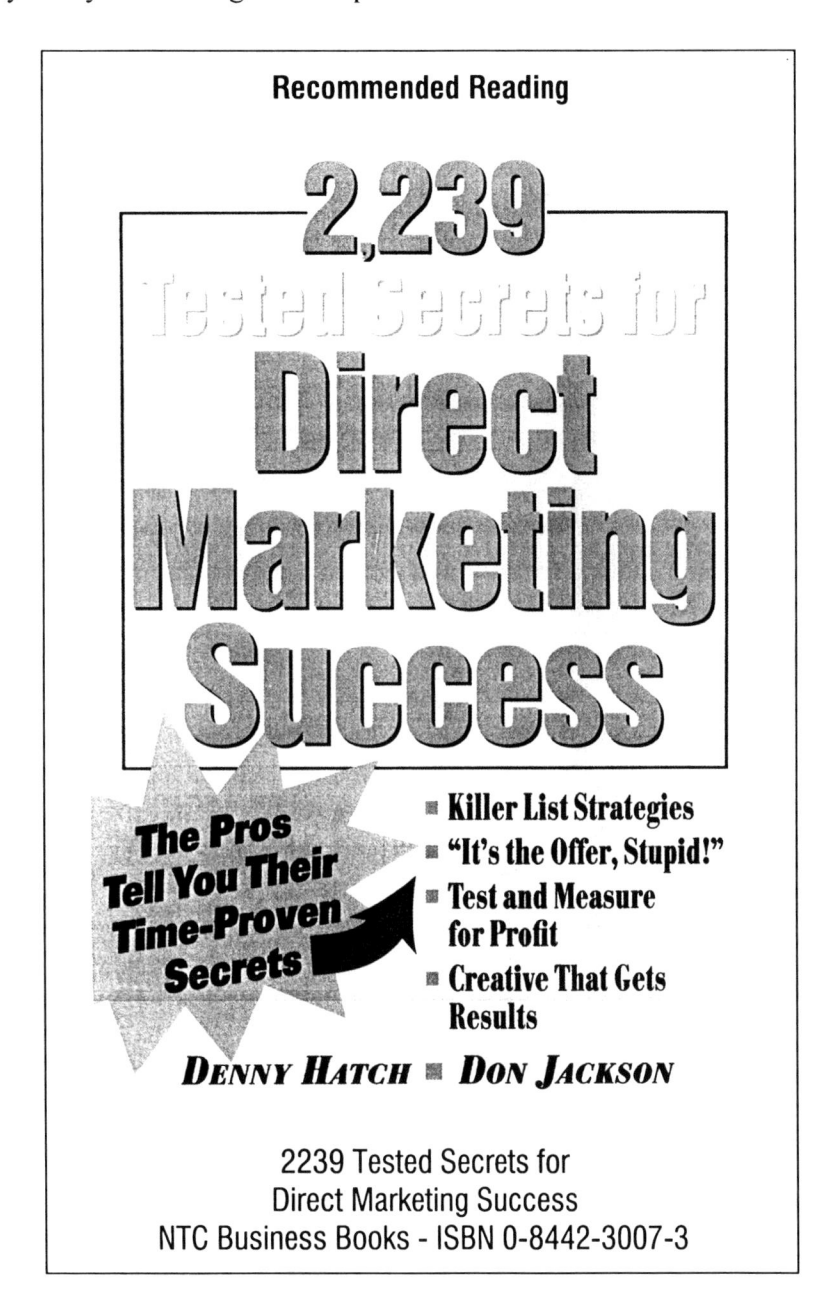

Recommended Reading

2,239 Tested Secrets for Direct Marketing Success

The Pros Tell You Their Time-Proven Secrets

- Killer List Strategies
- "It's the Offer, Stupid!"
- Test and Measure for Profit
- Creative That Gets Results

DENNY HATCH ▪ *DON JACKSON*

2239 Tested Secrets for
Direct Marketing Success
NTC Business Books - ISBN 0-8442-3007-3

Direct Response Advertising & Promotion

I feel very strongly about advertising and promotion;

Every dollar you put into advertising and promotion should be an investment that draws a solid return. If your promotions aren't making sales, or at least drawing new leads, something's got to change.

The reason many promotional campaigns don't get acceptable response, is because they just say;

> "Here we are, we're a wonderful organization. I hope you'll remember our name if some day you might happen to want what we sell."

Direct response advertising, on the other hand says;

> "You're business will be 63% more productive when you use this product. Try it for 30 days. If you don't like it, return it for a full no-questions-asked refund. Pick up the phone right now, and get two for the price of one. Here's who we are and how to reach us."

Direct response advertising sells the benefit first, then backs the promise with some kind of proof(like the guarantee), implores you to act immediately ... then finally, tells you who to call.

You'll learn how to do this effectively in this manual ... guaranteed. If you don't get it after reading this manual, call me a 888 224-0236, and I'll arrange a refund. I know this technique isn't for everyone. It's only for people who want their business or professional practice to be profitable.

Some people are just in business for a tax loss – effective advertising would just bring in annoying revenue they would have to spend.

Some people aren't bright enough to follow a simple formula – if they can't master the simple techniques in this manual, it's hard to imaging they can run a business.

I want you to demand response to your promotions.

It's like this; Say you hired a sales person. You put them out on the street for six weeks. After six weeks, you couldn't track one sale to them specifically. What would you do?

You would either fire the salesperson, or make some changes. More training, new sales scripts, new materials or samples. But you wouldn't just keep writing checks.

Unfortunately, that's what a lot of businesses do. They keep writing checks for ads, mailings, promotions of all kinds that don't make the phone ring. They just hope that people are remembering their name when they finally need whatever it is they sell.

At the very least, go for lead generation.

OK, you can't motivate people to buy your product today. If you run a funeral home, you're not going to get far with "call today and get two for the price of one." So, what do you do?

You offer free information – valuable information that will help people make intelligent decisions about their funeral needs when the time comes. "Don't wait until you need our services. Know now what to do and how to proceed. Call today for this valuable special report: *12 Questions You Don't Want To Have To Ask Your Parents' Funeral Director*. It's yours for the asking, and there's no obligation. Call now 555-999-9999."

This would draw calls from people whose parents are getting up there in years. You now have a name and mailing address of a person who is at least thinking about this enough to request some information.

You promised "no obligation." But get this; People feel obligated to anyone that gives them something valuable for free.

There is a natural law of reciprocation, whereby we all want to give back to people who have given to us. They will remember the nice people who gave them that valuable special report.

This name is now a "lead." A lead is someone who looks like a good prospect for what you sell. They have at least raised their hand and said "I'm interested enough to want to know more."

Now, you can methodically work to establish a relationship with this individual, one-to-one. A long list of this kind of quality of prospect makes for mailings with virtually no overflow.

Imagine, everyone who receives your message is a likely buyer … at least, some day.

Your business or practice might not have much in common with a funeral home, but if they can use direct response marketing, surely you can.

You'll read more about this technique later. But the important point here is that I want you to demand response from your promotions.

Never be satisfied just to get your name out there in front of a lot of people, especially when a lot of that "lot of people" will never buy from you anyway.

Customer Centered, Emotional Appeals

In the Appendices later in this manual there are lists of emotions, words and phrases that you should use to create and construct your marketing pieces.

The reason for the list of emotions, is because people make their buying decisions based on emotions. They will back their decision with facts and information. But the decision is emotional.

You've walked out of a store because you didn't like the salesperson, right? Heck, you even needed what they sell, but weren't about to buy it from that jerk. Emotional decision.

You've also bought something from a salesperson just because they were so nice, so persuasive … you didn't need a new shirt necktie to go with that suit. But the salesperson went out of his way to find you a shirt and tie that look smashing with it. You came in for a suit and walked out with a complete ensemble. Emotional decision.

What emotion will make people want your product or service?

> **IMPORTANT LESSON:** *All emotions fall under one of two categories: Fear and Greed.*

Before your sit down to design and write any marketing communication, you should know what emotion you are going to appeal to. Are you going to save them from some potential loss or danger? Or, are you going to help them hold on to more of their hard-earned money … or get more for it?

What makes people decide to buy what you sell? You might think it's features and components, but it's not. It's an emotion, and you need to know which one it is. There may be several.

I bought an SUV because I feel safer in it. I don't really need the space, I like being inside a large steel box. I bought a leather interior because it's A.) More comfortable, and B.) Prestigious. And I'm not ashamed of that!

Understand what makes people get excited about your product. Scare the bejesus out of them if you have to. Work them up into frenzy with your words and pictures – you'll learn how in the coming pages.

Yes, they need facts, features and components. But don't fool yourself. They use them to justify the emotional decision they've already made. Maybe they have to convince the boss, the spouse … even themselves … that it was a good decision. But the decision was based in emotion.

Write your copy and choose photos that tug at their emotions.

Testing

There's a whole chapter on testing, so I'm not going to say a lot here.

<u>Never</u> <u>be</u> <u>satisfied</u> with the return you're getting from your advertising and promotion. It can always be better.

The fear is, it can always be worse, too. So, when you've got things working well, you may be tempted to leave them alone.

Well, even the most successful ads and mail promotions can get stagnate after time. Some day, you're going to have to try something different.

Testing is a scientific approach to improving the response to your marketing communications. You do it by changing just one component of an ad or piece at a time. You won't totally overhaul something to try to come up with something better.

I know, the big companies like Coke® and Budweiser® do that all the time. But they probably have bigger budgets that you do. (NOTE: If you have a budget like theirs, please call me - I'd love to help you invest it!).

You should be methodically testing your ads and promo pieces, with the constant goal of improving response ... and sales.

This is all about growing your business profitably. That means you have to be effective and efficient with every marketing communication and every promotional dollar.

Chapter 3

The Magic Formula for Persuasion

This is the longest, and the most important chapter in the manual. "Most important," because it is the basis for everything else you will read.

The article you just read gives you this chapter in a nutshell. I included it because I wanted you to have a good feel for the formula before giving it to you in detail. This chapter is the detailed version.

The Magic Formula is referred to often in the coming pages. It, and the approach this manual takes, are based on one simple idea;

Selling is a sequential process

And the fact is, advertising, brochures, web pages … promo pieces of all kinds are simply a sales presentation put into print.

People make the decision to buy your product or service based on their emotional attachment to its benefits, their understanding and applicability of its features, and whether those factors make it worth more to them than the hard-earned money they'll have to part with in order to buy.

Often, you are taking a prospective buyer from the stage of being a total stranger, to someone who trusts you enough to give you their credit card number. It's a bigger leap with some people than others, but the process is the same for everyone.

The Magic Formula is designed to be an outline for your promotional copy. It is also a template for your graphic design. (In fact, you can apply this formula to sales scripts, too. That's a whole 'nother book!)

No matter how clever and effective your copy is, if the layout pulls your reader's eye out of the formulaic sequence, you've lost them. You'll notice that the chapter on graphic design follows this same formula. It's the designer's job to make the piece attractive and legible, and at the same time, to move the reader's eye sequentially through the message.

You may be both the designer and the copy writer. If so, make sure the copy and design work together to start the prospect at the beginning of the copy, and walk them step-by-step through every detail of the sequence.

If you are one or the other(copy writer or designer), it's important that you work closely with your counterpart to make sure the message is received in the proper order. That means both of you have to understand *The Magic Formula*;

Copy is King

The graphic designers in the crowd might not agree or appreciate it, but it's true.

Your graphic design may draw attention, and may work to guide the eye through your copy in the proper sequence. In fact, it must. But it's the copy that provides the information upon which your prospect bases his/her buying decision.

So, if you are in a position of hiring a separate copy writer and designer, go for the expensive copy writer and have them work with your graphics person. They know how the message should be received, and can help even the most elementary of graphic designers turn out a piece that will facilitate reader reception and comprehension.

This chapter is the foundation for the rest of the book.

This same *Magic Formula* can be applied to virtually any marketing communication. This chapter is first because it will be referred to in almost every other chapter. Whether you are working on a web page, a sales letter, a space ad ... it doesn't matter. The buyer's decision-making process remains the same.

Keep Holy the sequence, and thou shalt be set free!

So, here is the sequence;

>Attention – Emotional Appeal

>Promise – Lead With Benefits

>Proof - Eliminate The Risk

>Proposition - Motivate Them To *ACT*

>Call To Action - Make It Safe ...And Easy To Respond

Why it works ...

Imagine that you are about to buy a new car. You stop by a dealership, and before you've even narrowed down the field of vehicles you are considering, a salesman sachets over and says; "I'll take two thousand dollars off the window sticker if you buy today."

Clearly, that is a Proposition, maybe even a fairly good one. But are you ready for it yet? No! The salesman has committed the deadly sin of presenting out of sequence.

Every promo piece you create is nothing more than a salesman in print. If the "salesman" presents information out of sequence, the prospect is offended, she turns and walks away immediately.

You might be more polite than to turn on your heal and walk away from the car salesman, but you will certainly turn the page or click to the next web site without hesitation.

Think that's an exaggerated example of a promotional message presented out of sequence? Take a look at the Yellow Pages in your local telephone book. Go ahead, do it now if you can. Open to any classification. Now take a look at the display ads. Keep in mind that these businesses are paying hundreds, possibly thousands of dollars per month to vie for your attention.

Read the headlines of any four ads. I'm willing to be that three of them were the name of the business. Let's say you're looking at the "printers" classification. Do you decide which printer you're going to buy from based on the name of the business? Probably not.

You probably choose a printer based on any number of criteria; Convenient location, pricing, specialization, quality, ability to deliver on time. That's what you care about, not the company name. So why are they telling you their company name first?

EGO! We all love to see our name in print. And we like to think that prospects want to know our name, or may recognize it because we're famous in our community.

Your reputation may be a factor later in the game. But the prospective buyer perusing the Yellow Pages, the newspaper, their stack of daily mail, or the world wide web needs a reason to stop and read more. Your name ain't gonna' cut it.

Step One: Attention - Emotion

Think about the way you read a magazine. How do you decide which articles you read? You scan the headlines, looking for stories that may be of interest to you. If the headline gets your attention, you stop and read. If it doesn't, you scan on. Nobody reads every story.

When you're surfing online, which sites draw you in? The ones with interesting company names? The ones with the prettiest color schemes(that someone spent hundreds of hours creating!)? Of course not. You're looking for one that has something that's important to you.

You look at your mail the same way. You go through the stack of envelopes and cards, looking for something that looks interesting. If it doesn't look interesting, it either goes in the "maybe-I'll-read-it-later-if-I-don't-have-anything-better-to-do" pile ... or straight to the trash.

How (and Why) To Write Headlines That Get Your Pieces Read...

People are basically lazy. They will read and do the bare minimum to get by unless you do something to pique their interest, and then maintain it.

Each of us have fears and desires we are yearning to satisfy. The messages that get our attention are the ones that address those fears and desires. Maybe you're trying to lose a few pounds. You might be working on a promotion at work. Maybe you lose sleep over your kid's college tuition.

Every day, we're exposed to thousands of messages – messages from advertisers, from co-workers, family, friends, radio and TV commentators or programs … you get the idea. The point is, your message has to compete with all of the other messages that are vying for your reader's attention.

Your headline ... the first line in your communique ... must tell the reader that the weight is good-as-gone, the promotion is in the bag, and tuition bill will never haunt them again.

The headline has to "sell" them on reading the rest of the ad.

So it has to deal directly with the emotions that motivate people to buy.

Buying is always an emotional decision. The decision whether to even read your promo piece is also an emotional one. You must know what emotion will motivate the typical buyer of your product or service to take action, and address that emotion in your headline.

And, by the way, the decision NOT to buy is also an emotional decision. The emotion that keeps people from buying is usually a nagging fear of making a wrong decision. "I'll look foolish if buy this thing and it doesn't do what I thought it would." That has little to do with your product, but it has everything to do with whether your prospect decides to buy.

Even at first exposure, when they decide whether to stop and read your message, they're driven by the fear of being "suckerred" into your little "trap."

> **LESSON**: *It's much easier to NOT buy that it is to buy, at every stage of the relationship. So that line at the head of your promo piece has to make an emotional connection with the reader.*

You have to know who you're talking to before you can make an emotional appeal. An that's where too many businesses go wrong. They talk to the entire universe. Your "universe" may mean your local community, all women, everyone on the Internet. But not everyone in your universe is a realistic prospect for what you sell, product or service.

You have to clearly define the target customer for whatever it is that you sell. When you try to talk to an entire universe, you speak in broad generalities. In trying to appeal to "everyone," you're actually appealing to "no-one."

Get focused on a particular kind of prospect.

For me, it's business owners, marketers, and professionals. YOU! You own your business or practice, or are responsible for bringing in enough revenue to pay the bills and yourself. I want to help you build your sales … and profits. I'd like you to enjoy life in the process, so I try to make it as simple as possible to do that so you have time and money left to share with your family. So, everything I do is aimed at you, and I make no bones about it – that's why you bought this manual!

So you have to identify who your business is designed to serve.

That's who you talk to. You have to directly address an individual representative of your **clearly defined target customer**.

When they read your headline, they will see that you specialize in serving their unique needs. There will be an emotional connection because you understand their situation, and address their concerns and ambitions directly.

THAT'S what a good headline will do for you.

What Do Your Headlines Talk About?

Here's a single idea that will make this manual worth your investment;

Most marketers write headlines about themselves, their product, … whatever it is they're trying to promote. Your readers really don't care about you or the details of whatever it is you're trying to sell – they care about what you or it's going to do for them … how it will make their life better, make them more successful, more profitable … whatever. (Don't feel bad, that's just the way it is!)

> **LESSON**: *Start writing your headlines about your prospect, and what your product or service is going to do to make their life better. Make an emotional connection that stops them in their tracks and moves them to keep reading.*
>
> (You'll find a list of possible emotions you can appeal to in Appendices. And there's more about writing to emotions in the chapters on headlines and writing killer copy. My goodness, the

value to come in this manual is unbelievable!)

Be sure you know what emotion you are trying to appeal to before you ever write a word. If you're not addressing an emotion, you're not likely to grab your prospects' attention very effectively.

In my workshops, I get ads and promo pieces in advance from a handful of participants. I do "makeovers" on them to demonstrate how simple changes can make them much more effective. You'll see makeover examples throughout this manual, each demonstrating a particular point.

So, here's your first one.

This was a headline for a market research firm specializing in the association market. They help associations pinpoint what their members want from them. The "before" headline was based on a "curiosity" hook. You'll find a whole chapter on headline hooks later in the manual, so I won't go into that here. But the idea is to appeal to the reader's curiosity, hoping that will make them read more.

Although it was successful in raising curiosity, it didn't do much to strike an emotional chord;

Is there something you need to know?	**Can you afford to GUESS what your members want?**
Before	After

Too many association leaders are guessing at what their members want, just as too many business owners guess what their customers want. The "After" headline hits on fear much more effectively than the original.

Take a look at your latest ad or promo piece. Is the first thing your reader sees an emotional appeal? If it's not, you should go to the list of emotions in the appendix, and decide which one you want to appeal to.

You can see that the change in the before and after example was a small change. You probably don't have to scrap everything you're using – try to make small changes. Otherwise, you risk changing your whole "personality."

Small Changes

That's an important point. As you go through this manual, don't be thinking you have to scrap everything you're doing. When I do makeovers for my consulting clients and for workshop participants, I try to work with what they already have as much as possible.

In most of the makeovers I do, I have to put the message into the proper sequence, then add a few power words here and there. In many cases I have to change to copy from "ain't we grand" to "you will enjoy us because…"(see Killer Copy chapter). But I keep the changes small.

It's especially important if you've already been advertising for some time. Rather than totally change your look and feel, hold on to the recognition you've already achieved.

The Rule of Seven

Don't change everything about your advertising in one fell swoop. Make minor changes without totally changing your "look and feel."

IMPORTANT LESSON: *If you roll out a totally new look, you'll be starting over with your public.*

The "Rule of Seven" says that your prospect has to see you seven times in an eighteen month period just to remember you. But if your ads and promo pieces don't all look the same, the repetitions don't accrue.

If you're reading this manual, and thinking you have to totally start over, resist the temptation.

Make incremental changes over time so you don't throw away the recognition you've already established. In the chapter on "Testing," you'll see what components you should start with. Things like borders, colors and type styles are last. And when you do get around to changing those things, change them one by one, and gradually.

OK, back to the sequence ...

Step 2: Promise a benefit

This may be included with step one in the headline or photo. The emotional connection may well be in the form of a promise. You'll look better, feel better, make more money ... they're all promises that make an emotional connection.

In fact, if you can do both in a few words, make the emotional connection with a promise of a powerful benefit, and you get double duty out of your "prime real estate." Prime real estate is what I call that first 1/4 to 1/3 of your space. It's the first thing the reader sees, and it what they base their decision to "read on" or "toss" on.

What's a "Benefit?"

A benefit is something that your product or service does for the owner or user.

Makeup makes the owner feel more attractive. You've seen people who really don't look any better because they wear makeup ... but they feel more attractive! Pay attention to makeup ads today. When you read the newspaper or magazines, when you watch TV. Do they tell you about the ingredients? To they spend a lot of space or time talking about colors? No! They promise the prospect that they will be more beautiful. They even show photos of beautiful people to prove it! It's an emotional appeal. And that's what makes them buy.

Before you give your prospect "feature" information, things like horsepower, weight, number of years you've been in business … promise the results they'll enjoy when they own or use your product/service. The features can be included in the next step(Proof), but first you have to get them to envision the better life they'll enjoy after they buy.

You may think I'm being a little conniving with this sequence. After all, I'm saying you should play on your prospects' emotions. You're getting them all excited or scared.

Well, that's how people make buying decisions. They buy what gets them excited, not necessarily what's practical or necessary.

I'm not suggesting that you mislead the prospect in any way. Just the opposite: Don't ever make a claim or a promise you can't deliver on.

Am I saying the makeup ads are deceptive? Well, they do tend to give false hope at times! But why do people buy Corvettes? I used to own one, so I'm not slamming the car – they're dynamite. But half of the people who buy a Corvette buy it because they think it will improve their luck with the opposite sex. Is that any reason to buy a car? Is that a realistic promise? Do people buy BMW's because of their quality, or to impress their neighbors?

BMW could sell on safety, mechanical quality, attractive design, comfortable seating. But people buy snob appeal.

Don't be subtle about benefits. If using your product or service will make your buyer's life more satisfying in some way, play it to the bone. If not, then why should they buy it?

"But Larry, I'm an accountant. How can that make my clients' lives more satisfying?" You can allay fears of scrutiny by the IRS, or not knowing how your business is doing. You can enhance your business clients' profits through proper cash management, save them money, help them retire comfortably."

Think of how you can help your clients enjoy a better life. Do you help them look better? Feel better? Make more money? Attract admirers? Lead the pack? Sleep better?

> **Important Point**: *Your benefit should be one that you provide uniquely. Your competitors can't match it.*

If there's no difference between what your buyer gets from you, and what they get from your competitors, they have no clear reason to choose you.

Ideally, you'd like to offer a benefit that your competitors can't.

But I don't have a unique benefit ...

At the very least, you want to be the first to claim a benefit, even though your competitors may be able to say the same thing. If you're the first to say it, and you say it loudly enough for everyone to hear, the competitor who comes out an says the same thing looks like a copy cat. If you are going to be the first, don't be shy about it. Someone else can come in and drown you out with an aggressive campaign.

Hang your hat on something you do very well, even if you're not the only one that does it.

Roll out a big program to establish it as your "turf." Inundate the market with your claim, then continue to emphasize it in everything you do. Volvo hangs their hat on "safety." Do you think their cars are significantly safer than, say Mercedes or BMW? I think not. But since they established the "safety" beachhead first, they own it.

You have to be the first one to tout this specific benefit. Think about the benefits you offer, particularly the ones you do exceptionally well. List them in order of how well you do them. Is number "1" on your list something none of your competitors mention in their advertising and promotion? If so, move on to number "2."

When you get to a strong benefit that nobody else is talking about, consider using it as your preeminent benefit. "Preeminent" because you grab it first. You beat everyone to it, so it's yours.

But you can't execute this strategy it in a small way. You have to really saturate the market when you roll it out so anyone else who tries to grab it looks like they're just responding to you ...the now-established leader!

Benefits are what people buy. They will use features(facts and details) to justify their decision, but it's the benefits that make them buy.

Buying is always an emotional decision, not a rational one.

That's why we started with an emotional connection. We want to get them into the buying decision right away. If they read your headline and subconsciously say "that's me," then see a benefit that turns them on, they're already most of the way into a buying decision.

But wait, people are skeptical. There's a tendency to think: "This may be too good to be true … how do I know they can really deliver on this promise?"

Time for Step 3.)

Step 3.) Prove Your Claims

It's easy to make wild promises, and the buying public is jaded. You have to show them that you really can deliver what you say you can.

> **IMPORTANT LESSON**: *"Proof" is all about removing risk.*

People are terrified that they are going to make a wrong decision. Remember, buying is an emotional decision. Look at all of the emotions that discourage people from buying;

> "What if I send in my hard-earned dollars and the product doesn't do what they said it would? Then what? I'm out my money? I own a useless product? My friends and neighbors will laugh at my foolishness? My wife will leave me? My kids will disown me?"

You have to remove all risk to the buyer. They have to be confident that, if this buying decision doesn't work out, they can back out of it(saving money … and face!).

So you want to give them rational information to back your promises, plus an "out" in case all else fails.

Now's the time to roll out some of the features we talked about before. Your prospect makes their buying decision based on emotions. Then, they need some rational data to back it up.

Hey, what if they have to explain this purchase to the wife when it arrives? When I pulled into the driveway in my new Corvette … never having mentioned to my wife that I was in the market for a car, let alone a Corvette … I had some 'splainin' to do!

So, how can your prospect 'splain their buying decision? What can you give them to rationalize the buying decision?

Some of the things you can include in your communications;

- Guarantees
- Years in Business/Experience
- Case Studies
- Photographs Of Real People Enjoying Your Product
- Surveys/Studies
- Articles by or about you
- Reason Why
- Customer Education
- Customer List
- Delayed Billing
- Free Trials (See for yourself)

Guarantees

If you can promise that your product does everything you promised, or it can be returned for an immediate, no-questions-asked, full refund ... it's a lot easier for the prospect to pick up the phone and order.

Too many advertisers shy away from making strong guarantees. Fact is, very few people ever take you up on a guarantee.

And, ironically, the more liberal your guarantee is, the fewer people take advantage of you! If you're now offering a 30 day guarantee, try making it a year. How about two years? Am I making you nervous? You shouldn't be. With a 30 day limit, people are considering the first month a trial period. They will be very conscious of the deadline. With a two year term, the deadline is totally forgotten. Even if your product ends up on the shelf, the guarantee is forgotten. Besides, how many people do you think return a product after 729 days?

The longer and stronger your guarantee is, the more effective it is as proof.

The merchant who offers a 30 day guarantee doesn't sound very confident in their own product, now do they? If you can only promise I'll be happy with your product for a month, I'm not going to rush to buy it. If you tell me "return it any time … forever … if it doesn't do everything I promised," I feel pretty good about your integrity.

Years In Business

People tend to believe that, if you've been in business for twenty years, you must be doing something right.

Plus, it provides a sort of stability argument. People will subconsciously project your longevity into the future equal to your past. A new, upstart company's 10 year guarantee doesn't carry as much weight as the same guarantee from a fifty-year-old company. If you've been around for fifty years, they can be pretty confident that if have a problem with your product two, three years from now, you'll still be around to make it right.

Better Than Money Back Guarantee

I threw this in just in case you're a young upstart, wondering how you can compete with the old-timers' longevity. Hey, even if you're the old-timer, a better than money back guarantee can be a powerful proof step. This is actually becoming a "proposition," but it takes the guarantee a step further, so I've included it in the "proof" step.

You've seen this used, but maybe didn't realize what was happening. The proposition(next step) includes an extra gift for fast action; "Order within the next 7 days, and receive this valuable bonus gift absolutely free." The better than money back guarantee then says; "Even if you return the product, the bonus gift is yours to keep - our way of saying thank you for giving us a chance."

Not only is there zero risk in ordering, they'll have something to show for their efforts even if they return the product. Isn't that even better than "your money back if you're not satisfied"?

Make sure the gift has something to do with the item you're promoting, so it will be of value to the same target customer. Don't give away free cookware when the main item is a boat. The buyer isn't going to be enticed. Maybe a fishing rod, or a ski rope(depending on what kind of boat it is) would work.

And, try to pick a gift that costs you next to nothing, but still has great value to the target customer. If you've got a box of last year's ski ropes in the back, give them away as bonuses in stead of letting them gather dust in the store room.

Case Studies

If your promise is something measurable, and takes a significant length of time to achieve, a detailed case study of a past client's experience can serve as backing for your claim.

For example, say you promise that your product will help the buyer increase production efficiency in their factory. A promise like that will take time to come to fruition. And, in that time, the buyer is taking a leap of faith. They have to be patient as they implement your product and wait for results to accrue.

Case studies(the more, the better) can show the starting point and month by month statistical progress other customers have enjoyed. The more case studies you offer, the more likely it is the prospect can find one involving a business similar to their own.

Articles by or about You

If you have been published as an expert source, copies of your article add weight(in more ways than one) to your media kit or direct mail package. If a respected publication has printed your article, they serve as a third-party endorsement.

Better yet, if a publication has written an article ABOUT you.

If they sent someone to interview you, and they took the time to write an article, you must have something going for you. If the publication thought their readers could learn something from you, they have declared you an expert. You can even use short quotes from the article, listing the publication as the source. What a great endorsement!

If you have a local business journal or business oriented newspaper, they may be willing to do an *advertorial* about your business, and sell you reprints of the article. Ask your advertising representative.

Photographs

There's a whole chapter in this manual on effective use of photographs. A good photograph can provide all of Steps 1.) through 3.), in the Magic Formula. A model who looks just like your target prospect makes an emotional contact by being "one of them," and by looking them straight in the eye.

If the model is demonstrating the primary benefit you are promising, it covers Step 2.). Plus, photos of people using your product serve as proof. <u>Photos represent reality</u>. The prospect can see for herself that your product works. Hey, it's in the photo. It must be true.

Same caveat I mentioned in Step 2.): Don't exaggerate – don't make claims or promises you can't deliver on. And don't "create" "proof" that isn't real and accurate. Airbrushed photos are like fudged survey figures: They're lies.

Don't ever, EVER lie to your prospect. It will come back to haunt you ... possibly bankrupt you ... possibly put you in jail ... eventually.

Research: Surveys and Studies

It's hard to argue with scientifically-assembled statistics.

> **IMPORTANT LESSON**: *If you use statistics, use real numbers. "78% of 978 cases" is much more effective "three-fourths of nearly a thousand cases."*

You can survey customers who are already using your product or service to find satisfaction levels. You can conduct scientific tests to confirm the reliability or strength of your product.

For surveys and studies to be believable, they must be conducted by an unbiased, independent source. It doesn't have to be Consumer Reports®. Any independent research firm will do. But don't compile your own figures and use them as proof.

If you belong to a state or national trade association, they may have statistics supporting your claims. Sure, they would apply to your competitor, too. But if your competitor isn't using them, you're the one who brought the information to light. It's hard for them to come out later and say "me too" in their advertising, now isn't it?

Free Trials or Samples

This one crosses over to the next step: Proposition. It's a proposition in that it makes it exceptionally easy for the prospect to respond. It's still proof in that they get to see for themselves that your product or service does what you say it can ... before they actually buy.

A free trial allows the prospect to try your product or service for a limited amount of time, or in a limited capacity, before they actually buy. Many software manufacturers offer demo versions that lack the full capability of the product. They provide enough features for you to experience the software, but not enough for you to just use the demo version to suit the intended purpose. A demo of a database program may have full functionality, but only capacity for 20 records. You get to try it, play with it, experience what it can do to automate your business without spending a dime. But it will only take you so far before you have to buy the full-function version to continue to enjoy its benefits.

A service business may offer the first consultation for free. You get to meet your service provider, see what it's like to work with them and what kind of solutions they can come up with. The consultation should be a full-scale consultation that really delivers results. The prospect can see that the fee for future consultations will easily pay for itself. You are getting your prospect "hooked." (I don't use this one – so please don't call and ask for a free consultation!)

Why do food manufacturers hand out free samples in grocery stores? Getting people to try a new product is not easy. They have to be motivated to pick up that new package with no guarantee that they're going to like it. The risk of disappointment stops them in their tracks. But wait, what's that smell?

Customer List

279 satisfied customers can't be wrong. All the better if they're names your prospect will recognize.

Testimonials

Whether it's a short quote from a testimonial letter, or the whole letter, positive comments from past customers are powerful proof.

In fact, a testimonial quote can make a great headline. If you can pull a sentence out of a wildly enthusiastic letter from a happy client, it can be the emotional connection that draws readers in.

> **IMPORTANT LESSON**: *Always show the writer's name, company name(if you're selling business-to-business) and city. And don't ever*

use a quote without the writer's permission.

This is one time that the language of your copy will stray from the "you" copy format. This time, the voice is that of a happy client talking directly to the prospective client. Don't paraphrase to make it sound like you telling your prospect the story. Let the happy client talk directly to them.

In other words, use the actual text of the testimonial letter. If you want to make some changes in the way it is worded, maintain the voice of the happy client. Be sure to ask for their permission to paraphrase. Make sure they agree to the new wording before it goes into print for the whole world to see.

The idea here, is that the prospect reads the happy client's story, and surmises that "he had a great experience with the XYZ company. I'm sure I will too.

Implied Testimonials

An implied testimonial quotes a (usually well-known) source that wasn't talking directly about your organization, but whose comments support your message. Although they were not talking about you specifically, they did say that your product or service is important/viable, whatever.

For instance, say you are a chiropractor. The Surgeon General of the United States makes some comment about the importance of regular chiropractic care(I know, don't hold your breath waiting for this one to happen!). You could use a quote from that statement, and show it as coming from the Surgeon General of the United States. Although she wasn't talking about you specifically, the quote would support your message. That's an implied testimonial.

> **NOTE:** *You can also use research results that did not measure you specifically, the same way. If there is a significant medical study whose results recommend regular chiropractic care, you could pull statistics from that study and quote them in your promo materials.(Of course, check copyrights or get permission first.)*

You can cover a lot in a short headline

It's even possible to cover the proof in the headline, along with the emotional appeal and the promise of a benefit. Now we're getting into some serious copy writing!

No Ants ... Guaranteed

In three words this headline makes an emotional connection, a promise, and offers proof. Now that's efficient copy writing!

If you have fire ants, you hate them. You've tried getting rid of them yourself, but you just haven't quite gotten the job done. (If you've never lived in the South, you might not know about fire ants. They are the Devil incarnate! It's almost impossible to kill them. They have a bite that you will never forget. Amazing little beasties.) When someone comes along and guarantees that they can make them disappear, you've got to be interested.

Proposition

This is the difference between "Direct Response" advertising, and "Institutional" (or, "Ain't we grand") advertising.

Direct response says exactly what it does; It talks directly to a specific kind of prospect, and motivates them to respond.

The proposition step is where you offer a reward for fast action.

"Fast action" is important. You've grabbed their attention. You're already winning against all odds, just by getting them to stop what they're doing and read your ad or piece. You've promised a benefit, and they are apparently interested … otherwise, they wouldn't have gotten to the next step; You proved that you can deliver on your promise.

Most advertising drops the ball here. It kind of leaves the prospect with "Well, please give us a call some day if this might be something you could use and you happen to remember who we are." You don't want to do that.

You want the prospect to pick up the phone right now and call. Or, you want them to jump in the car and come down. Maybe you want them to surf on over to your web site, send a fax … a carrier pidgeon.

> **IMPORTANT LESSON:** *You've got them all lathered up for the benefit you've promised. NOW is the time to either close the deal or get them to take the next step in the dance.*

Motivate Them To Act Fast With A Compelling Proposition

It's easier for your prospect to throw a brochure, letter, ad or memo in the trash than it is to act on it. If you accept the premise that people are basically lazy, you have to accept that they're far more likely to turn to the next page ... or throw your beautiful marketing communique away ... than they are to take the action you're hoping for.

Hit them between the eyes with a compelling proposition!

A compelling proposition is the difference between getting a response and getting tossed. Even if you aroused their interest in the headline ... even if they're sold on your offering ... They still have to be motivated to take action.

A proposition gives the prospect some extra benefit, or helps them avoid some loss, if they
act right now. Some examples of what you might use as incentives(more to follow);

- Fast-action discounts - "Early Bird"
o Limited Availability - "First 20 To Call Get
- Bonus or Premium - "Ginsu Knives"
o Free Samples - Trial Offers
- Coupons
o Free Special Report - Educate prospects.

Fast Action Discount

Let's get this one out of the way first, because I don't especially like it.

I don't like it, because I don't like to use discounts as propositions. Discounts are for distressed merchandise, not for a regular way to bringing in business. Simply lowering your price gets your buyers into the habit of waiting for you to discount.

Go to any mall, and look at which stores have the traffic. The ones with "Sale" in the window are busy, the others are not. Retailers have trained their customers to wait for sales. I haven't seen any statistics, but I would bet that the percentage of mall store merchandise sold at full retail price is relatively small.

If price is the only way you can differentiate yourself from your competition, you have a tough row to hoe(my Midwestern upbringing comes out!) to generate profits.

Maybe you've played this game: You lower your price, the competition goes a little lower. So, you go a little lower. And on it goes until nobody's making any money.

As I said, discounting is a good strategy for getting rid of distressed inventory without giving it away(although the tax benefits of donating it to charity are worth considering), but as a day-to-day come-on, I think it stinks.

Limited Availability

Scarcity, for some reason, makes things more attractive.

You've heard it; Only 3 left at this price.

The only thing wrong with this one, is that you may get four people to respond ... when you only had three. Now what? Do you hope to upsell the fourth person to the full price? Don't bet on it.

Or, maybe you really have 5 left. So, when number four calls, you can still sell at this price. She doesn't know she's the fourth to call. You can play this game all day, right?

Don't use limited availability unless you really do have a limited number. Maybe you're selling the last five of a discontinued item. Maybe you're holding a seminar in a room that only seats 40, so only the first 40 to register will be accepted.

Or, you could just be using this to build interest, and you want to limit how many you'll sell at the reduced price.

It's an effective proposition, but should only be used when there really is a limited supply.

Bonus or Premium

I can hear Billy Mays in the OxyClean ad now: "Call during this program, and we'll supersize your order to this giant 6 pound tub."

Throwing in "something extra" is a strong motivation to act fast. Of course, the fear is that they'll miss out on the free stuff if they don't call now.

Go into any department store, and look at the cosmetics counter. You can get a free tote bag, or a free watch, or a free makeup mirror ... all kinds of premiums are offered with minium purchases.

The premium is often so attractive, people will buy the cosmetics just to get it!

This strategy is one of my favorites, because you're delivering extra value rather than lowering your price. The original item, coupled with the premium, is now worth far more than the purchase price – make that the full retail purchase price.

Deferred Billing

With this tactic, you ship your product, promising to wait 30, 60, 90 days ... again, the longer the better for "proof" ... before you charge their credit card.

Then you get to say "Try it, use it for 90 days. If you can't see that the information in this manual is worth 100 times the cover price in increased sales ... and PROFITS, return it and your credit card will never be billed. That's right, you can start building your business before you pay a dime, or you never will!"

Special Terms

What stops people from buying your product? If it's lack of cash, which is often the case with big-ticket(expensive) items, offering favorable payment terms can be the answer.

Twelve payments of $19.95 sounds a lot more palatable than $239.40.

Coupons

If you've ever clipped a coupon, you've responded to direct response advertising.

I go through the coupon inserts in my Sunday paper with a fine-toothed comb. Once I've clipped a coupon, I'm committed to buying the product.

If you can get people to cut out your coupon (you can make the whole ad a coupon), you've got them. Most ads just hope the prospect remembers. The coupon makes sure they do.

Coupons, as all propositions, should have an expiration date. They can come back to haunt you later.

Free Information

Later in this manual, you'll learn about 2-step advertising and lead generation.

Offering free information ... provided it's information that's truly valuable to your target prospect ... is a great way to get people to "raise their hand" and identify themselves as qualified, interested prospects.

You'll get a lot more on that in future chapters.

Reason Why

Have you ever seen an offer that was so good, it made you say: "Why would they do that?"

If your proposition is going to look like the Ginsu Knives'(Remember those? As the commercial went on, they kept adding knives and adding knives. Pretty soon, it looked too good to be true.), you'd better have a good reason for giving away the farm ... and you'd better explain it to your potential buyer.

If they're thinking "this is too good to be true," they're also thinking "if is sounds too good to be true, it probably is" just before they tune out.

But occasionally, you will make a proposition that is so good, people will be highly skeptical. It's dangerous to make a proposition that strong, but sometimes it works.

Here's what I mean; In 1995, I had a pretty dismal year in my speaking business. I spent a lot of the first half of that year writing my book: *Shoestring Marketing*. So, I was writing in stead of marketing myself. I only spoke 19 times that year – not a good thing for a guy who is trying to make a living by speaking.

About June, of that year, I came to realize that my cash flow was not looking good. I needed some new bookings, and I needed them fast.

At that time, almost all of my speaking business was with associations. Now, I work more with corporations who have me do programs for their dealers, agents, distributors, brokers, franchisees ... you get the picture. The corporations understand that a good product is going to cost money. So when I quote my fee, they understand the value they're getting for the investment.

Associations don't all understand that. Most do, but not all. So, I decided to go after all those associations that can't afford me, and offer a lower fee. That should generate some business fast, don't you think?

Now, offering a lower fee is not generally a strategy I recommend. People tend to think they "get what they pay for," so a cheaper speaker is not a very appealing proposition for the average meeting planner. Even the planner with a small budget is skeptical of suppliers who suddenly come down to their level.

A number of associations have low speaker budgets. Some have not money at all. But there are a number out there who have some, but not much of a budget. I ran into them all the time making my sales calls. They'd get out the violins when it came time to talk about money. "We're a non-profit organization, and have to use our members' dues and convention registration money prudently." As I wiped the tears from my eyes, I would think to myself: "… so give them the worst speakers you can find at your convention. Better yet, don't even hire speakers – ask for volunteers who have been pretty successful(or who like to let everyone think they are) get up and tell the crowd how they did it."

Oops, I digress. Point is, I had a whole list of associations that didn't have a lot of money for speakers. Shouldn't they jump at a chance to hire me for half my normal fee? The proposition would give them a very short time to make a decision. Heck, I needed cash flow. I ask for a retainer to hold every new booking, so even if it's months away I get some cash right now. So that was the deal: Make a quick decision, save 50%.

Well, there were a couple of problems with that idea;

First, I had to feel at least a little guilty about charging my full fee to those who can afford it. I mean, pricing shouldn't be based on "ability to pay." If I'm selling the same thing to a non-profit organization as I am to a successful corporation, is it right to charge the corporation more? OK, that's a whole 'nother debate. Suffice it to say, I didn't like that idea.

Second, the offer sounded too good. Why would he cut his prices by 50%? Is he having problems? Is he offering us a watered-down version of his program? Half price is enough of a discount to make people wonder why.

> **LESSON**: *If your proposition may sound too good to be true, give them the reason why you're offering it.*

Now, I couldn't very well give the whole truth, the fact that I was broke and would work for half fee to generate cash flow. That sounds like those guys you see on street corners with signs that say "will panhandle for food," or something heart-rending like that. I didn't want to come across as a panhandler, and I certainly didn't want to admit that my business wasn't going well. Hey, who wants to hire a marketing guy who can't market his own business?

So, I decided to make the proposition more restrictive. The half-fee offer was only good for speaking engagements in the month of December. December sucks. Not in general, but in my business. There just aren't many organizations that hold substantive meetings in December. They have a Holiday Party, but rarely a business event. But I had a pretty good list of organizations that met in December, and for whom my program would be approptiate.

So the proposition to just that list was: "Half my normal fee for any December date. You must confirm your date within two weeks of receiving this offer." The *Reason Why* was: "December sucks. Every year I sit home staring at an empty calendar. There are thousands of business owners, marketers and professionals out there who truly need my programs ... especially at the end of the year as they prepare for 1996. Bring me in this December, and I'll fill what would have been empty dates, so half fee is like gravy to me."

OK, I didn't say "December sucks." But I did explain that December was a dead month for me, and that I'd rather be out there helping their members at half fee than sitting home, staring at an empty calendar.

Now, my corporate and larger association clients could understand why I was offering someone else half fee. It was only during a low-demand period. Heck, they could bring me in for half fee in December, too. In fact, in retrospect, that's who I should have gone to first. "Schedule a special year-end seminar this December, for half my normal fee. December sucks, and I'd rather be in Cleveland helping your dealers prepare for 1996 than sitting home with an empty calendar. So, I'm making this special one-time offer to you, my loyal corporate client."

But I wasn't that smart. I went to all the people who couldn't afford me otherwise. But to them I could say: "I know you can't afford my normal fee, and I understand that. But for just one month, you have the opportunity to bring in the same program I charge $XX for all year, for just $X."

By the way, the proposition got me three bookings in a month that would otherwise generate zero or one. So, it was successful as far as it went. Now, I like having some down time in December. It doesn't suck anymore. I can get my business closed out for the current year, get my tax act together, and get ready for the next year. I can take a vacation without turning down any business. Hey, life is good in December … now.

But here's the point of a *Reason Why*: If your proposition is so generous that it will make people skeptical, you have to explain why you're doing it. "We're moving to a new location, and I'd rather practically give this stuff away than have to move it." "New inventory arrives next week, and I have to clear this stuff out to make room."

By the way, don't give a bogus *Reason Why*. Every year, thousands of stores hold a "Memorial Day Sale." What's up with that? I know, it's time for the new seasonal merchandise to come in, so we have to get rid of the old Winter stuff. Well, tell me that. Don't tell me you're having a sale just because it's Memorial Day and you want to do something nice for the country's economy. Horsepucky. If you give a reason for discounting, make it believable … and the truth.

You'll find a lot more on propositions in the chapter on Testing. The only way to be sure which proposition will work best for your product, service and market, you have to do some semi-scientific testing. (I said "semi" because I don't want to scare you off!)

The purpose of the proposition is to induce *FAST ACTION,* so don't give them a lot of time. Make the deadline clear and soon. And don't be flexible. I even say; "snooze you lose – why not call right now so you can't forget later?".

Action!

OK, you've got your reader salivating for your product or service! They know they have to act right now, or they'll miss out on your fantastic offering and proposition.

I can't tell you how many ads, letters, web sites … all kinds of marketing communications … fail to tell the reader how to get hold of the company. Or, just as bad, they make it difficult.

Give them as many ways to contact you as you can.

Phone Number

Toll Free Number

Web Site & Email Address

Fax Number

Toll Free Fax Number

Mail/Walk In Address

And when they do contact you, respond immediately.

If your telephone callers are greeted with "please press one if you're using a touch-tone phone …" stop advertising – you're wasting your money. You're getting your callers all excited, then letting them down. Trust me, at least half of the callers that get that recording hang up. Maybe not in the first :10 seconds (like I do), but within two minutes they're gone.

If you give an email address, check your email at least hourly, preferably twice as often. Send back confirmation that you got their message so they know they got through … and got in on the deal.

Better yet, use an autoresponder – instant gratification for your customer! These technological marvels respond automatically (hence the title!) 24 hours a day, 365 days a year, instantly.

When your prospect requests information, it is sent back immediately by email. Your brochure, product information, rate sheet … any document you want to make easily available … can be in your prospect's hand within seconds. And you didn't have to lift a finger.

Plus, you'll get a list of everyone who requested information from the autoresponder so you can follow up. This is one of the great marketing tools of the new millennium (whenever you may believe it actually starts!).

Make it easy. Make it fast. Make it painless. Make it cost-free. And be ready to field their response immediately. It would be a crying shame to take them this far, then lose them because the last step was a pain.

Chapter 4

Directors and Distractors

If you want your prospect to read every word of your communiqué ... and read them in the proper sequence(the Magic Formula) ... your graphic design must pull their eye to the first word. It must then take them by the hand, and walk them visually through every step of the sequence.

You do that with what I call "directors" and "distractors."

We are used to reading from top to bottom, and from left to right. That is a natural director. Anything that pulls us out of that pattern is a "distractor."

Distractors

<u>Your headline should be the first visual focal point of your communiqué</u>.

No matter whether you're writing a display ad, a sales letter ... even a web site ... the first thing the reader sees has to cut through all of the clutter in their minds and stop them in their tracks. Why? You want your reader to start at the beginning of your message and take the whole thing in ... in the proper motivational sequence.

So, your headline must be graphically distracting, appeal emotionally to the target prospect you're addressing, and lead them in to the next line of your message.

Graphically distracting means it gets top billing in your allotted space, and the typeface stands out from the rest of your copy.

Don't get into fancy, hard-to-read fonts. I've tested exotic fonts in the headline, thinking they would grab more attention. If they did, they didn't get more response … probably because they were harder to read.

And be careful with acronyms and abbreviations – be sure your audience knows what you're talking about.

I made the dual mistake of using a goofball font, and a term my audience didn't understand. I thought everyone knew what "R.O.I." meant. (In case you don't it stands for *Return On Investment*.)

I ran an ad in a magazine read by association management types, with R.O.I. as a headline, and got zero response. You know, to me that's just about enough to make me go slit my wrists. ZERO.

So, next time I spoke at one of their functions, I just flat out asked my audience; "Why did this ad draw zero response?" All at once, about a fourth of the audience said; "What's R.O.I.?"

I thought it was probably just the weird type that made them ignore it. I'm sure that didn't help, but when they don't know what the letters mean on top of it, you don't have a chance!

Important lesson learned; Keep it simple and clear.

If you are creating an ad that will be surrounded by other ads and articles, you want your distractor to pull your prospect's eye from the rest of the page, to the top of your ad. If you are writing a web page or a direct mail piece, you want your distractor to draw their eye to the beginning of your message so that they will receive your information in the proper sequence.

Remember that the first step in *The Magic Formula for Persuasion* is the "Attention" step. You have to break through all of the competing messages and mental clutter to get your communiqué noticed and read.

Your graphic "distractor" is a visual effect that you will use to draw your prospect's eyes away from all of the competing messages and into yours. There are a number of different kinds of graphic distractors you can use.

Which you use will depend on what media you are working with, and on space limitations.

If you are creating a print media advertisement, you will be paying for every square centimeter of space you occupy. If budget is a consideration for you(and I assume it is!), you have to use your space as efficiently as possible.

In direct mail, you can be more generous with your space. The distractor for any given page within the mail package can cover as much of the page as you think you need to grab the reader.

The three we'll concentrate on here are;

>Typographic
>Graphic Art
>Photographic

Typographic

The simplest and most efficient distractor is a headline set in a stand-out typeface.

In print media advertising, where every square centimeter has to be used efficiently, the bold type headline serves the dual purpose of providing a graphic distractor, while providing words for your message at the same time.

When you read a newspaper, your eye scans the page for information of interest to you. The eye becomes trained to look at photographs and headlines.

Keep in mind that people read type they are comfortable with first. As they scan the page, they're looking for news and information. Ads with goofball borders and shapes may be distracting, but the eye is repulsed by them! The eye is looking for photos and headlines, not advertising.

So, if your ad is going to be all text, the text should be the kind the readers' eyes are looking for. In most print media, that means large, bold headlines followed by 11 or 12 point type like you're reading right now. This is Times New Roman type. It's what you see in most magazines and newspapers. Your eye is comfortable with this type because you see it every day.

People read what they're comfortable with. Don't try to reinvent the printing press. You may think you're being very clever with modern or mystical type faces. And you may even create an artistic masterpiece ... but nobody's going to read it.

Hey, don't shoot me. I'm just telling you the way it is.

So you want your all-text ad to look like the other text your reader is scanning. You don't have to make your ad look entirely like an article. But you must draw the reader's eye, and make it easy for them to stay with you once you have.

Your headline should be set in a type face similar to the type the publication uses for its headlines.

Jump-start your sales...

New 8- tape audio program shares secrets that will lift response to your marketing communications of all kinds, *guaranteed*.

$50,000 Business Makeover

Try it, use it for 60 days. If you don't see 100-times the $97 price in value, return it for a full no-questions-asked refund.

Order before 10/15, and receive a free copy of the book *Shoestring Marketing*. Keep it as a gift ... even if you return the tapes.

Full details and secure, online order at:

MagicFormula.com

Jump-start your sales...

New 8-tape audio program shares secrets that will lift response to your marketing communications of all kinds, *guaranteed*.

$50,000 Business Makeover

Try it, use it for 60 days. If you don't see 100-times the $97 price in value, return it for a full no-questions-asked refund.

Order before 10/15, and receive a free copy of the book *Shoestring Marketing*. Keep it as a gift ...even if you return the tapes.

Full details and secure, online order at:

MagicFormula.com

For the moment, I want you to look just at the headlines in these ads. We're talking about distractors here. Which one do you think is more effective?

The ad on the left uses the same type as the body text, but bold and slightly larger. This is the way many newspapers set their articles. Of course, there is information in an ad that would not be present in an article. But this looks enough like an article to keep the reader comfortable, yet enough like an advertisement that the reader doesn't feel duped.

The ad on the right uses a heavier bold, in a sans serif type. There is a whole chapter about type faces, so I won't go into the differences here. But visually, you can see that the ad on the right has a stronger distractor with just that difference.

It's a heavy type face, plus it takes up two lines. So, it uses more of the space you're paying for, but it does grab the eye very effectively. Even if this is not the way the publication sets their headlines, it still looks like a headline from other publications, and it's still comfortable for the reader.

What a difference a simple change can make!

In brochures, flyers, or on web pages, you can use bold type headlines the same way. The idea is to pull the reader's eye to the beginning of your message.

Graphic Art

A clear graphic can make an excellent distractor. If you use a graphic as a distractor, that graphic becomes your headline.

So make sure you're using the graphic to start telling your story, not just to draw the eye. You see it all the time: advertisers use some cutesy graphic to draw your eye, but it has nothing to do with the product or service being promoted.

One of the worst I ever saw was a checker board design with three pairs of shoes in the middle. It was a "curiosity" headline for a bank. Problem was, the graphic has nothing to do with banking! The readers that would be drawn to that graphic are people looking for new shoes, or possibly, for linoleum tile.

Once a reader is drawn in by a graphic, then disappointed because the advertiser just used it to draw them in, they feel duped and they're gone.

What, you don't think people are that sensitive? Believe me, it doesn't take much to insult your prospects' intelligence. And if they're insulted, they're gone.

Photographic

Nothing, but nothing, works better than a good photograph to draw the eye. It is the ultimate distractor … if you do it right.

There is a whole chapter on photographs elsewhere in this manual. It's that important, and they're that good as distractors.

The down side, is that you have to use a lot of your space to make a photograph effective. It's usually worth it, but you have to balance your budget, too. Plus, good photography is not inexpensive. Whether you do your own photo shoots, or buy stock photography, it's going to add significantly to the cost of your ad or piece.

Captions

If you do use a photo, you absolutely must give it a caption. Promise me you will?

Why? It's natural for people to scan their newspaper page looking for interesting articles and stories. As they scan, they will be drawn to photographs: Especially photographs of people just like themselves.

When their eye zeros in on the photograph, the next natural step is to look beneath it to read the caption. If there is nothing there, they will go back to their scan pattern.

> **IMPORTANT LESSON:** *If your photo gets their attention, they will automatically look under it for a caption. Don't miss that opportunity to keep and build their interest.*

If you use a photo as your distractor, it becomes your headline. It is the attention step.

The caption is then the next step in *The Magic Formula*. Ideally, the photo demonstrates the benefit you are promising. The caption reinforces what they just saw, or explains it if it is at all unclear.

I mentioned that there should only be one real distractor in your ad or promo piece. The reason for that, is that you want your distractor to start the reader at the beginning of the message. If there are other distractors scattered around, their eye doesn't know where to go first.

If they are drawn to a point other than the beginning, they start receiving your message out of sequence. They get confused, and they leave.

Directors

Once the reader is drawn to the beginning of the message, you want them to receive every word of it, and in the proper sequence.

Directors are graphic elements that help keep the eye in a "normal" flow.

Some of the things that you can use to keep the eye in sequence;

> "Normal" flow
> Type faces
> Bullet Points
> Spacing
> Indentation
> Justification

Notice that none of these directors are tricks or slight of hand. You don't have to get cute to draw people in and keep them reading. Using graphic elements that your prospect is comfortable with will get you a lot farther than balloons and stars.

People read what they're comfortable with, so keep it simple.

Our normal flow, or natural director, is the pattern of reading left to right, top to bottom. If everything you write is just riveting, the reader will want to start at the beginning and follow that natural pattern.

But, alas, not all that you write is riveting. Don't be insulted – it's just that your prospects are not nearly as fascinated with what you have to say as you are. So, you have to use graphic design to keep their eye flowing through your message. You don't want them to just jump around and read the message in random sequence.

You already know that selling is a sequential process. What you're trying to do here, is keep them in that sequence. You went to all of the effort to put your message in the proper order, you want them to receive it that way.

Notice how the type and graphic design help your eye flow easily through the sequential message in this ad;

> # Live Your Dream!
>
> ## "The acreage you've always wanted may be more affordable than you realize."
>
> - Generous credit limits stretch your buying power ...
> - Low interest rates mean affordable payments ...
> - Pre-approval lets you negotiate with cash in hand ... from $50,000 to $2.3 Million
>
> These Low Rates Won't Last Forever
> Call Beth Gordon <u>Today</u>
> or have your realtor make the call for you.
>
> **Community Mortgage**
>
> *Here To Help You Live Your Dream*
> Community Mortgage Services, Inc.
> Beth Gordon - 770-410-4950 Ext 226
> Pager - 404 871-8927
> www.liveyourdream.com
>
> Georgia Residential Mortgage Lender

The largest, single element is the headline with it's subhead. The headline "Live Your Dream" is in the largest, boldest type – probably on the whole page, if this is in a newspaper. That should draw readers in, and start them automatically at the beginning of the sequence.

There is plenty of white space around the copy, both to make it easy to read and to make this ad stand out on a page that will be jam packed with competing ads and articles.

The headline and subhead provide the "attention" and "promise" steps of *The Magic Formula*. Of course, those are the first two things we want them to read.

Then, the bullet points take the eye from the subhead into the "proof" step. One by one the eye is led through these short bites of information, easily flowing from one to the next with the help of bullets as guide posts.

Please, don't get too cute with your bullets. If you have a graphic design program … even just a word processing program … you have access to dozens of bullets. Actually, any graphic can be turned into a bullet. I've seen people use their logo as bullets. Come on!

If you get too cute, like with that pointing finger bullet (☞), or the ever-popular arrow (➜), or any of a thousand other possibilities, you're adding graphic elements that have nothing to do with the message, and that can actually become distractors. They can pull the eye into the bullet points before you mean to.

I recently spent a day with a consulting client, almost half of which was spent on reworking their old ads. After about three hours, the client looked at me and said; Your designs look really simple. Is that what you're trying to get us to do? Yes!

> **IMPORTANT LESSON:** *Simple is better. Don't be tempted to use all of the tools in your graphics or word processing program. They clutter the space, draw the eye out of its normal flow, and make your ads and pieces look amateurish.*

Remember that people are lazy. They will only read what they're comfortable with.

They're used to reading bold headlines, then 11 or 12 point serif body text. Headlines in goofball fonts scream "ADVERTISING." They're not there to read the advertising, so they immediately filter the goofball fonts out.

A photo followed by an explanatory caption is normal reading. A headline above a photo will probably be missed altogether. They see the photo first, then look under it for a caption. That's just normal eye flow, and the reading pattern they're used to.

Bullets that gently guide the eye are normal. Balloons, fingers, airplanes, stars … those things all interrupt their normal flow rather than facilitate it. You want to keep them flowing smoothly through your message, not stopping to admire your word processing expertise.

White space gives the eye rest at the beginning of each line. If your text is jammed into a little box, with little or no margin, the eye has a hard time finding starting points to begin each new line.

That's why centered text is more difficult to read than left justified text. When the text is all justified left, it's easy for the eye to find the beginning of each line.

Breaking extensive text into small blocks gives the eye a guide to follow. This page is broken into paragraphs to help your eye keep its place. I use a blank line between each paragraph to separate them. Where text must be jammed into smaller space, you would want to indent the first line of each paragraph to help the eye.

None of this is rocket science. Yet, I see ads, letters, brochures … you name it … that are so disorganized, the eye doesn't know where to start or where to go next.

Over-designing makes a piece difficult to read. Don't assume people are so fascinated with what you have to say, that they're going to be willing to work at reading it. It won't happen. They're gone by about the second paragraph.

Keep it simple and clean. Use recognizable fonts and graphic elements to keep the reader comfortable and flowing in sequence. Don't interrupt that flow once you've drawn them into your space. If anything is going to distract their eye, make it the first element in your space, and make it the "attention" step of *The Magic Formula*.

Then take them by the hand, and walk them step-by-step through the rest of the message … in sequence … and you'll hold more people through the "proposition" step, and get more response.

Chapter 5

Layout

The human eye is automatically attracted to larger blocks of space over smaller blocks of space.

So, as you consider the layout for your page, space ad, or web page, keep in mind that the spot where you want they eye to start should dominate the page space-wise. Remembering *The Magic Formula*, you want the reader to start at the beginning of your message.

Eye Patterns

Research has shown that, when confronted with a new page, people start at a point about one-third of the way down the page, just right of center. Then, they go to the upper left-hand corner, and scan in a "Z" pattern unless a distractor stops them. (You read about Directors and Distractors earlier in this manual.)

The distractors most likely to draw the eye are 1.) Photographs, and 2.) Large blocks of space. A photograph that occupies a large block of space is by far the best distractor.

So, if you want to stop the eye, especially on a printed page filled with competing messages, the ideal layout for a space ad is the 2/3 - 1/3 grid, as shown here;

The photo or graphic would be centered in the upper 2/3 of the space. It doesn't have to occupy all of the space ... in fact, it's best if it does not. A photo or graphic surrounded by a large block of white space will draw the eye from almost anything else on the printed page.

"But Larry," you say: "That uses up most of the space I'm paying for – there's hardly any room left for copy!" You are correct, grasshopper.

Keep in mind that the "attention" step is the most important. The hardest part of advertising is getting your prospects' attention. I have no problem with using two thirds of my space to grab attention.

So you have to write tighter copy – most writers get too wordy anyway. It's a good exercise to have to say the same thing with half as much copy!

What your kids don't learn in school...

Imagine, classes your kids look forward to! Get them in on the action at Twin Dragons, and they'll learn more than just martial arts skills;

- **Self-confidence**
- **Perseverance**
- **Respect**
- **Fitness**
- **Discipline**
- **Flexibility**

Summer special - FREE uniform with prepaid 3-month membership. You can start this afternoon!

Twin Dragons Tae Kwon Do Institute
More than just skills ... character traits
1145 Hwy 12(@ I-10) • **Vidor** • Call 783-9332

Another alternative that is a close second to the 2/3 - 1/3 grid, is the opposite. Use the upper one third for your photo or graphic, and the lower two thirds for copy. This is especially useful in a tall/narrow layout;

It's important to maintain the character of the photograph. If you are using a smaller format, the natural assumption would be that you simply reduce the photograph. Not so!

Remember, the best photographs are humans making eye contact with the reader. If you simply reduce a photo, you may reduce the face to the point where eye contact is lost. It is wiser to crop the photograph – too leave the face as large as possible, cutting out peripheral details ... as long as doing that does not change the character of the photograph.

Here's the same photo from the first ad, reduced then cropped;

By cropping this one, it definitely lost some of the character of the original. But you can see what I'm saying about eye contact. In the sample on the left, it's reduced to a point where eye contact is lost. In fact, is can get difficult to tell that the model is a young man. The sample on the right makes eye contact, gives the reader a model they can identify with, and still demonstrates a karate move.

The point is, if you are trying to put a photo into a smaller space, try cropping in stead of just reducing so you don't lose the emotional connection with the reader.

The 2/3 - 1/3 and 1/3 - 2/3 grids are not the only possible grids. You can split your space up any way you want. But remember, the eye will be drawn to the dominant graphic feature. The largest block of space will usually be the first visual focal point. That's where your reader will start. That graphic feature should serve the purpose of drawing the reader's attention – the first(and critical) step in the Magic Formula.

Text Only Ads

Don't get me wrong. You don't always need a photo or graphic to draw attention. You may not be able to afford the amount of space it takes to run a photo. But the same rules of graphic design apply. Even though your ad is made up completely of text, it will still consist of blocks of space. Those blocks have to be planned carefully to draw the eye to the beginning of your message, then walk the reader by the hand to the next component, and so on.

What your kids don't learn in school...

Imagine, classes your kids look forward to! Get them in on the action at Twin Dragons, and they'll learn more than just martial arts skills;

- Self-confidence
- Respect
- Discipline
- Perseverance
- Fitness
- Flexibility

Summer special - FREE uniform with prepaid 3-month membership. You can start this afternoon!

Twin Dragons Tae Kwon Do Institute
More than just skills ... character traits
1145 Hwy 12(@ I-10) • **Vidor** • Call 783-9332

This ad is all text, yet it still fits the 1/3 - 2/3 formula. The headline is the dominant feature. Just those seven words occupy one third of the space we're paying for. That's OK. Remember, the headline or first visual focal point is responsible for up to 80% of the success of the ad. If it doesn't draw readers, the rest of the space was a waste altogether! To only use one third of the space you're paying for is a bargain!

As the space gets smaller, you have to start editing out text. You can't keep reducing your type size until it's illegible;

> **What your kids don't learn in school...**
>
> Imagine, classes your kids look forward to! Get them in on the action at Twin Dragons, and they'll learn more than just martial arts skills;
>
> - Self-confidence • Respect • Discipline
> - Perseverance • Fitness • Flexibility
>
> Summer special - FREE uniform with prepaid 3-month membership. You can start this afternoon!
>
> **Twin Dragons** Tae Kwon Do Institute
> More than just skills ... character traits
> 1145 Hwy 12(@ I-10) • **Vidor** • Call 783-9332

If you reduce this as to a smaller size, the text starts to get difficult to read – especially for people my age. When you go to a smaller size, you have to reduce the amount of text rather than the size of the text.

Therefore, your objectives for the ad will probably change. The ad above tries to sell the concept of Karate as a positive force in the child's life, then makes an offer of a free uniform with a 3-month membership. As the ad gets smaller, you may have to simply sell the proposition;

> **Free Uniform**
>
> Summer special - FREE uniform with prepaid 3-month membership. You can start this afternoon!
>
> **Twin Dragons** Tae Kwon Do Institute
> More than just skills ... character traits
> 1145 Hwy 12(@ I-10) • **Vidor** • Call 783-9332

Now we're getting really small. But you can see that the headline still occupies one third of the space. The type is still legible. But there's a lot less of it.

Actually, this is smaller than I would want to go. There comes a point where you're just not buying enough space to deliver a message and still give the reader enough response information.

Again, the cardinal rule: You must give your prospect all the information they need to make an intelligent decision about the action you're asking them to take. Do you think the last ad gives enough information to send a reader in ready to make a three month commitment? I don't.

But, how about this;

Free Pass

Try one class on us - no obligation. See for yourself how you can build self-confidence, fitness and flexibility. Stop in today: 5:30PM

Twin Dragons Tae Kwon Do Institute
More than just skills ... character traits
1145 Hwy 12(@ I-10) • **Vidor** • Call 783-9332

We have a small space, so we're asking for a small commitment. This sells the offer first, with a brief reference to the overall benefits of Tae Kwon Do. But we're not going for a three month commitment like the earlier ads did. We just don't have enough space to explain that offer sufficiently.

Be realistic about what you can reasonably sell in the space you're buying. The smaller the space, the less copy you can fit in, and the less of a commitment you can ask of your prospect.

Notice that this small space ad still uses the 1/3 - 2/3 grid. Three blocks of text, each occupying one third of the space. But the headline is large and bold, making it the dominant feature. Anyone who sees this ad will surely start at the words "Free Pass." Not only is it a visual focal point, it has the added strength of the power word "Free." There's more about that in the chapter titled *Killer Copy*.

The relationship between designer and copy writer

I've worked with a number of newspaper groups, and there's always a common problem: The advertising sales people have a completely different idea of how an ad should look, from the graphic design people.

Often, the sales person (sometimes with input from the client, sometimes not) writes the copy. They've met with the client, and they have sold an idea. But, when the production people get hold of it, the whole thing changes somehow. The ad they come back with looks nothing like what the sales person and the client envisioned.

So, the sales person has to either go back and sell the new ad, or have a thumb-wrestling match (usually 2 out of 3) with the designer to get them to change the ad. With deadlines looming, production people are anxious to get on to the next project. The sales person is worried about the next sale … or if there'll ever be one with this client!

Or worse: The sales person brings in some concept that production person knows sucks. It's an abortion. Now, there's a diplomatic standoff; The graphics person knows this ad shouldn't come to fruition, yet he or she is hesitant to tell the sales person that he is a ninny for dreaming it up.

Usually, the sales person wins. After all, sales is who brings in the revenue.

You've seen the ads that were designed by an overly-creative sales person. Maybe the client came up with the idea … but a sane sales person would have (at least, should have) talked them out of it.

You're a team

Whether you're the copy writer or the designer, whether you come up with the concepts or have to execute for someone who did(I know, sometimes you'd like to execute *them*!), it's important to work together with the singular goal of making your ad SELL.

If it doesn't motivate the prospect to act, it doesn't matter if it wins awards for graphic excellence, or conceptual superiority. All that matters, is that people are drawn to the ad, read it, understand the message, and ACT. Nothing else matters.

Sequence

I give my graphic designer a script. Just like in a broadcast ad.

Now, when you write a script for a broadcast ad, you expect your talent to read it in the sequence in which you wrote it, do you not? The listener/viewer has no choice but to receive your commercial message in the sequence in which it is presented. There's no skipping around or going back. Boom, boom, boom. That's the message.

What I want my graphic designer to do, is to present my script so the reader will have no choice but to read it in the proper sequence. Her job is to draw the reader's eye to the top of the space and read my headline or check out my photo. Then, I want their eye drawn to the next line of copy, then the next.

This is simply *The Magic Formula* you've already seen. If you agree that selling is a sequential process, you have to agree that the designer's job is to direct the eye through that sequence.

> **By the way:** *This all applies to other promo pieces, too. I'm talking primarily about ad layouts here, but your brochure has to stand out in the pile of mail. Your flyer has to make them stop and look.*

You want your ad to stand out in the crowd.

So, the designer's first job is to create something that will pull the reader in, even if it is surrounded by other ads.

In a sea of "creative" ads, the best way to stand out is with simple, clean ads. Surround your headline or headline photo/graphic with lots of white space. Make it take up at least 1/4, up to 2/3 of your space.

Remember; that first visual focal point, your headline or photo/graphic, is 80% responsible for the effectiveness of your ad. Don't handicap yourself by making it too small to be noticed in a sea of competing type and designs.

That's the attention step. If it doesn't work, nothing else matters … because nothing else will get read!

Then, you have to take the reader by the hand, and walk them step by step through your message. And you want to keep them in the sequence so they get it all … in the order in which they need to receive it to be able to make an intelligent decision.

Don't leave it up to them to find their way around. Direct them through the text with bullets, type changes, and some of the other tricks in the chapter on graphic design.

Take a look at the ad on the next page;

> # Let 'em run wild.
>
> *Give them room to grow, trees to climb and places to explore. All without wreaking havoc on your pocketbook.*
>
> *With interest rates as low as they are now, there's never been a better time to move to the country. Whether you're planning to build or buy a home, we know where to begin.*
>
> *We've been lending money for farms and homes in the country for more than 80 years. Call us, we're the experts.*
>
> ## Country Mortgages
> by Farm Credit

This ad was done by someone who gets it.

Notice the alignment of elements(see chapter: Layouts that look like C.R.A.P.). The graphic, the text, and the company name are justified and aligned to the left, but that whole block is indented by 1/3 of the space. The headline is centered.

But, look at how much of the space the graphic and headline occupy. It's more than half of the ad – I like that. Hey, the headline and graphic are what determine whether it gets read or not. Half or 2/3 of the space is a fair investment to me.

And, notice how much white space there is in this ad, particularly around the graphic. This will make this ad stand out on a page full of ads and articles. It will be an oasis of calm in the storm.

So, their grid made a margin down the left side. The headline interrupted the margin, but everything else aligned with it. It's attractive, organized, easy to follow.

And, it follows *The Magic Formula* ... although, it leaves out a specific proposition. It ends with "Call us, we're the experts." Well, ain't we grand? I would like this a lot more if it said "You'll be one step closer to owning your dream home when you get together with our mortgage experts."

OK, I've digressed. There's more on how to say "we're experts" without saying "ain't we grand?" in the chapter titled Killer Copy.

Get Organized

Before you start to lay things out on the page or in your space, set up a grid pattern you can use to align the elements. It should start with the largest, single block of space at the top left. Then, use it to work the eye sequentially through your message.

Copy writer, give your designer a script – give them the message in sequence, and tell them you want the thing set up so the reader's eye is drawn through the message in sequence. You don't want them bouncing around, getting your message out of order.

If they get a step out of sequence, the odds of making a sale or getting a response go down the tubes fast.

Chapter 6

Photographs

Do you like this photo?

Don't make the classic mistake ...

It was a bit of a trick question. It really doesn't matter whether you like it or not.

It's a mistake to choose photography ... or any other element ... based solely on your personal preferences. The only thing that matters is whether the photo will draw your prospects' eyes, and make an emotional connection.

First, a reminder: The first step in *The Magic Formula* is to grab your prospects' attention with an emotional connection.

When you use a photo in an ad, it becomes the headline. It is the attention step.

Nothing draws the eye like a good photograph.

Needless to say, a good color photograph is ideal. But I understand budgets. A good black and white photo will outsell a bad color photo any day, so don't be intimidated by competitors who spring for color.

The decision whether to use photos is a strictly economic one. Photographs, whether color or black and white, take up considerable space. If you're talking print advertising, the photo can take up 20% to 50% of your space. In fact, I like to use up to 2/3 of the space for the photo.

When you're paying by the inch, the space a photo occupies is clearly more expensive than just a strong headline.

Add to that the cost of the photography itself, and you're talking a big difference in expense.

Where to get good photographs

Your own shoot

This is definitely the expensive way! But if you want to show a model using and enjoying your product, it may be the only way to get the shot you need. The best photos show a model enjoying the benefit you are promising in the ad. A custom photo involving your product may very well be worth the expense.

Stock Photography

If your product doesn't look any different from your competitors', you may be able to find stock photography that conveys your message.

For example, I recently did an ad for an optometrist. We needed a model in glasses. You can't see the brand on a pair of glasses. We found a perfect stock photograph we were able to use for a lot less than it would have cost to hire a model and photographer for a shoot. (It's the photo at the beginning of this chapter.)

You may have stock photography in your graphics or even word processing program. Read the conditions of use very carefully before you use them in print. Just because they're on your hard drive doesn't necessarily mean you're free to use them in commerce. You usually have to pay a per use fee for stock photography.

Unauthorized use of a professional photographer's work can result in a lawsuit … and you will lose. Don't do it.

More people will be drawn to a good photo, and believe the story it tells, than just a headline.

Photos represent reality to the reader. Deep down inside, they have to know that the people are models, and that it's really not a slice of somebody's actual life. Nonetheless, people see photos as the truth.

IMPORTANT LESSON: *Graphics and cartoons represent*

fantasy, so don't think that cute clip art that came with your work processing software will accomplish the same thing as a good photo.

(Exception: Technical drawings, where appropriate, can be very effective.)

Once drawn to the photo, they will go directly to the caption. Your photo becomes the headline, the caption explains and drives the benefit home.

Always include a caption under the photo. People are used to looking for the caption under photos. Don't let them down.

And don't think you can change their reading pattern.

Don't place your headline above the photo. Most readers will continue down from your photo. You spent all that money to get a great photo, and you bought all of that ad space to run it.

Don't make the mistake of losing your momentum by placing the first text you want them to read in the wrong place.

The first text you want the prospect to read belongs directly below the photo. Nowhere else.

Is it worth the expense?

Will the extra readership make up for the cost of the space? Again, test carefully - do the math.

Photos of humans will increase readership <u>IF you use them properly</u>;

1.) The model should be looking directly into the "iris" of the camera.

A good model working with a good photographer can make direct eye contact … and therefore, an emotional connection with the reader. As your prospect scans the pages in their newspaper, or the pieces in their mail, the photos that look them strait in the eye will grab their attention first.

There's a certain level of trust in people who look you in the eye. (Yes, it applies to photographs, too.)

2.) The model should reflect the emotional mood of the piece.

If you're playing on the emotion of fear, your model would be cowering in a corner. If your emotional appeal is greed, they should be enjoying the wealth they attained when they started using your product.

The emotional mood of the piece is something you should have planned before you even think about photography. It will affect what kind of scene you want to set, what type of model you'll look for, how they'll be dressed and posed, and what kind of facial expression they'll show.

3.) Make sure the reader can see the models' eyes.

If you have limited space, crop the photo, don't reduce it. You want that direct eye contact with the reader.

If you have to use a small photo, don't try to use a full-length view of the model. You may have to zoom in on just a head shot to capture that eye contact. You can't make the emotional connection, nor establish trust, if the reader can't clearly see the model's eyes.

4.) The photo should directly demonstrate your key benefit.

How many photos have you seen that had nothing to do with the product or service the ad or brochure was trying to sell? Don't use photo's just for their attention value, use them to directly sell your product or service or not at all.

Don't just show your product, show it in use by a satisfied "customer." The model should be operating or using your product, with their facial expression reflecting the emotional appeal. Will people be happy, excited, satisfied, relieved ... whatever they will feel when they use your product or service, they should see in the face of your model(s).

5.) The model should be someone just like the reader you want to attract.

If your product or service is gender-specific, the models should be the same gender as the prospect. You may think that attractive women would attract a male audience to your male-specific products' ads. They may attract male readers, but not for any reason that has anything to do with your product.

Exception: Victoria's Secret attracts a male audience very effectively. But, they're selling the products the models are wearing. I don't know how many men really think their wives or significant others are going to look anything like the models when they put on the lingerie, but I know I notice their ads!

Don't get caught up in the idea of using super-models(or similarly "beautiful people"). If the image in the ad is too different from the prospect, they will see it as fantasy and not as reality they're willing to plunk down money for.

And, if you use a celebrity, it should be someone they can relate to. Wilford Brimley was easy to relate to in the series of ads he did for a diabetes medication. It's a little harder to relate to Suzanne Summers selling exercise equipment.

In the chapter on layout, you'll see more about where and how photos should be placed in your pieces.

If you use a good photo, it will be the first thing your prospect sees. And that is as it should be. You used the photo to draw their attention.

So, if the photo draws their attention, you have to understand that the photo is where their eye begins to take in your message. It is the attention step in *The Magic Formula*, and they will make it their geographic starting point.

The photo must be placed at the beginning of your communique. Otherwise, you will draw the eye to the wrong starting point. In other words, if you put the photo halfway down the page or space, their eye will start there and move down. Anything placed above your photo will probably be missed. You are asking the reader to leave their normal pattern, and they will resist.

So, they will start in the middle of your message, missing the important first steps. They're lost and confused from the get-go. Once they're lost and confused, they're soon gone.

Don't expect the reader to work hard to read your piece and to get your message.

And, don't over estimate their interest in what you have to say. If you start them at the wrong starting point, and they get lost as a result, they lose interest in your message real fast.

A good photo is the ideal way to start them at Step 1. It's the attention step. At the same time, it can deliver the promise and proof steps. They're expensive, and they use a lot of space. But, done correctly, they can convey most of your message very powerfully.

Stock Photography Sources

wonderfile.com

masterfile.com

brandxpictures.com

gettyimage.com

Chapter 7

The "Art" of Typography

The type you use in your marketing materials determines whether it will be easy to read ... or some degree of difficult.

So, let's start with a question; Do you want to make it difficult for your prospect to read your message? Well, duh. Of course you don't. Yet, I see perfectly compelling copy destroyed by the improper or inappropriate use of type faces and styles.

The Battle

There seems to be a battle for control between copy writers and graphic designers.

Time and time again, I see perfectly good copy destroyed by graphic design. And, in many cases, the design component that destroys the copy is the type.

Take a quick glance at the headline below, and tell me what you read;

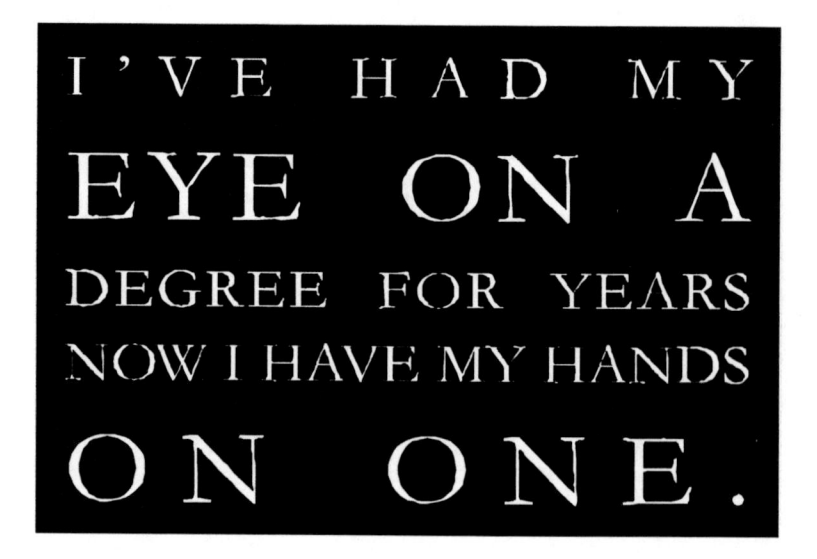

> **I'VE HAD MY EYE ON A DEGREE FOR YEARS NOW I HAVE MY HANDS ON ONE.**

When I put this up on the screen in my workshops, and people invariably read;

Eye on a on one.

Now, imagine you're reading the morning paper. You're looking for stories that interest you, and you read "Eye on a on one." What do you do?

Do you stop and read the ad to find out just what the heck they're talking about? NO! It has no meaning, so you pass it by.

This was an actual headline, set just like they had it(with the dreaded reverse type). It was for a major university, directed at adult learners. Unfortunately, it only spoke to dyslexic adults!

The designer laid the type out in an attractive design, but in the process, made certain words stand out. The words "eye on a on one" jump out at you, while the others nestle into the background.

I'm sure the designer was very proud of his or her work. Heck, the university spent thousands running the ads, so they must have thought it was clever too.

What are these people thinking? Doesn't anyone actually look at this stuff, and say: "Wait a minute, I thing "eye on a on one" jumps out at the reader, and the message is lost."? Apparently not!

Here it is again: The dreaded;

REVERSE TYPE

Graphic designers seem to love this stuff. Check your morning newspaper, and you'll see it in all kinds of ads.

The thinking is, it's the reverse of most type on the page, and will therefore stand out. Again, grasshopper; people are reading the morning paper for the news. They're not looking for something "different." In fact, their eye is repelled by something "different," because they know it's not news; its advertising.

Reverse type is hard to read. The eye has to turn itself inside-out to make the stuff out. That makes reverse type a doubly-whammy: Hard to read, clearly not the news the reader is in the paper to read.

"But," you might ask: What about using reverse type to make certain points stand out in my brochures or flyers, where the reader is not looking for news. (They must be fascinated with your info, reading your brochure in great detail to learn all they possibly can about you, right?)

Reverse type creates a graphic "distractor." Yes, it draws the eye, and can be used to help guide the eye through your text. But simple black headlines and bold subheads, with a bullet point here or there, will do it just as effectively and still be easy to read.

If you absolutely must use reverse type, limit the text to a very few words. Use a large, extremely bold type face so it shows up clearly. Otherwise, it will be difficult to read.

EASY TO READ should be your meditation mantra. Just before you sit down to "create," close your eyes for twenty minutes and quietly whisper: "Easy to read, Easy to read." Because, when it comes to selecting typefaces and styles, that's the most important factor.

Typefaces can add personality to a piece, yes. But be careful that the "personality" isn't too cute and too difficult to decipher.

There's a great typeface called "Pepita." You've undoubtedly seen it or a similar typeface on menus in Mexican restaurants.

Here's what it looks like in a short sentence.

YOU'VE PROBABLY SEEN THIS ONE IN ORIENTAL RESTAURANTS. IT'S CALLED MANDARIN.

One or two words in a headline is enough of this kind of thing to give your piece some personality. But don't overdo it. Large blocks of text would be nearly impossible to read.

Even at that, I've seen many Oriental and Mexican restaurant signs you can hardly read because of the typeface. People are driving by at 30, 40, 70 miles an hour. They'd better be able to understand your message at a quick glance.

Headlines

The headline ... that first handful of words your reader sees ... can be 80% responsible for the success of your marketing piece. Why? Because, if it's not compelling to the reader, they have no reason to drop what they're doing and read the rest of your piece.

But good copy alone cannot a powerful headline make. It has to be legible, and it has to draw the reader's eye. Remember *The Magic Formula*: Your reader has to receive your information in the proper sequence if you want them to respond. The headline is the first step in the formula. So, you want to make sure they read it first.

There are a number of things you can do to draw the eye to the beginning of your message: the headline. You can use photography or graphics if you can afford that extra space. Or, you can simply print it in type that dominates the space and demands attention.

Will it pass "The Indy 500 Test?"

In 1998, Indy car owner and drive Eddie Cheever Jr., was having a hard time finding a primary sponsor for his entry in the Indianapolis 500.

In case you're not familiar with that race, it is the largest sporting event in America. Between the live and television audiences, millions of people are glued to the action for over three hours. The potential exposure for a sponsor is enormous ... IF their team is competitive in the race. If your car gets eliminated through mechanical problems or an accident, your exposure ends. If your car runs at the end of the order, your exposure is limited at best.

Back to Eddie Cheever Jr. He found a major sponsor in Rachel's Potato Chips just two weeks before race day. You are probably aware of the fact that "Rachel's" is not a household word. Well, it wasn't in 1998, either. Sponsoring Eddie in the Indy 500 was to be their springboard to fame and fortune. A one-time investment in a primary sponsorship at Indy had to take their whole marketing budget for the year.

"So," you might ask, "what the heck does that have to do with type faces?"

If you go online, you can still find photos of Eddie Cheever's Gforce Rachel's Potato Chip car. The primary side panel is emblazoned with the name: Rachel's.

Oh, by the way. This car dominated the television coverage of the race. Eddie Cheever won the race. Yeah, the big one – he won it with his last-minute sponsor's name on the car's side. It was a Cinderella story.

He didn't just win it, he led 76 of the 200 laps. He was on the television screen more than any other car in the race. Good news for Rachel's, right?

So, why aren't they a household word?

Some day, go online and find a picture of the car(It's easier to find a picture of the car than it is to find Rachel's Potato Chips!).

You'll see that the name "Rachel's" is in a modern, cutesy type face that's hard to read standing still. Imagine how hard it must be to read it when it goes by at 200 miles per hour!

> **The Lesson:** *Imagine that your headline will be on the side of an Indy car, and that you'll be paying hundreds of thousands of dollars to put it in front of that huge audience. Will they be able to read it?*

PS: You may be wondering why I didn't just go ahead an put a picture of the car in for you. The Indy Racing League is very protective of their photos. Copyright laws made it prohibitively expensive to include a photo.

A Case Study

A few years ago, a program participant submitted a brochure for me to critique. In my *Marketing Makeover* workshops, I always get pieces in advance from audience members to use as examples in the program.

As always, I had made the brochure over prior to the presentation, so I could show "before" and "after" versions.

This was a simple, two-color brochure. Since I'm printing in black on white here, you can't see the color. But you don't have to to be able to understand the importance of clear, simple, easy-to-read type in the example.

The cover headline on the original brochure looked like this;

Is there **SOMETHING** *you* **NEED TO KNOW?**

When I first saw the piece, I had two thoughts: 1.) Vague headline, and 2.) Graphic disaster.

I digress from type here, to talk about the vague headline ... but it's important to the story, so bear with me.

This company does market research for associations. This is how they find out what kind of products and services their members want them to provide. They make major decisions about the content of their product and service offerings, conventions and education programs based on this research.

The original headline was an obvious attempt at "curiosity." Tease the reader to look inside and find out what it is you're talking about. "Is there something you need to know" doesn't even tease, in my opinion. It's vague, not talking specifically to anyone.

So, I rewrote the copy to say: "Can you afford to guess what your members really want?"

By the way, at the presentation, the audience agreed that my headline was much more powerful. So, even though is was "my opinion," it was endorsed by 100 seminar participants!

I also reset the type to a straight-forward, sans serif type. I kept the underlines in, just to give it a little graphic interest without obliterating the type.

My makeover turned out like this;

Can you afford to GUESS what your members really want?

Well, they decided they liked the new headline … for the most part.

But, they gave it back to the same graphic designer, apparently charging them with the challenge; "Take this well-written text, and make it as difficult to read as you possibly can."

And they made it look like this;

Can You AFFORD to GUESS what YOUR MEMBERS WANT?

Never mind that they took out one word of the text to make it fit neatly in their little box shape. That alone is a sin.

> **IMPORTANT LESSON:** *Copy is king, in my world. Never cut words to fit space. Change the space, don't change the words.*

But taking out the word "really" didn't totally destroy the copy. I've seen cases where designers edited the copy to the point of totally changing the meaning to make it fit a space. At least they didn't go that far.

But they went back to the original, cutesy, hard-t-read style they had in the original brochure.

The battle between copy writer and graphic designer rages on!

Dominate the Space, Don't Confuse It

Your headline has to be crisp, clear, simple. The type should draw the eye inexorably to the top of your page or space.

The headline should contrast significantly with the rest of the copy. There's more on that elsewhere in this manual, so I won't get into contrast here. Suffice it to say; the headline should be different from the body copy.

Type Faces, Type Styles

"Type faces" refers to families of type. One of my favorite sans serif types for headlines and subheads is the family called "Swiss 721." You can't tell it from Helvetica(another type family), but I have a lot more styles available to me with the Swiss.

"Type style" refers to the appearance of the various character styles within the same family. Bold, condensed, and italics are all styles that may be applied to any type family.

In one of my favorite type families, Swiss 721, I have all of these styles available to me.

Swiss 721 bold condensed outline

Swiss 721 bold outline BT

Swiss 721 bold round BT

Swiss 721 black BT

Swiss 721 black condensed BT

Swiss 721 black extended BT

Swiss 721 black outline BT

Swiss 721 black round BT

Swiss 721 BT (normal)

Swiss 721 condensed BT

Swiss 721 extended BT

Swiss 721 heavy BT

Swiss 721 light BT

Swiss 721 light condensed BT

Swiss 721 light extended BT

Swiss 721 medium BT

Swiss 721 thin BT

You can also add bold or italics style to most of the same type faces. For example;

Swiss 721 BT

Swiss 721 BT Italic

Swiss 721 BT bold

Swiss 721 BT bold and italic

Look at all of the different effects you can achieve within one type family!

When I say you should stick to maximum two type faces in any piece, remember that you can apply all of these different styles to those type faces. Don't get carried away, though. You can see that if you used more than a few of these type styles, even though you're using the Swiss 721 type family, you can make your copy look like a ransom note!

You can also use different type sizes, kerning, letter spacing, word spacing, line spacing and leading. Stay with me here, it's not as complicated as it sounds. And you don't have to try to use all of these effects. In fact, it's best that you don't try too much.

Remember, you want your ad or promo piece to be clean, simple, and easy to read. You want to use type faces and styles to start your reader at the beginning of your message and guide them step by step through the sequence you want them to receive the information in.

Type size is just what it sounds like: how large each character is. Type size is measured in "points." This body copy is in 12 point type. It's a very readable size for body copy. 11 point is OK, 10 is getting too small. If you go to 13 or 14 for body copy, your type looks too "open."

A much larger type size will make your headline stand out, pulling the reader's eye to the top of your message. That's a good thing. Large or very bold type in the body copy can distract the eye out of your sequential message. Be very careful not to overdo type styles.

Kerning is the space between any two characters. It's a minute adjustment for the rare occasion that two characters didn't fall together well as a result of your computer's standard spacing. Unless you're an experience typesetter, you will probably never use this. But you may use overall letter spacing, which affects all of the characters in a block of text.

Letter spacing is just what it sounds like: the amount of space between characters. To show you an example, here are two copies of the same sentence, one with normal letter spacing, the other at 120%;

> Letter spacing refers to the space between characters. (Normal)

> Letter spacing refers to the space between characters. (120%)

You might play with this a little bit with your headlines. You can space your characters more or less than normal to make them fit the space allotted. If you have limited height, but width to spare in your layout, you may use a smaller type size in bold or black, and use letter spacing to make it occupy more width without using up height as a larger type size would;

Headline in 18 pt black

Headline in 18 pt black

Headline in 22 pt black

The first line is normally spaced 18 point type. The second is the same type at 125% letter spacing. It's the same height as line one, but occupies more horizontal space. The third line is what happens when you try to occupy more horizontal space with a larger type size. It also takes up considerably more height.

By the way, if you have height to burn, but you're limited on width, you can use less than normal letter spacing, or you can use a "condensed" style of your type face. Note this example occupies the same amount of width as the first 18 pt example above, but uses much more vertical space(height);

Headline in 36 pt black

This example is 36 pt black condensed BT at 60% of normal letter spacing. It's twice as tall(36pt vs 18pt) as the first example, but the same width.

I wouldn't use this, by the way – I think it's difficult to read. Condensing like this only works well with serif type faces. If you do it with a sans serif face, the serifs can bleed together(especially if you're preparing an ad to appear on newsprint) making it downright illegible;

Times Roman 36 pt condensed

OK, that's really hideous! Just wanted you to see what would happen.

Leading (pronounced: ledding) and Line Spacing are equivalent to Kerning and Letter Spacing, only you're affecting the distance between lines in stead of letters. You could use line spacing in stead of larger type to make your headline occupy more vertical space if you think it looks better. Just don't let lines get too far apart. The eye has to moved smoothly and comfortably from line to line just as it does from character to character. If you throw a big gap into the middle of a single thought, they may disconnect.

You can see the tremendous flexibility the designer has at his or her fingertips just using different styles of the same type face. When you look under "fonts" in your computer menu, you have dozens … some people have hundreds of type faces and styles available. Add to that leading, letter spacing and the rest, and you have more options than you could ever possibly use.

> **Important point:** *Don't mess with letter or line spacing in your body copy. "Normal" is the most readable spacing. Mess with it, and you'll make your piece harder to read. You know you don't want that.*

The examples I've shown you with the Swiss family(not Robinson) alone give you all the options you could ever need for headlines. To be honest with you, Swiss 721 is about all I use for headlines. And I don't use half of the styles that are available to me.

Occasionally, I do use a serif type face for a headline, especially if it will appear in a publication that uses serif type for their own story headlines and I want to keep the eye flowing to my ad as it would to the next story. You have to consider the other type you'll be either competing with or trying to fit in with.

Typically, I would use a progression to guide the eye through my type. Here's how most of my own ads make the progression;

Headline in Swiss 721 Black, 18 points

Subhead Swiss 721 Black 16 points

Body copy Times Roman 12 points

body copy Times Roman 12 points

body copy Times Roman 12 points

Action step Swiss 721 Black 14 points

See how your eye is naturally drawn to the top line, then eased through the message in sequence?

Typefaces, used properly, can add a mood or attitude to your marketing piece. They can make a party invitation look fun, an investment offer look solid. In the wrong hands, they can make the party look boring, and the investment offer frivolous … or worse.

Some rules;

1.) Keep it simple. (Is there a simpler rule than that?!)

Your type face should, at the very least, make it easy for your reader to comprehend your message. It should not interfere with or alter the intent of the message.

T t M m E e   T t M m E e

Serif   Sans Serif

2.) **Sans Serif** vs Serif Type Faces

Read this paragraph printed in two different typefaces, and tell me which one is easier to read;

> "Serif" typefaces have little "feet" at the bottom of each character. These "feet" help guide the eye from one character to the next. Serifs make it easier for the reader's eyes to flow through blocks of text. Times Roman is the classic serif typeface. It's worked for hundreds of years … I say stick with a proven winner.

"Serif" typefaces have little "feet" at the bottom of each character. These "feet" help guide the eye from one character to the next. Serifs make it easier for the reader's eyes to flow through blocks of text. Times Roman is the classic serif typeface. It's worked for hundreds of years … I say stick with a proven winner.

For some reason, you see more and more people using sans serif type in full pages of text. Many of the business letters I receive, brochures, even some newer magazine titles have given in to the temptation of looking modern in stead of being readable.

Just because your computer gives you the capability of using literally hundreds of type styles doesn't make it advisable. Every time you add a new type face to a printed piece, you detract from its readability. That's right, every time. Here's how your piece progresses from "clean and legible" to "might as well be in Greek";

Use more than two fonts within the same piece, and you start to look disorganized.

> Three - amateurish
> Four - sloppy
> Five - ransom note

Three typefaces make the reader shift gears too often. You piece begins to look like you just couldn't decide which type you liked, so you compromised yourself by using three.

Four typefaces make a piece look downright sloppy. Never mind that it's difficult to read. It looks disorganized. Remember that type is a graphic element, too. If you have a graphic or photo, a logo, plus four different type faces, the task of reading your piece is downright daunting!

People are used to reading black type on white paper. They're used to a bold headline, then an 11 or 12 point serif type face for body copy. Any time you stray from that format, you ask the reader to step outside their comfort zone at least a little.

Why do you think they will be willing to do that for you? You're intruding on their day to begin with when you push a promotional message in front of them. The least you can do is give them a comfortable, easy-to-read format.

If you look at the chapter titles in this manual, you'll see that sans serif typefaces called Swiss 721 Black BT. It's very bold, to make it stand out from body copy. So, you see a kind of hierarchy in the titles; I wanted you to read the titles first, then draw you in to the content at the beginning of the message. I don't want you to skip around.

Some type faces add a little whimsey, or make the page a little more casual;

Some "Comic" type face can add a little fun to the look of the page. Again, it stands out when used for just a few words. But how would you like to read a whole page of text printed in this same type face? The eye has a hard time following from character to character. When the eye has to work hard, the reader is less likely to read the whole message. Can you afford to let the reader decide what to skip?

Typefaces are designed with specific applications and "moods" in mind. A few popular typefaces that you may want to consider are;

Times Roman - the classic serif text typeface.
        Great for blocks of text.
        Mood - business.   Normal - **Bold**

Palatino - If Times Roman is just too formal for you,
        Palatino is a more modern yet very readable serif.
        Mood - modern business.   Normal - **Bold**

`Courier` - Looks like a typewriter, doesn't it?
        That makes it ideal for letters.
        People are still used to letters coming out of typewriters.
        This one is a must for all sales letters.
        Mood - typewriter (done by hand!)   `Normal` - `**Bold**`

Helvetica - The most popular sans serif typeface.
        Great for headlines, bold or normal.
        (Equivalent to the Arial typeface on your computer.
        Excellent for web page and email body copy in 12 point size.)
        Mood - clean, organized. Normal - **Bold**

AvantGuarde - A <u>more modern</u> sans serif typeface.
> If you just can't stand to use the more conservative Helvetica,
> this one is an updated style.
> Mood - modern, yet clean.   Normal - **Bold**

<u>A note about Courier</u>: no other statement causes more controversy in my workshops than "Courier is a must for sales letters." The younger the audience, the more argument I get over that one.

Here's the deal: You have to test with your own audience. In my experience, and in the experience of many of the top direct mail businesses, Courier is the "written by hand" look for sales letters. It's a proven winner.

There's considerable information about testing in another chapter of this manual. You will notice that "type face" is not on the list. Test the more impactful items on the list first.

If you like Times Roman for your letters, go ahead and use it. Get a great headline, benefit, promise, proposition and easy action step established. Then, and only then, should you mess with type face. It won't make an earth-shattering difference in response by itself. A badly written letter in Courier will not outpull a great letter in Times Roman.

But here's my recommendation: Start with Courier type for your sales letters. Get the other pieces down pat, then mess with the type. Why fight what direct marketers in a broad range of businesses have already tested and proven?

Here's why people fight me on this one: They personally don't like the look of Courier. "It looks like a sales letter." Yes it does … it is a sales letter. Duh! Do you think you're fooling your reader into thinking your communiqué is not a sales letter because it's in Times Roman, or Heaven forbid, Arial? Get real.

You can't disguise a sales letter. It is what it is. But the more you can make it look like a personal, one-to-one communication, the more receptive the reader will be. A nice piece of letterhead that looks like it was individually typed in a typewriter makes a more personal connection than something that looks like a graphic masterpiece.

But you can test it if you want. Reinvent the wheel at your own peril. I'm trying to help you sidestep the pitfalls that successful direct marketers have already solved. Why not cut straight to the stuff that's already been proven for you? Especially such a small issue.

Use Courier in your sales letters until all of your components are tested and working. Then test the type. 'Nuff said?

There are many more type faces to choose from, and that's the danger! Remember, you want your communiqué to be easy to read. You want your reader to be comfortable, otherwise you lose them before they get your message.

Another important point: Use large enough type so people my age can read it! If the text won't fit on the page, edit the text, don't use a smaller typeface to jam it in.

> **The Exception:** *The rule of Serif type for body copy does not apply to web pages and email. Tests have proven Sans Serif type (such as Arial) is more readable.*

Why? The resolution of the computer screen is much lower than that on the printed page. This page was printed a 300 dpi(dots per inch). Your computer screen is more like 72dpi resolution. The newer flat screens are a little better, but still no match for the printed page.

In the lower resolution medium, the serifs – those little feet on each character – tend to run together in the lower resolution. Looking at this page, each character is clearly separate from the others on either side. The serifs guide the eye comfortable from character to character. In a lower resolution medium like your computer monitor, they cause a bit of a blur at the bottom of the line.

It's not something real noticeable, but it does make a difference in readability. Again, anything you can do to make it easier and more comfortable for your reader will make it more likely they will stick around to read your entire communiqué.

It should go without saying that, for the same reason, small type is not effective for web pages and email. If you go below about 11 points, you're really taxing your readers' eyesight … especially if your target customer is my age or older!

Don't make it a challenge for your prospect to decipher your message. Use clear, simple, familiar type faces for ease and comfort of readability.

SPRING IS SPRUCE-UP TIME!

C̶̶̶̶̶ Bay Weekly readers will be having their homes remodeled, RENOVATED, LANDSCAPED, *painted*, *redecorated*, UPDATED and if you're in the Home Improvement field, they'll need YOUR HELP!

Starting March 16th. CBW will feature:
The Spring Spruce-up Directory

◇ Don't miss this opportunity to put your ◇
business name in front of this
important audience.

Reach 77,000 Greater ▬▬▬ residents
for as little as $26.00 per week!

Issue Dates: March 16th through June 8th.
Deadline: March 10th.

Call Today!
7▬▬-▬34 or ▬▬▬-▬▬▬-6601
C▬▬▬ Bay Weekly - Advertising That Works!

Ransom Note Copy

Every once in a while, I come across and ad that so clearly demonstrates a concept for me, it speaks much more loudly than I ever could. (The name has been obliterated to protect the innocent. I have permission to use this, but didn't have the heart to print their business name.)

There are eight different typefaces in this single ad. And the scary thing is; this ad was prepared by a weekly newspaper's advertising department! Certainly, they should know better.

Limit yourself to two type families in any one piece. You may use bold and italics to accent select words or phrases, but don't let your marketing piece look like a ransom note! It makes it difficult for your reader to get through the information.

And remember; any time you make it difficult for the reader, you increase the odds that you'll lose them long before the "call to action."

Chapter 8

Layouts that look like C.R.A.P.

Most of us are stronger in one of the two disciplines I talk about in this book.

Many are pure copy writers who write the words, then completely turn them over to a graphic artist. Even if you are responsible for both copy writing and graphic design, I'm sure you'll admit that you are considerably stronger in one pursuit than the other.

Well, I'm a copy writer who decided to study graphic design later. Some years ago, I bought my first graphic design book. The first book I bought is still my favorite, and I recommend it highly: *The Non-Designer's Design Book*(see sidebar).

Recommended Reading

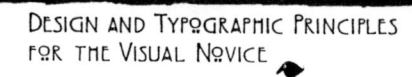

Non-Designer's Design Book
by Robin Williams
Peachpit Press ISBN 1-56609-159-4

The author is a woman by the name of Robin Williams(no, not the male actor/comic).

She came up with the acronym C.R.A.P., although she doesn't go so far as to use is as an acronym. Her publisher must just be more conservative than mine! It stands for the four graphic design principals her book concentrates on;

>   **C**ontrast
>   **R**epetition
>   **A**lignment
>   **P**roximity

Contrast

Contrast is what draws the reader's eye to your promo piece. Out of all the ads on a newspaper page, or the pieces in a pile of incoming mail, the one that uses contrast most effectively will jump out at you.

Contrast with competing messages ...

When you read your morning paper, you scan the pages looking for items that interest you. When you come to the part of the page that is mostly advertising, you tend to scan more quickly.

Hey, you didn't pick up the paper to read no stinking advertising!

So, advertising has to go out of its way to grab your attention.

The Anti-Contrast

Sure, some ads try to disguise themselves as news stories. You've seen them. They use a news hook headline, set in the same type the paper uses for news stories. They look just like the rest of the stories you scan carefully for the content you're looking for.

That layout fools the eye - you don't go into the fast-scan mode you usually apply to the advertising section of the page. It does get you to consider the ad within the same framework that you consider article titles. And, if the headline appeals to you personally, you will be drawn into the ad.

In other words, it uses lack of contrast to keep your eye in its normal flow through the page. It's the Anti-contrast.

Or, you may call it "stealth advertising." (It tries to sneak under your radar. Get it?)

Standing Out In The Crowd

But most ads make at least some attempt to stand out in the crowd. When you place an ad in a print media publication, you don't know where it will land on the page nor what will surround it. It could sit between two news stories, or be completely surrounded by other ads. Each of the other ads is competing with you. Oh, they may not sell competing products or services, but they're all competing for the attention of the reader.

Many do-it-yourself advertisers think the key to drawing attention is using some graphic trick.

One contrast trick you see all too often is the black background with all reversed (white on black) type. It works if you use it only for a headline, and only with a very few words.

You've seen whole ads or large blocks of text in reverse type. They stand out in the crowd, but they're hard to read. When your ad is on newsprint, you run the risk of ink filling some of your white spaces, making it practically impossible to read.

It doesn't do any good to grab readers' attention if they can't read your message. If you must use reversed type, use it only for a short headline in very bold sans serif type. You don't want any part of the characters to be thin enough that ink can bleed and fill them up. Then, leave the rest of the ad background white with black type to make it readable.

Another contrast trick is to use a line drawing or cartoon-type figure to draw the eye. The contrast from the rest of the page is effective - it does stand out in the crowd. But it shouts "advertising," and immediately sends the reader into that fast-scan mode.

If you must use clip art or graphics, make sure they have something to do with the product or service you're promoting. Just because it draws attention doesn't make it a good start for your piece. It has to appeal specifically to the emotion you are playing to in the rest of the ad. It must marry with the copy to establish a mind-set in the reader, to get them started on the right foot.

To draw their attention with some unrelated graphic element is to dupe them into your space. And that's how the reader feels when they realize they were drawn in by trickery: duped! Do you think they're going to stay with you for very long after you've slapped them in the face?

The best attention-getter is a good photograph. Since they're discussed at length in another chapter, I won't go into the use of photographs here. But suffice it to say that good photographs get the first shot at the reader's attention.

As they scan the page for that first time, photos of human beings get the most attention. Photos represent reality. As long as the reality in your photo demonstrates a benefit that you are offering in the ad, they're the ideal distractor.

Typography can provide contrast

If you don't want to use a photograph or cogent graphic as an attention-grabber, you have to depend solely on your headline. Remembering *The Magic Formula*, your headline has to reach out to your specific target reader with an emotional appeal - something that matters to them.

For the headline to be noticed, it has to either look like the news story headlines: same type face and length, or stand out from everything else on the page.

If your intent is to match the publication's headlines, you simply select the same type face and size they use. You will then be included in the readers' more meticulous "news scan" of the page … as long as your piece is not surrounded by other ads. Of course, you can't control that, so you're taking some risk.

If you're in a publication that doesn't carry a lot of advertising, as is often the case in trade journals or association publications, you're probably safe. If, however, you're in a metropolitan newspaper, the odds of being buried among competing ads go up significantly. In that case, you have to head your ad with a graphic element that draws the eye from all the other ads.

Slab serif typeface, in very large and very bold styles are excellent. They only work if you're writing very short headlines. Or, they may force you to break your headline into two parts.

Here's and example: "Fast, Easy Access To Your Home Equity" is a headline I wrote for a mortgage broker for a home equity loan promotion.

To use that headline in its entirety, you could make it look like the other story headlines in the publication. It might look something like this;

**Fast, Easy Access To
Your Home Equity**

To use a bigger and bolder type face, you would have to break the headline up into several lines to fit the same column width;

Fast, Easy
Access
To Your
Home Equity

It fits the same column width, yet would really stand out on the page. Of course, it uses more line space, but pretty much guarantees it will get noticed. I believe your headline should be the dominant focal point in your space. And, your space is an ad among other ads and stories, it must dominate the page. So it's not unusual for the headline or photo(which actually serves as the headline) to occupy 2/3 of the ad's space.

> **IMPORTANT LESSON:** *Your headline(or photo) is 80% responsible for the success of your ad. If it only uses up 2/3 of your space, it's a bargain!*

The typeface is bigger and bolder than anything else on the page, so the eye is drawn to it.

Would it work to make the headline shorter, so we use less space? We could say "Fast, Easy Home Equity Loans." That's a little shorter, but I don't like the copy as well. We could just say "Home Equity Loans." Now, I really don't like that copy, but it would take up about half as much space. I'd rather use the longer headline, make it the visual focal point of the page, and work to write tighter copy underneath.

See, it's always a balancing act between copy and graphic design. Should you change your headline copy so you can use a certain type face? Should you change your contrast strategy to accommodate the headline copy?

Copy is King

I believe the copy is the most important element. The graphic designer has the job of drawing attention to the piece, and making the target prospect want to read it. Then, the graphic elements should walk the reader by the hand through the Magic Formula sequence. You want them to read all of your copy, in the proper sequence.

To change the copy so it will fit the graphic design risks destroying your message. I've seen it happen too many times: A copy writer turns in excellent copy that will *Sell Like Hell*. Then, the graphic designer edits or rearranges the copy to fit their layout, and the message is diluted.

Contrast within your message ...

We designed a attention-getting headline, graphic or photo to pull the targeted readers' eyes to the top of our space. Whether "our space" is a space ad on a magazine page, a sales letter, a web page, a classified ad ... it's all the same. We want to pull their attention from everything else in their purview, and start them at the beginning of our sequential message.

So, the copy in that attention-getting headline, or the subject in the photo must convey the thought we want as step one: An emotional appeal. We want them to think "they're talking to me!"

BE BOLD
But don't get stupid

When you want to mix typefaces, like the example above, make sure you create a bold contrast between the two. This is a technique you will see incorporated in logotypes. It also works for headlines.

You can see that this example use one very large "slab"(very bold) type face, plus a very light/small one. The contrast between the two makes a very attractive combination.

This draws the eye to the beginning, then to the second word, line or tag line. In the example, your eye has to start at: **BE BOLD**. That large slab type dominates the space. In fact, when you turned to this page in the manual, it was probably impossible to not look at this example before you could go back to the top of the page and start reading again! After your eye was drawn to: **BE BOLD**, it was irresistible to read on, and get the second half of the message: But don't get stupid. That's exactly what you want to accomplish with your graphic design.

If you are going to use split type contrast, make sure you use it on a splittable combination.
(Yes, my spell checker says "splitter" is not a word. It's not a typo - I just talk this way.) Be bold, but don't get stupid is a very splittable thought.

In a logotype you might use the same technique like this;

SMITH MOVING AND STORAGE INC

This is the same technique used quite differently. First, the name: **SMITH** is in a serif type face, and: MOVING AND STORAGE INC is in a sans serif. That's the opposite of the first example. There's no reason why ... I just liked the way they came out! Look at both of them reversed;

BE BOLD But don't get stupid   **SMITH** MOVING AND STORAGE INC

Hey, if you like one or the other this way, go for it. Graphic design is part personal preference. But be careful: **DON'T GET STUPID**. Now I'm talking to you – I'm not talking about the examples anymore!

Don't let your personal preferences lead you to create pieces that are difficult to read, or just don't make sense. Remember the reader. They must be drawn to the very beginning of your overall message. Then they must me taken by the hand and walked step by step through every line, in sequence. If you start drawing the eye out of the sequence, you're getting stupid.

You don't want the reader's eye wandering around the page. You want it in your message, in sequence, all the way through. Bad graphic design will destroy good copy.

Step by Step

Now, we have to move their attention to the next step in the sequence.

Just grabbing their attention is not enough. That's why unrelated graphics, photos or cutesy type faces don't work. They don't get beyond the cute and get down to business.

To move them to the next line, there has to be a graphic element that keeps them from skipping through the ad. So we want to direct them to the next line, then the next. Each line should move them to the next, leading them inexorably to the final step: Action.

Now, you have to move to an easily readable type face. You can't write the whole ad in that big, bold style we used for the headline. Now it's body copy, and you want it to be comfortable for them to read. Typefaces are covered in more depth in another chapter, but the typeface you're reading right now is the only one you need for body copy.

Argue with me if you wish - I love to create controversy! But Times Roman is the typeface we grew up reading. Books, magazines, newspapers ... most use this same type face or one very close to it. Don't make your reader work at understanding your message.

I like to use a drop-cap at the beginning of the first line of body copy.

Drop-caps make a transition from the big headline type into the body copy. This one starts slightly outside the paragraph, a contrast point that grabs the eye after it's finished with the headline. You can see it's the same type face I used in the headline.

Drop-caps help the eye transition from headline to body copy. Remember, the goal is to keep the eye flowing comfortably through the Magic Formula sequence.

Fast, Easy Access
To Your
Home Equity

Hey, it's your money...
You shouldn't have to jump
through hoops to get your
hands on it when you need it!

See how the drop cap pulls you into the next line? You can take it a step farther by including the first few words in the drop cap style;

Fast, Easy Access
To Your
Home Equity

HEY, it's your money...
You shouldn't have to jump
through hoops to get your
hands on it when you need it!

Remember the contrast rule from earlier in this chapter: Don't split words up with typography unless they are splittable thoughts. This just wouldn't work;

HEY, IT'S your money...
You shouldn't have to jump
through hoops to get your
hands on it when you need it!

That's just not a sensible splitting point in the sentence. If the first one to four words don't split off as a separable thought(splittable), just apply the drop cap to the first character.

Can you see how this would stand out on a page full of other ads? The headline dominates the space. The drop cap contrast technique pulls the eye into the first line of copy. You've hooked your reader and started to reel them in!

Repetition

Now, as the ad develops, we want to use repetition of elements to keep the reader comfortable and involved.

This is why you don't use five different type faces. Each change makes the reader shift gears and refocus. Every time you ask them to work, you invite them to leave!

In fact, any more than two type faces make your ad or piece look amateurish. I know, it's fun to play with all of those different looks. And some are even quite attractive ... at least, by themselves.

For example: Look at the type used in this manual. The same type is used for all chapter titles. Wouldn't it look a little silly if each chapter title was in a different type? You would think I'm totally disorganized. (You may think so anyway – I do tend to skip and/or repeat things at times – but that's another issue.)

The body text is all in Times Roman. The subheads are all just the same type in bold. The "Important Lessons" all look the same.

That repetition of elements helps you know what's coming. You know when an "Important Lesson" pops up, because of the way it's set up – it's consistent throughout the manual.

Repetition of elements also makes for a more attractive piece. Here's an exaggerated example;

- Two hotel nights
- Breakfast daily
- Saturday dinner

- Two hotel nights
- ☞ Breakfast daily
- ❖ Saturday dinner

Face it, pieces that look disorganized are not attractive. They may even be more difficult to read. Throwing in type faces, bullets, graphics and borders that don't look like they belong together will make your piece downright uninviting.

You want to be consistent with your design elements. Repetitive use of the same components makes for a clean, consistent look.

Simple repetition and consistency makes your piece easier to read, and more attractive to the eye.

That means more readers, which should translate eventually into more BUYERS.

A note about repetition:

Be careful not to repeat any one element too often. For instance, ten bullet points in a row become monotonous and hard to read. It's hard to read because, since they all look the same, the eye has a hard time spotting which comes next.

Bullet points are good for three, even four short items. For any more items than that, use a numbered list. It's still consistent and repeats the same element(a number), while making it easy for the eye to see where it should go next at the end of each.

That's also true if your points are longer than just a few words each. The next number is easy to follow.

Alignment

Jump-start your sales...

New 8- tape audio program shares secrets that will lift response to your marketing communications of all kinds, *guaranteed.*

$50,000 Business Makeover

Try it, use it for 60 days. If you don't see 100-times the $97 price in value, return it for a full no-questions-asked refund.

Order before 10/15, and receive a free copy of the book *Shoestring Marketing*. Keep it as a gift ... even if you return the tapes.

Full details and secure, online order at:

MagicFormula.com

Jump-start your sales...

New 8-tape audio program shares secrets that will lift response to your marketing communications of all kinds, *guaranteed.*

$50,000 Business Makeover

Try it, use it for 60 days. If you don't see 100-times the $97 price in value, return it for a full no-questions-asked refund.

Order before 10/15, and receive a free copy of the book *Shoestring Marketing*. Keep it as a gift ...even if you return the tapes.

Full details and secure, online order at:

MagicFormula.com

Here are two versions of the same ad. The border is the same, the copy is the same. There are minor differences in the type faces.

The biggest difference between the two is the way the text is aligned.

The text in the ad on the left is all centered. This is a very typical alignment scheme. Most amateur graphic designers(do-it-yourselfers, in other words) start with this type of alignment.

There's nothing wrong with having everything centered. It looks nice. It doesn't make the text terribly difficult to read.

But it does confuse the eye a little bit. Each line starts and ends at different points than the previous line. So, as the eye goes from line to line, it has to adjust to that minor change. It's not real hard work, but it is work.

And remember: People are lazy. If this was much longer, it would get tiresome, and the reader would bail.

But, for this short block of text, it's no big deal.

Now, examine the ad on the right. Can you see the difference in alignment? Your eye automatically starts at the top left – which is where you normally start reading text.

Each line starts at the same point on the left margin. That's what margins are for – alignment!

The beginning of each paragraph is signaled by an indentation. Just like when you read a book or a magazine. It's what you're used to and comfortable with.

Then, the product title is centered, and in the same type as the headline. Some people will not read the text. They'll only read the headline and the bold type. They will get enough message from the headline, the product title and the web site address to buy if they're so inclined.

The web site address at the end is aligned to the right. If you read just the bold lines, they go left, centered, right … moving your eye in a comfortable left to right, top to bottom pattern.

Alignment of text + graphic elements

Your ad or piece should never look like anything happened by mistake.

Any graphic element(that includes the text) should be aligned with some other graphic element.

It may help to use a grid system in your piece. For design purposes, draw a grid over the page, and use it to lay out and align your graphic elements.

If you look at newspaper and magazine pages, you can see the grid they used to lay out each page. You'll see that publications use more than one grid throughout their pages, but the grids all fit a common theme.

For instance, look at these layout grids;

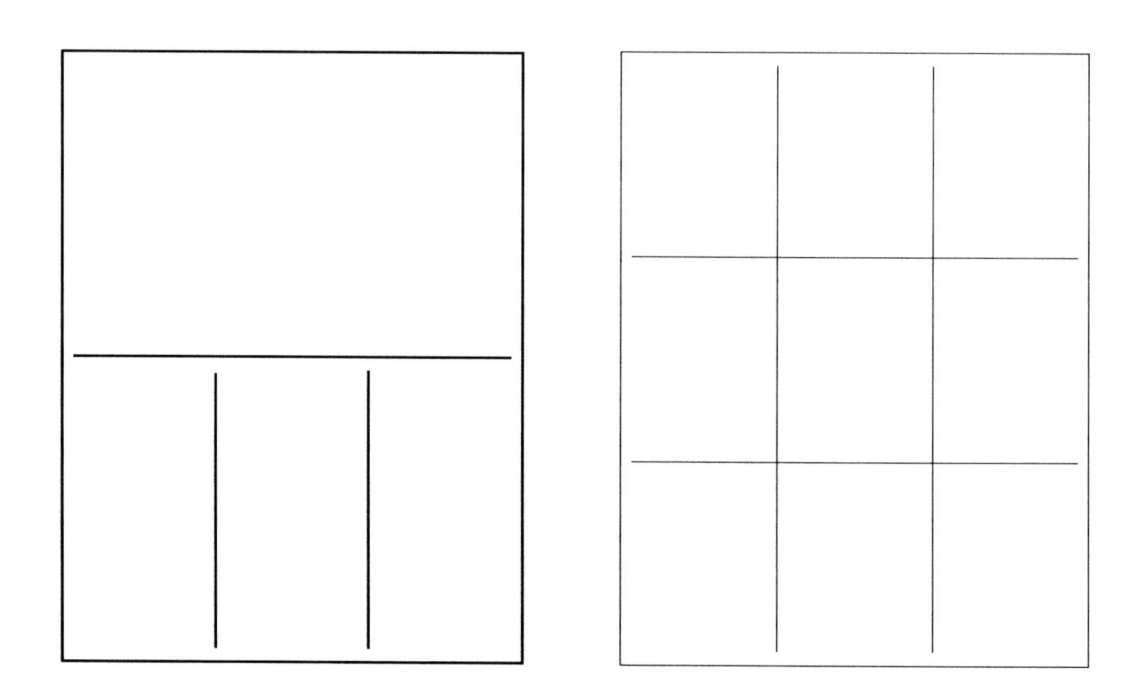

Both are based on a three column grid. One page may feature a half-page photo with three columns of text underneath. Another may include three or four 1/6th-page photos with blocks of text in between.

In a long document, you would want to vary the page layout to keep the reader interested. But don't use two-column, then four-column, then three-column grids. It looks disorganized and gets more difficult to follow. And you know how I feel about making anything difficult!

Proximity

Remember the bullet points I used in the example under Repetition?

• Two hotel nights
• Breakfast daily
• Saturday dinner

They would have been three included features in an ad for a travel package.

It only makes sense to put those three items together. What if I scattered those three elements all around the ad? You would have to pull them together in your mind – a leap many readers would not make.

Look at the before and after versions – albeit, with a very minor change – of this ad;

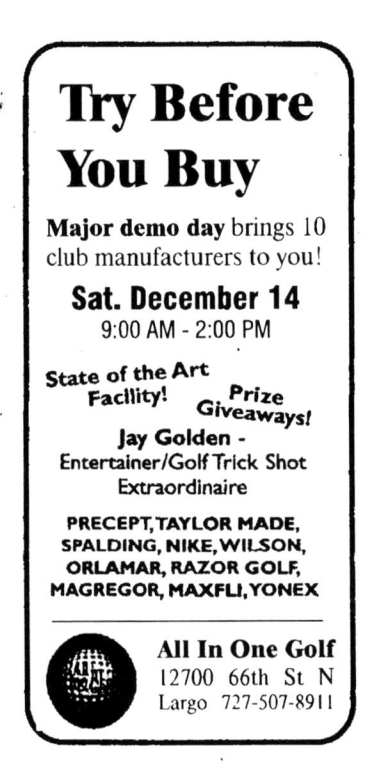

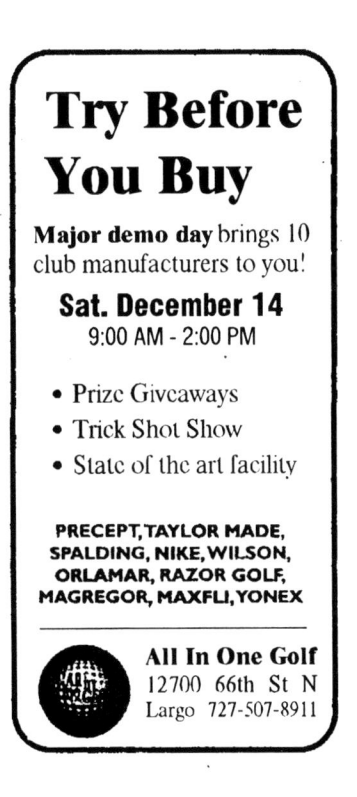

Try Before You Buy

Major demo day brings 10 club manufacturers to you!

Sat. December 14
9:00 AM - 2:00 PM

State of the Art Facility! **Prize Giveaways!**

Jay Golden -
Entertainer/Golf Trick Shot Extraordinaire

PRECEPT, TAYLOR MADE, SPALDING, NIKE, WILSON, ORLAMAR, RAZOR GOLF, MAGREGOR, MAXFLI, YONEX

All In One Golf
12700 66th St N
Largo 727-507-8911

Try Before You Buy

Major demo day brings 10 club manufacturers to you!

Sat. December 14
9:00 AM - 2:00 PM

• Prize Giveaways
• Trick Shot Show
• State of the art facility

PRECEPT, TAYLOR MADE, SPALDING, NIKE, WILSON, ORLAMAR, RAZOR GOLF, MAGREGOR, MAXFLI, YONEX

All In One Golf
12700 66th St N
Largo 727-507-8911

The very small change of arranging the three features into bullet points in stead of throw helter skelter around the space makes the ad easier to read.

Another example; Look at the Table of Contents in the front of this manual.

It just makes sense that the chapter titles would be listed in the order in which they appear in the books. I've also listed some subheads in a few of the chapters. It only makes sense that the subheads would appear in direct proximity to the chapter title under which they fall.

What if I had made the chapter titles and the subheads the same size, and all justified to the left? It would be much harder to find your way around.

The subheads within the same chapter are kept together. But they're indented as a group, kept in proximity to their parent chapter name.

That may seem like a really basic example, and it should be. But you see some pretty disorganized arrangements of thoughts in too many pieces. Don't let that happen to yours.

Practice makes perfect

Look at the ads in your morning paper, read the direct mail pieces on your kitchen table. You'll see lots of ads that could use major overhauls in all four areas; Contrast, Repetition, Alignment and Proximity.

Redesign them in your mind. You're practicing a skill that will help you make your own ads look polished, professional ... and most important: Easy to read.

Chapter 9

How to write killer copy

You may feel like writing copy is some mystical art. Although there is a degree of artistry involved, it's really as much science as art.

You must understand a few important ideas before we start;

      1.) Advertising and promo pieces are sales in print,
      2.) Selling is a sequential process,
      3.) People buy based on their emotions.

Sales in Print

When you sit down to write the copy for your ad or promo piece, you are really writing the script for a one-sided sales conversation.

If you were face-to-face with your prospect, you would have the advantage of a dialog. You could ask probing questions your statements and questions. You would be able to establish rapport with the communication skills sales people learn in their training.

The challenge when selling in print is to present your message in language and style that the prospect will respond to. You have to talk specifically about the prospect's "hot buttons," without input from them.

So, how do you keep your prospect interested? How do you keep them engaged in the sales "conversation," when you don't have their reactions to work with? You talk about their favorite topic.

Talk about their favorite topic, and they'll be compelled to read every word.

How do you know what their favorite topic is? Here's the good news. Everyone's favorite topic is the same; It's themselves.

Take a minute right now … yeah, take a break from this material for just a minute and read some of your current promotional copy. Doesn't matter whether it's an ad, a brochure, a web page, or any other promotional material you may be using. Now, who does it talk about?

If it says things like "We've been in business for 25 years," or "The largest dealership in the state," it's about yourself. Your prospects really don't care about you. Sorry, but they don't. It doesn't matter to them how long you've been in business, how many units you sold last year, how attractive your staff is, how many dragons you've slain. They don't care about you.

> **IMPORTANT LESSON:** *Count how many times you've used the word "you" vs the words "I" and "we" in your copy. If the "yous" don't outnumber the "Is" and "wes' by two to one, you have to go back and rewrite it.*

Your prospect only cares about how your experience/size/etc. is going to make their life better. Will your size help them save money because you can offer volume pricing? Does your experience give them some advantage they can't get from your newer competitors?

Good copy talks about benefits. It presents the information about he seller in terms of what it does to make the prospect's life easier or better. In stead of saying "We've been in business for 25 years," you might say "You'll enjoy the guidance of an experienced …".

If you really want to do some soul searching, here's an exercise I use in my workshops: It's called Red Light/Green Light. Take out a pink(representing "red") hi-lighter marker, and a green one. Grab any promotional copy you're using right now, and read it one sentence at a time.

Any sentence that is about yourself, the business, or your product/service and it's features, you will hi-light in RED. Those sentences that are about your prospect, and benefits to them, you will hi-light in GREEN.

Don't be surprised to find that more of your page is red than green. It's natural to want to tell your prospects all about you and your product or service. And, of course, they need to know about you and your product/service to make an intelligent decision. But first, they have to make an emotional decision to be interested. Address the emotional decision first. Get them excited, and it will take a lot less information to make a buying decision.

Be brutally honest with yourself as you read and hi-light. It's easy for you to see why your 25 years' experience is a benefit to your customers. But unless the copy is worded so that they can clearly see why that's a benefit to them, they aren't going to make the connection. They want to "enjoy the security that comes with being guided through the process by an expert with 25 years' experience."

Here's an easy way to analyze a sentence: Any sentence that begins with "We, I, or Our" is almost definitely about you. If the sentence begins with your company name, the owner's name, or the name of the product, it's probably about you.

If the sentence starts with the word "You," it has to be about the reader.

Magic Words, Phrases and Emotions

Of all the words in your copy writing vocabulary, the word "you" is the most important. If you start a sentence or a headline with "you," you have to write about the reader. It's the first word listed in the Appendix listing because it's the most important.

Of course, you can't start every sentence with the word "you." But please strive to use the word "you" at least twice as often as you use "I, We or Our." In fact, go for three to one.

One-to-one conversation

When sit down to write this "you" copy, remember that you are writing to one individual human being. You may actually be writing to 10,000, but only one will read your copy at a time. So, it's important to write in one-to-one, conversational language.

It may help to picture a particular customer, and write as though you are writing the communiqué to them specifically. Choose a customer you know well, one you wish you could clone because they're the kind of people you'd like to do business with every day.

Then write like you would talk to them face-to-face. "Conversational" means "just like you talk." You would never say "enclosed for your perusal" in conversation. Why would you ever write that way? If you were sitting across the table from this specific prospect, what would you say to get them emotionally involved in the product or service you're trying to sell? Would you start with how long you've been in business? I hope not.

Pepper your copy with the words listed in the appendix. They'll make your copy more compelling, more interesting, and more emotionally-charged. Remember, people make buying decisions based on their emotions.

By the way: This applies to business-to-business promo pieces, too. You're not addressing some corporation, or government agency ... you're talking one-on-one with an individual human. Talk directly to that human ... and talk like a human ... and you'll be more likely to hold their interest.

An Example

Here is some actual promotional copy written for a construction company. Here are just two short paragraphs, both before and after being rewritten in "you" language;

> **BEFORE**
>
> J.P. Cullen & Sons, Inc., founded in 1892, is one of the oldest construction companies in the nation. Founder John Patrick Cullen gave birth to the company's standard of pride in workmanship.
>
> **AFTER**
>
> If experience and longevity in business are important to your choice of a construction company, you'll want to partner with J.P. Cullen & Sons, Inc. You'll be

associated with one of the oldest construction companies in the United States, founded in 1892 by John Patrick Cullen. You'll experience a pride in workmanship that harkens back to the 19th Century, and has never changed.

BEFORE

The Cullen organization maintains its vitality through energetic, forward-thinking, aggressive leadership. Cullen's reputation as an innovator has enabled it to attract and retain top-notch professionals for its management team.

AFTER

Why not put your project into the hands of a widely-reputed construction industry leader? You'll work side-by-side with Cullen's top-notch management team. Forward thinking, innovation and vitality are qualifications for employment here, and at the same time, motivation to perform exceptionally for valued clients like you.

A close second …

"You" is the most important word in your vocabulary.

Right behind "you" on the power scale, is the word "Free."

Want a two-word prefix to a power phrase: "Yours Free;"

Two things you must keep in mind if you're going to use free offers;

1.) People are skeptical – everyone knows "there is no free lunch."

What you give away must be of enough value to the specific target customer to arouse interest. To give something of no value, especially of no value to the specific prospect, will do nothing to lift your response.

Banks are famous for giving away useless, unrelated premiums for opening a new account or taking out a new loan. Toasters(cheap ones), cameras(cheap ones),

Radios-in-headphones(cheap ones) … get the picture? I have a toaster, and it's not a cheap one. I have a camera … I have no use for a radio built into a bulky headset. Who responds to this stuff? I guess it must be people who can't otherwise afford a toaster – that's not the new account I would want to attract if I were a banker!!

Or how about the "Free Vacation" offers? Do you really think they can afford to give away a "luxury cruise" with a car loan? Besides, if you just bought a new car, you probably don't want to take a cruise right now. And you really won't want to when you find out how "luxurious" it actually is, and how much of your own money you're going to have to spend to turn it into a decent vacation.

> **LESSON:** *Don't make your Free offers too good to be true. People know better.*

2.) Your Free offer should attract prospects for the next sale.

So, what do you offer so you can use this powerful word "Free?"

I think the best "free" item to give away is information. It doesn't cost you anything to produce, but it can be of tremendous value to the prospect. I've used my *Special Reports* as free offers on many occasions. You may have responded to an ad offering a *Free Special Report* as a lead-in to this manual. That's an example of a "two-step" process (discussed in another chapter in this manual).

The *Special Report* should be of value to the prospect, and should attract the kind of prospect who is likely to buy the product you are leading up to.

A few years ago, I wrote a *Special Report* titled "How To Boost Meeting Attendance By 37%." I used it as a free premium, hoping to add association meeting planners to my prospect list. Later, I would approach them to consider me for future speaking engagements. Well, all association meeting planners want to know how to boost attendance, to the *Special Report* was a big hit. Unfortunately, fewer than 10% of the meeting planners who responded ever hire professional speakers for their events. So, I got lots of names, very few of whom were qualified prospects for the product I was leading up to. Important lesson learned!

So, I wrote another *Special Report* titled "How To Stretch Your Speaker Budget." Everyone who responded to that offer actually hires speakers. Not all hire speakers like me, and a lot of them had low speaker budgets(so, they didn't hire speakers like me). But the percentage of respondents who were live prospect was much higher, more like 60%.

> **LESSON:** *Your "Free" premium should be of specific interest to the type of prospect you want to attract ... and not of interest to non-prospects.*

There are lots of other uses for "Free;"

    A.) An extra premium to get them to buy now.
      "And if you order today, you'll also receive ... FREE!"
    B.) Volume bonus
      "Buy three, and you'll receive the fourth FREE!"
    C.) Two for one
      "Order now, and we'll double you shipment"

They're all bribes. And that's OK. If you want people to respond to your advertising and promotion, you have to motivate them to act now rather than set it aside.

So, the word "FREE" serves two purposes; Not only does it grab the reader's attention, it can set the stage for a proposition that will motivate them to buy now.

Use the "Words That Work" in the Appendix. I keep that page in front of me every time i write copy, just to remind me to pepper the page with power words. They really do make a difference.

Emotions

The emotional appeals listed in the same Appendix are just a few of the possibilities. Give some thought to what emotional appeals apply to your product or service. What will get people excited about owning/using what you sell?

That excitement can be a positive or negative charge. By that, I mean that all emotions fall under one of two categories; Fear and Greed.

There are a lot of different emotions, but all of them are some form of either fear of losing or being left out of something, or desire for more of something. That's fear and greed.

And most products or services can be sold from either angle.

For a fear angle on your product/service, think about what your prospects will miss out on if they don't buy. Will they suffer through the Summer heat if they don't install one of your swimming pools? Will they be left out socially because they're not keeping up with the Jones'? Will they have a hard time selling their home when the time comes because it's missing this important accouterment?

For the greed angle, think of all that they will enjoy after they do buy. "Now, you'll look forward to the Summer heat because you'll be cool in your backyard pool. Your neighbors can't help but admire your taste when they see your ABC pool. You'll be amazed what a backyard pool can do for your home's resale value."

Envy is a greed hook. Jealousy is a fear hook. Get it?

The important thing is to know which emotion you want to appeal to before you ever start writing.

Features vs Benefits

Most writers think in terms of features. After all, you know what went into the development and design of your product. You know how important the selection of materials, the attention to detail, and the control of the manufacturing process are.

But your prospect doesn't care.

Features are facts, details and components. How your product was built or designed, who designed it, how much it weighs – how many have been sold. Your prospect wants to know how all of that translates to a better world for them.

A "25' by 16' pool" is all about features. Steel-reinforced concrete is a feature. "Now, you can include healthful lap swimming in your exercise program," and "Durability and low-maintenance make your ABC pool a pleasure to own" are about benefits.

Speak In Grade-School English

It doesn't matter what level of education you or your target market has acquired. You're always better off speaking simply, clearly, so everyone can understand you.

If you make your communications simple, it doesn't matter who reads them. Everyone will understand. If you try to show off your vocabulary and prose, you will lose … even offend …at least some of your readers.

Why take a chance on eliminating anyone from your audience? The professors and lawyers still understand simple English … even if they don't use it when they speak.

Not everyone that reads your materials understands the professorial or legalese.

The Magic Formula

This manual is built around the simple template for compelling marketing communications of all kinds; *The Magic Formula For Persuasion.*

It's the sequence in which people want to learn about you and your products or services.

Get used to writing "you" copy, using headlines that grab attention, and following the sequence. You'll write more effective marketing communications.

You'll soon be writing ads and promo pieces that get noticed, get read, and get *RESPONSE.*

Chapter 10

One-step vs Two-step proposition

Here's the difference between the two;

The One-step proposition attempts to close the sale with a single communication. An ad or promo piece asks the prospect to make a buying decision right now, and respond with their credit card in hand.

The Two-step proposition asks a little less of the prospect. The first ad or promo piece asks the prospect to simply respond. It may be to get additional information, often accompanied with a premium or discount voucher to thank them for responding. The second step, then, is to contact the prospect after they have received their information, and close the sale at that time.

How do you decide which will work for you?

Generally, the price of the product or service determines whether a One-step approach will work. If you're selling a $1,000 product, it's going to be hard to get the prospect to make a buying decision based on one contact.

If you're selling a product priced at under $50, a one-step approach may well work.

If you have enough space in your ad, you may even do well with a $99.95 price point. Much more than that is a lot for people to part with based on the information you can provide in a less-than-full-page ad.

You may be able to stretch that price point by promoting a "payment" amount; "Four payments of $47" keeps your dollar figure under that $50 radar prospects seem to have!

Direct mail is different. Why? In a direct mail package, you can provide a lot more information than you can in an ad. Plus, direct mail can be more targeted – your piece will only go to pre-qualified prospects.

That also makes direct mail ideal for the second step of a 2-step promotion. You can put all of the information they need to make an intelligent decision right in their hand.

Space limitations

> **Remember my rule governing copy length:** *You must give your prospect all of the information they need to make an intelligent decision on the action you're asking them to take.*

I you're running a classified or small-space ad, or mailing out post cards(possibly in a card deck), there's a limit to how much information you can give, and how much you can expect your prospect to give up when they respond. Their name and address are about as much as you can hope for.

> **LESSON:** *Most small space ads should be designed and written with the intent of eliciting a response. They are step One of the Two-step process.*

By the way, an ad that motivates the prospect to come to your place of business for step two is Two-step ad. So your objective with the ad is "get them to come to the store," not "get them to buy."

The buying step happens at the store, so your sales staff has to be ready to take them to step Two.

The Two-step proposition

This is the solution if you want to get prospects to raise their hands and say "I'm interested." While a One-step ad goes for the jugular, this approach allows you to compile a list of interested prospects so you can focus your serious efforts on them. You spend considerably less on the ad or mailing, leaving your marketing budget free to reward your sales people for closing the deals.

The *Magic Formula* applies to these marketing communications, too. You have to start by grabbing their attention with and emotional connection. Then promise a benefit and prove you can deliver it. Then comes the proposition. If the free information you're promising doesn't get the kind of response you want, try throwing in a free gift;

The Free Gift

You can even offer a free gift as your "thank you for responding." This gives the prospect even more incentive to take that first step;

Low Payments • Fast Approval
Your house payments shouldn't leave you too broke to enjoy your new home! I've been helping people just like you get the most for their money for over 22 years. <u>Call me before 3/1/</u> and receive a FREE payment calculator – know what you can afford before you make that offer! There's no obligation. It's my way of saying thank you for your interest. 501 222-2222 Hometown Finance

---

Do you see each step of the Magic Formula ... in sequence ... in this ad? This walks the prospect from "total stranger" to "hot prospect" in just 70 words. I could have made it even shorter - can you?

> **BRAIN TEASER:** Try getting the copy in the above ad down to 50 words without losing any of the message.

The gift should be something of value, and it should have something to do with your product or service. Don't give away coffee mugs unless you sell coffee ... or drinking coffee is somehow related to your business.

The sample ad offers a loan payment calculator as reward for responding. If you've ever bought a house, you know you could have used one of these things. Imagine being able to calculate your payment based on currently-available rates, the price of the property and your down payment, instantly. Then you could play "what if" with different down payment amounts, different offers - this is a valuable gift to the property-shopping home buyer.

Of course, if you say "no obligation," you can't call people later and act like they owe you something! A little tact, please.

But the "universal law of reciprocation" does leave the recipient somewhat beholdin'(as they say in Texas.) It's not up to you to call this to their attention – they know it deep down inside.

The Three-step proposition

There is actually a three-step proposition you may want to try, especially if you are selling a fairly expensive product or service with a very limited promotional budget.

An ad as small as a classified can be used to make the emotional connection, and arouse enough interest to get them to make a very low-risk response. If people are skeptical at all, they don't want to pick up the phone and get stuck talking to a slick sales person.

So, step One is the small ad, or possibly a post card. It can also be those automatic-dial recorded telemarketing callers. It teases the prospect enough to get them to make a one-way response, one-way meaning they don't have to talk to a human.

What they will do is "call toll-free for a recorded message". They can hang up any time during the recording. No risk. If they like what they hear in the recorded message, they have to take the second step too: there is time at the end to leave their name, address and possibly phone number or email address to receive more information. Then, after the information has been sent, the sales department takes it to step Three.

Any small business with an answering machine to do this one. Just make sure you have enough lines and machines to handle the volume at your peak call-in time. If people get a busy signal, they probably won't try again more than once or twice. All that work to get responses, and you lock them out! Put in several phone lines with a rollover from the listed number. You can buy answering machines for about $20 now, so get as many as you have lines. Heck, borrow machines from your friends and neighbors if you have to.

But don't let your prospects run into a busy signal.

A Three-step classified: **Boost your 2003 sales -**
Free recorded message tells how.
Call toll-free 888 222-9999.

There is no risk in responding to this ad. And who doesn't want to boost their sales?

Another no-risk response is a "fax on demand." They call a toll free number, enter the document number and their own fax number, and the information magically appears on their machine. The drawback here is that not everyone has a fax machine. Or, they may not be near the fax machine when they make the call, so your information goes into the general fax stack. By the time they get to it, the urge may be forgotten.

Another drawback with fax on demand: You don't get their mailing address for future contact. If the info you fax to them doesn't motivate them to act, you don't get another shot at them.

You can set up fax on demand right on your computer with the right software. If you anticipate heavy response, there are well-equipped services that can do this for you. They have enough lines to handle huge volume. Again, Heaven forbid that your prospects get a busy signal. When they're hot for the information, you want to respond immediately.

Talk about immediate response: Why not refer them to your web site, with full information available by auto-responder? These technological marvels are exactly what the name implies. The prospect puts in their email address, and the auto-responder instantly emails the document.

The problem with this approach is that: 1.) It asks the prospect to do more of the work, and 2.) If the prospect is not online … or if their computer is not even turned on … they have to put your ad aside and do it later.

> **IMPORTANT LESSON:** *Any time your prospect has to defer action for any reason, the odds of them following through drop through the floor.*

Once they put it aside, it can get buried in a pile or forgotten. Or, when they do get around to it, the excitement has passed. The great thing about the recorded information is that everyone has a telephone, and they can respond any time from anywhere and get the information immediately.

It's called "strike while the iron is hot." OK, you may not be old enough to remember that one – it means; "Hey, they're salivating for your information. Get it to them before they lose the urge."

Another problem with fax on demand and auto-responders, is that they are very hard to follow up on. You can make them fill out a form with their contact information before they get the auto-responder document, but people may decide it's not worth is after all … or, if they're clever, they'll just give you a false address and phone number.

The Follow-up

In a One-step, the prospect calls to order. In a Two-step, the prospect calls for more information, or comes in to see the product in person. In a Three-step, they call for information, then raise their hand to say "I'm ready to talk to a sales/customer service person." Then, you have to make the second and third step.

The third step is the follow up call. You ask; "Did you receive the information you requested? Did it answer all of your questions about …?" That opens a dialog that may or may not lead to future business. That third step puts more pressure on your sale staff(or your sales skills).

In all three scenarios, the sales or customer service department has to close the sale at some point. Make sure your people know about the proposition, know how to close the sale, and are well-rewarded for doing so.

> **IMPORTANT LESSON:** *Don't run lead generation ads or mail out post cards without training and rewarding the people in your store or phone center.*

And don't ever … ever greet your prospect with "please press one if you're using a touch-tone phone."

> **BRAIN TEASER:** Here's my 50-word version of the ad you saw in the brain teaser;

> **Low Payments • Fast Approval**
> Your house payments shouldn't leave you broke! For 22 years I've helped people just like you get more home for their money. <u>Call now</u> and I'll send you a FREE payment calculator – know your payments before you make an offer! No obligation. 501 222-2222 Hometown Finance

OK, now try to get it down to 35 words. But keep Holy *The Magic Formula* – don't leave out any steps in the sequence. Isn't this fun?

Another example;

Here's one I did for a travel agency that specialized in honeymoon travel.

> # Your honeymoon should be the fun part...
>
> **FREE Booklet:** 10 Potential Honeymoon Disasters, and How You can Avoid Them
>
> Honeymoon travel expert Mary Jennings shares secrets cruise lines and resorts won't tell you! **Call NOW!**
>
> ## 288-0700
> **Honeymoons in Paradise**

Look how specifically the headline targets honeymooners. Then, we strike a little fear into their hearts. "What, the honeymoon isn't automatically the fun part?" Heck no! There are potential disasters out there, and you need to know about them before you start planning.

Would this ad draw a list of qualified prospects for honeymoon travel? You know it!

And that's all we're trying to do at this point. This is designed entirely for lead generation. It doesn't attempt to sell anything. That comes as the second step in the 2-step process.

Direct Mail Takes Over

"Why," you might ask, "did you not send them to a web site for the free information?"

It makes sense – then I wouldn't have to spend any postage to mail the free booklet. They could just download a .pdf of the report.

But then I would have no way of contacting them again. I want their mailing address so I can follow up with a sales letter. I want a phone number so I can call later and ask "Did the booklet answer all of your questions?" and start a dialog with the prospect.

And, here's an important plus: I'll find out when their wedding date is, and contact them in a year for their anniversary trip. What, you didn't think of an anniversary trip? What better way to celebrate?

Patience!

The two-step approach requires patience. The first step is simply to get a qualified prospect to raise their hand. Out of that huge universe out there, you want to find the relative few who might be good prospects for whatever it is you sell. Offering free information … that would only be of interest to your target prospect/and that would definitely be valuable to your target prospect … is a great way to flush them out.

And give the information in the spirit of caring. Don't harass them after you send it. Follow up, but don't be a pain.

The Reward

Patience has its reward. If your ad is written and designed like the examples I just shared with you. You'll be rewarded with a constantly-growing list of qualified, interested prospects for your products and services.

If you stay focused on the same target audience, both in terms of promotion and new product development, your new product launches with enjoy instant sales.

You'll promote them first to your list of qualified, interested prospects who already know you and trust you.

The more your list grows, the more your promotional messages will go direct to good prospects, with very little wasted on overflow.

Chapter 11

How to Write Breakthrough Headlines

The word "breakthrough" is the operative word here ...

> **Here's a bit of bad news;** *Your prospects are not combing the newspaper, sifting through their mail, and opening every one of their emails hoping to learn more about you or your business.*

That statement shouldn't surprise you. Yet most ... fully most ... advertisements and promotional materials are written as though they are. They seem to think that prospects are out there looking for the company name, or the name of the product.

Worse yet, many seem to think prospects are out looking for the names of the principals of the business.

Just the opposite is true; Your prospects are doing everything in their power to AVOID reading your ads, promo pieces and emails.

Believe it or not, they have more important things on their mind than you.

In fact, most people are in a bit of a fog. They float through life avoiding anything that may require any effort. At work, they do as little as possible to get by. At home, they settle into the Barcalounger to watch TV ... with a REMOTE control in their hand. (I just saw an ad for a recliner with a cooler built in. A cooler! Now all they have to add is a catheter and they can remain prostrate all evening!)

They're sort of on autopilot. They mindlessly drive the same route to work. They go through their motions all day. They drive home. You can fill in the rest.

At the end of the day, they couldn't tell you anything that happened in the past 12 hours. Hey, have you ever asked your spouse "what happened today?" Did they have a response? It's not that nothing happened. They just can't bring it up in memory because they did it on autopilot, and it's filed away somewhere deep in the dark recesses of their mind.

It's the headline, stupid ...

If you hope to have people read your promotional message, you have to break through that fog.

You have to slap them out of autopilot.

That job falls squarely on the shoulders of your headline.

Yes, those few words at the beginning of your communique have the responsibility of grabbing your prospects' attention.

> **IMPORTANT LESSON:** *It's been estimated that your headline is 80% responsible for the success (or failure) of your piece.*

Wow, that's a lot. 80%. How can that be?

Well, if the headline doesn't stop your prospect in his or her tracks, and make them want to stop and read your piece ... It just doesn't matter what else is in there, because they aren't even going to see it.

It's not the layout, the design, the colors ... it's the headline upon which they base their decision whether to "stop and read more" or to "move on to the next item".

Photos

There's a whole chapter on photographs. A good photo can be the "attention" step we're talking about. It becomes your headline.

But most of us really can't afford to use half of our ad space on a photo.

Even if you have a good photo, it's still important to caption it. You've got to draw them in deeper with the caption.

In this chapter, I'm just talking about text headlines.

In a classified ad, it's the first few words. In a brochure, it's the first thing people see on the outside cover. In an email, it's the subject line.

The key is; Your headline is the first words they read.

Since people in America read left to right, starting at the top of the page(or space) and working top to bottom, the headline must go at the top of your page or space. It's not just a graphics issue. It's a sequence issue.

You've already learned the *Magic Formula* for persuasion. The headline is the "attention" step. For it to work as such, it has to be the first thing the reader sees. Therefore, it goes at the top unless there is a photo. In that case, the photo would go at the top, and the text headline would appear directly under it as a caption.

How do you read your morning newspaper?

You don't read every word in your morning newspaper – nobody does.

You scan each page, looking for things that apply to your world. You're looking for things that are familiar, or relevant to your world.

When you see something of interest, you stop and read more.

As you read your paper, you're scanning headlines. Each story has one. It tells you what it's about, and gives you enough to decide if it applies to your world or not.

So, you scan the page, looking for headlines that are relevant to your world.

Question: Do you scan the advertising looking for information that is relevant to your world?

Well, you're not scanning the ads as closely as you are the articles. After all, you bought the paper for the articles, not the advertising. But, whether you realize it or not, you do see the advertising. You can't help it as you scan the page.

Your prospects do the same thing.

They scan the articles pretty carefully. They quickly (even if only subconsciously) skim the ads on the page.

The truth is, they really don't want to read the ads.

> **IMPORTANT LESSON:** *They don't want to read advertising. In fact, they're actually trying to avoid it!*

As they scan the page for articles they're interested in, they speed up when they come to the ads.

They don't want to read advertising, but they can't help seeing them at least for a second or two.

That's your small window of opportunity!

If your headline is relevant to their world, they will stop just as they would for an article headline. If it's not, they're gone ... *FAST*.

So, the key to writing **Breakthrough Headlines** ... headlines that break through your prospects' preoccupation and routine ... is to make them relevant to each individual's own world.

How do you do that? You're trying to talk to hundreds, maybe thousands of people. How the heck do you find something that's relevant to each one of them?

Focus

First, you should take a hard look at just how many you are trying to talk to.

Imagine you're a real estate agent. You have listings in the $50,000 range, and others in the $1,000,000 range. You probably have just about everything in between, too. What can you say that will reach the $50,000 buyer, the $1,000,000 buyer, and everyone in between?

What most people do, is try to talk to all of them. So, what happens is, they have a diluted message that doesn't really appeal to any of them. There isn't much you can say that will grab the attention of people at all levels.

That means you need to look at your promotional message, and give serious though to just whom it will address.

The more focused you can get, the more effective your headline will be.

Conversely, the broader your stroke, the fewer you'll hit.

People don't stop to read unless the headline addresses them specifically. Broad, general headlines don't address anyone. I know, you think you're addressing more people. But what's really happening is, you're not addressing anyone specifically enough to grab their attention.

You can't slap people out of their fog with general headlines.

You may have to get more focused than you are now. You may have to zero in on that $50,000 home buyer, and talk straight to them ... addressing their specific needs and concerns, and doing it in their language.

The natural question is; "But Larry, I'm paying for newspaper space. That paper goes out to thousands of people, most of whom are not in the $50,000 range. Don't I want to talk to all of them to get my money's worth?"

The answer is; "Do you want to sell a house, or not?"

If you want to sell a house, you have to decide who the likely buyer is, and what's on their mind.

You have to think about them reading the paper. What articles will they read? What language will connect with them? What's going on in their world? Why would they be buying a house ... or even considering it? What's the most important thing (to them) about that house?

My wife works for a big company that moves her every year or two. So, we've bought a number of houses. We know what we want, but it's not always easy to find it. Oh, it's not difficult because we're looking for something weird. It's difficult because realtors don't seem to be want to tell us what we need to know!

What do your customers need to know?

What are the most important things on their mind when they are getting ready to buy whatever it is that you sell?

When we look at houses, we want a dynamite kitchen. Failing that, we want the space and infrastructure to be able to build a dynamite kitchen. Then, we want entertaining space … of course, flowing from the kitchen. That's what's important to us. The real estate agents all tend to talk about what's important to them.

What do you talk about? Do you talk about the things you think are important about your product or service? Or, do you know why people buy from you, and tell others just like them that that's what you offer?

Grabbing Attention

I'm a big fan of advertising. It's fun to read ads, and try to figure out just what the writer was trying to accomplish. Unfortunately, in too many cases the writer didn't seem to know themselves!

The headline should grab your prospects' attention. It has to break through their mundane existence, and make them stop and want to read more.

Remember, the "attention" step in *The Magic Formula* is where you make an emotional connection with your reader.

Emotional Appeals

So, before you start to write, give some thought to what emotion you want to appeal to. Hey, the headline is the emotional connection – it makes sense to have an idea of what emotion you're going to connect with before you start to write, right?

Here are some of the emotional appeals most often used in advertising;

GREED	GUILT	FEAR
DESIRE	Safety	Popularity
Love	Sex	Escape
Wealth	Prosperity	Education
Profit	Ego	Something New
Exclusivity	Pride	Being First

Pity	Sympathy	Envy
Comfort	Release	Discovery
Pleasure	Fun	Opportunity

Of course, there are many more.

> **IMPORTANT LESSON:** *The top two emotional appeals are FEAR and GREED.*

If you think about it, all emotions are subsets of either fear or greed.

Another way to think of it, is that you are either motivating away from pain, or toward some kind of reward.

You're either helping them avoid some negative outcome they're likely to experience if they fail to take advantage of your product or service, or you're going to make their life better somehow.

That's all there is to it. Simple, huh?

So, your first challenge is to figure out what emotional appeal you want to make.

Make it One-to-One

Your ad or piece may be put before thousands of prospective readers. But remember, only one will read it at a time.

So don't write to "everyone" or "anyone." Write to YOU. Then, you're talking about one person – the one who's reading your piece right now. Nobody else matters to them.

Headline Hooks

There are several classic headline "hooks" you should be aware of. Some you might want to use, others, you really should avoid.

Here are the six you see most often in advertising.

Next time to read the paper, see if you can spot what hook they're using, and what emotional appeal they're trying to make at the same time.

You'll be surprised to find out poorly thought out most advertising is! There's often no hook, and no emotional appeal.

But that won't happen to your advertising!

1.) Self Interest

Remember I said you have to break through your prospects' preoccupation with their mundane, every day world. That world includes millions of commercial messages, all saying "pick our product" or "pick our company."

Most sellers of products and services talk endlessly about themselves. They tell the prospect all about the virtues of their company and the features of their products. What they fail to talk about is the most important thing.

If you want your headlines and copy to break through, and to stand out in the crowd of competing messages, the best way to do it is to talk about your prospects' favorite topic.

I know, you have thousands of prospects … all individual human beings. How the heck can you know what each one's favorite topic is? And, how can you cover all of them in one headline?

> **IMPORTANT LESSON:** *Everybody's favorite topic is **themselves**. Stop talking about yourself and your product or service, and start talking about how your prospect's life will be better after they own it or use it.*

Self Interest headlines talk about the prospect, and how your product or service will make their life better. Will it help them get smarter? More attractive? Wealthier? More popular?

So, to write self interest headlines, you have to be able to articulate what will be better about their life, not what's better about your product.

The nice thing about this, is that you don't even have to be better than your competition. Odds are, they're talking about themselves. If you talk about your prospect … and how their life will be better after they take advantage of your offer … you'll be talking about what really matters; Themselves.

Lower your Golf Scores

FREE Booklet: 10 Practice Tips To Improve Your Golf Game...*FAST*

PGA pro Doug Hendricks shows you how to get maximum results. No obligation - call NOW!

Tee It Up Golf

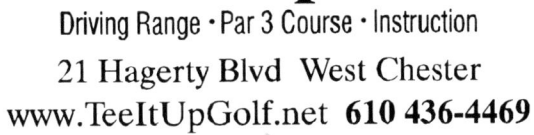

Driving Range • Par 3 Course • Instruction

21 Hagerty Blvd West Chester

www.TeeItUpGolf.net 610 436-4469

Rt 202 to Matlack, South to Hagerty Blvd, Left 3 blocks

Would you say this sample headline addresses a self interest? A specific kind of person?

Is it motivating the reader away from pain for toward some kind of reward?

Every golfer wants to lower their scores. Heck, Tiger Woods still wants to lower his scores.

> **An aside:** *Something else interesting about this ad ... It doesn't sell the actual product at all. It offers free information. This is a lead generation ad, designed to get the prospect to respond. Thousands may see this ad, but only golfers will respond. Now, we have a name and address of a known golfer. We can establish a relationship with them one-on-one now. (Read more about this strategy in the chapter on one-step and two-step advertising.)*

2.) News

I recently bought a bottle of Tide laundry detergent. I've bought Tide for as long as I've done laundry. My mother bought Tide, and I would guess that my grandmother probably did too. Talk about lifetime value of a customer!

Anyway, the Tide bottle had the word NEW in giant letters.

Wait a minute, how can Tide be NEW? If my mother and grandmother used it, and I'm still a loyal customer, what would they want to change?

This particular bottle had a NEW scent. Nothing else is different. But, it's NEW, and that's enough to put a NEWS headline on the packaging. (Yes, packages have headlines, too. What's the first thing your prospect reads on your product package?)

GOOD NEWS if you're considering Home Ownership ...

... By far the greatest wealth for all affluent households is the value of their home. 34 percent of the wealth of these families represents equity in their primary residence.

Consumer Federation of America

There's no better news than GOOD NEWS.

This example was one I put together for a makeover during one of my workshops. I was speaking for the Florida Association of Mortgage Brokers. Two days before the program, I heard a story on the Today Show about a report that had just been released by the Consumer Federation of America, stating that equity in the family home is a big part of personal wealth.

That's news!

The world is constantly changing. Your industry is constantly changing. Consumer preferences are constantly changing. All are sources of news.

But, make sure the news is important to your prospects. It doesn't matter if it's important to you. The only one that matters in the equation is the prospect reading your ad or piece. What does it mean to them?

By the way, what's the emotional appeal in the sample ad? Wealth? Is that not a subset of GREED?

3.) Fast, Easy Way

Who's not looking for a faster, easier way to get things done?

This hook works for all kinds of convenience products.

Think about TV Dinners. Is that not the fast, easy way to feed your family? " A Delicious Dinner Fast … and Easy" might be the headline.(Well, they were delicious when I ate them in college.)

I recently saw a bank ad, carrying the headline; "Shorter, Faster Easier." It was talking about their loan application process. Shorter forms, faster approval, an overall easier process.

I saw another bank ad that said; "The slow, boring way to wealth." It puts a different twist on the Fast, Easy Way hook … but that's what the writer started with.

> **Are you starting to have fun with this?** *You should be. Start looking for this stuff in the ads you read in print, see on TV, or hear on the radio. If you can learn to spot good stuff when you see it, you can learn to write good stuff faster and easier. (Get it … faster and easier??)*

4.) Curiosity

This one's difficult and dangerous(NOT, fast and easy!).

The idea here is to grab the prospect's attention by arousing their curiosity. Usually, a curiosity headline asks some kind of question. The reader should be so curious to find out what the answer is, that they'll stop whatever they're doing and keep reading.

Remember, we're trying to break through the prospects' preoccupation. It's a tough assignment to write a curiosity headline that will get them that involved.

> **IMPORTANT LESSON:** *Curiosity is hard to arouse. Only experienced copy writers should mess with curiosity headlines. Don't be insulted by this next one: If you bought this book, you're not experienced enough to use curiosity. (Nothing personal, OK?)*

In fact, I've seen a lot of failed attempts at curiosity headlines, written by big-time advertising agencies. Most just don't work, even when experienced (and expensive) copy writers and designers try to pull it off.

Many mislead the reader, or draw the wrong kind of reader. I use a bank ad in my workshops that show three pairs of shoes as their headline. (Yes, photos can be headlines - read the chapter about photos.) I cover the rest of the ad, just showing the picture of the shoes, and ask the audience what they thing the ad is selling. Nobody guesses financial services! So, the headline draws people that are looking for shoes, I guess.

Nice job ad agency! You drew a bunch of shoe buyers and foot fetishists to your bank client's ad.

5.) Humor

Listen to the radio for :30 minutes, and you'll hear at least a dozen attempts at humor headlines.

I say "attempts," because most are no more than that.

Jay Leno is paid literally millions of dollars to be funny. If he's that good, you would think all of America would stay up late – maybe even take an afternoon nap so they can – to laugh uncontrollably at this tremendous humor talent. But it is not so.

> **Important point:** *Half of the population really has no sense of humor.*

You know people who don't laugh at anything. Anything! What a way to go through life. But they're out there; the Grumpy, the Grouchy, the Humorless. Heck, it might even be more than half of the population.

Look at the increase in Road Rage. There's a phenomenon. People are traveling effortlessly, reclined in a luxurious leather seat, on the wings of a motorized, mostly automatic vehicle. They're carried in air conditioned comfort from point A to point B, at amazing speed. Yet, if one other driver doesn't fully cooperate in their free passage, they draw the rage of the impeded driver. Do you think those people have a sense of humor??

If half of the population has no sense of humor, humor headlines are lost on them. So, by trying to use humor in your ads and promo pieces, you automatically eliminate half of the population from your audience.

And, I have more bad news for you if you think you're being funny in your ads …

I don't stay up for Jay Leno. I don't find him all that funny. I saw him do standup years ago, and he was hilarious(So, you know I at least have a sense of humor). But now, he just doesn't do anything for me.

That's another point about humor: At least half of the people who do have a sense of humor, don't have the same sense of humor you do. Jay Leno has changed. I don't find him funny anymore. I have a different sense of humor than he does(or his writers do). He's doing fine without me, but none of the advertisers who buy time on the Tonight show get a shot at me.

> **Important point:** *Even if you've ignored my first point(half the population has no sense of humor), and still want to use humor, get this: Half of the people who do have a sense of humor don't have the same sense of humor you do.*

So, what you think is just fall-on-the-floor funny is totally lost on 3/4 of the population. That's 75%, all but 1/4th - whatever you want to call it.

Think about the last time you told a joke at a party. How many people laughed. Not courtesy laughed – really split a gut. You thought it was funny … probably your best joke … or you wouldn't have pulled it out for a public occasion. Unless you were laughing so hard yourself (because, of course, you thought it was hilarious!) that you weren't aware of how others were responding, you undoubtedly saw a number of people who either didn't think it was funny or just didn't get it. No sense of humor, or at least, not the same as yours.

> **IMPORTANT POINT:** *You're burning advertising dollars if you're trying to be cute.*

Maybe you're amused, but most of the human race isn't. And I can guarantee you that failed attempts at humor will not grab or hold many prospects' attention.

Listen to the radio again, and keep score. How many attempts at humor really make you laugh. You'll find it's not very many.

Besides, you're not in the entertainment business. Everybody on Radio seems to think they are. Let them do the entertaining. You want to do the SELLING, and humor won't make it happen for you.

Don't waste your time, energy ... and especially *MONEY* ... on humor advertising.

6.) Testimonial

Testimonial headlines are quotations from comments you have received from happy customers, clients, or patients.

Testimonial headlines are powerful, because they are a third-party endorsement rather than you talking about yourself.

Good testimonials are specific about results;

"Our sales increased 37% using Larry's promotional techniques."
> Bob Jones, Owner
> Bob's Boutique

If I wrote a headline that said "I can help you increase your sales by 37% with my promotional techniques," it wouldn't be nearly as powerful the testimonial version. When I say it ... even if it is true ... sounds like puffery.

People will believe an endorsement from people just like themselves. That's important. The person you quote should be representative of the people you're trying to address. If you're talking to business owners, the quote should be from Bob Jones, Owner of Bob's Boutique.

And, you should include the name, and if appropriate, position, organization, city and state. If you don't identify the source of the quote, it won't be accepted as truth.

> **IMPORTANT POINT:** *Be sure to clearly identify the author of the testimonial. That means it's important to get their permission to use their quotation.*

Good headlines are not that hard to write.

First, know exactly who you are talking to. Picture an individual who perfectly matches the profile of your target reader, and write like it's a personal letter to that individual. You'll be writing one-to-one, "you" copy if you do that.

Then, decide what emotional appeal you're going to go for. It should be appropriate to your product or service. You can use some variation of either FEAR or GREED to sell almost anything.

FEAR is great for automotive alarm systems. You could appeal to GREED by talking about keeping your valuable vehicle, but it's not nearly as effective.

Conversely, you can talk FEAR of failure in life to sell college admissions. But, you'll get more attention with a GREED tack that sells a brighter future for those who carry the sheepskin.

Then think of a hook that will grab the reader. I gave you a few to work with, and a couple to avoid. You may try humor or curiosity of you wish … but the odds are, you'll be burning precious resources(dollars!) in so doing.

This was a long chapter. There's a good reason;

> **IMPORTANT LESSON:** *Your headline is 80% responsible for the success of failure of your ad or promo piece. Give it the most attention in your writing process, and present it graphically so it gets the reader's first attention.*

Chapter 12

Where to Advertise

Where you choose to place your advertising is as important a decision as what goes into the ad.

The options available are almost overwhelming. And each sales representative can give you a pretty strong case for their publication, medium or station. And honestly, each of those can be valuable for different products, situations and reasons.

Who are you selling to?

The most important question in media selection is who your intended audience is. You want to choose media that reach the maximum number of the people you want to reach, without paying for a whole lot of people you don't want to reach.

Who don't you want to reach? Your product or service has universal appeal, right? I mean who wouldn't be able to find a use for your buzz-seeking fly eradicater?

No matter what you sell, it's important to know what kind of person is most likely to buy it. It's not enough to know that someone would see value in your product, or even want it. Can they afford it? Will they remember it, and look for it on the shelves at the store? Are they more likely to pick up the phone and have you deliver your product?

"Know thy buyer" is the key to media selection. Your media advertising representatives can generally give you a pretty good profile of their readers/viewers/listeners. If they can't sent them packing.

You can't afford to invest your marketing dollars to talk to the masses.

You have to zero in on your target customer, focus your attention on them, and spend as little as possible talking to the "overflow."

"Overflow" refers to all the people you're paying to reach who would never buy your product or service. "Overflow" is like "leakage." You pay for it, but it does nothing for you. You might as well have a bonfire for your money.

Market Research

Nothing can replace solid, scientific market research. Market research companies can help you identify exactly what type of person would be predisposed to buying your product or service, what their hobbies are, where they live, what they do with their spare time ... you get the picture.

But you're not likely to spend the money on that kind of research. So, you have to do the same thing with research that you do with most aspects of your business; Do it yourself.

Don't confuse "market research" with "hunches." Market research is scientific. It involves looking a past sales records, talking to people who bought and to people who didn't. It takes time and it takes effort. That's why market research firms charge a lot to do it for you.

But you already know something about your target customer. You have a feel for who buys from you now – at the very least create a profile of your current customers, and look to target people just like them. The more narrowly you can define your target prospect, the more efficiently you can select media that they're likely to see you in.

But it still takes pencil-on-paper market research. Don't tell me: "I know who my customers are," or: "I know who buys my products." Look it up, talk to them, quantify on paper/in the computer. Anything less is a hunch.

Don't ever "invest" in a "hunch." Save that for the trip to Las Vegas.

Advertising based on market research is an investment. Money thrown after a hunch is a gamble at best.

Broadcast Media

When you watch the Super Bowl, you can't help but be drawn by the glitz and glamor of television advertising.

The productions are so elaborate, the music so stirring. Some are simple cartoons, or even silent text messages. The actors' voices, the motion – maybe even dancers. You can do a live product demonstration, or show people enjoying the benefits you're promising. And, you can entertain people. Make them laugh, make them cry … make them thirsty for your product.

Now, how many products that you saw advertised during last year's Super Bowl did you go out and buy?

Television is a complex medium to work in. Yes, you have an enormous pallette of colors, sounds, movement. But, unless you have the budget to hire top talent, from actors and directors to musicians and camera operators, your ad is going to be a waste of money.

Your advertising representative will assure you that they have top-notch people in their production department down at the station. They can take your ad from concept to air. They'll write copy, secure the talent for every aspect of the ad, do all of the filming in their state-of-the-art studios right there in your home town.

They might even stroke your ego by suggesting you be in the ad in stead of paying for expensive actors (yes, they're expensive … even for locals). Heck, nobody can sell your product or service better than you, can they?

Odds are, your ad will scream out that it was done locally. It will make you look like a fool.

Don't believe me? Watch your local news tonight. Pay close attention to which ads look like they were done locally. Trust me, you can tell. More often than not, they make the business owner look like an idiot.

In my home market we have a local cell phone salesman that does all of his own commercials. Whoever told this guy he should be appearing on camera ought to be shot. When I needed a cell phone, I remembered the guy ... remembered that I would never do business with a goofball like him, and avoided his store like it was under quarantine.

His ads are a monument to his enormous ego. And as long as he's paying, the advertising sales rep is going to tell him the ads are wonderful. He's going to give him 237 reasons why he should keep it up.

> **Lesson:** *The advertising sales representative is not in the business of selling your product or service. He/she is in the business of selling advertising.*

The sales rep could care less whether your ads are getting results. The ad rep just cares that you keep buying advertising!

If you can't track specific sales directly to a medium, with sufficient dollars coming in to make the advertising profitable, you can't afford it. And if you're advertising on television, it's almost impossible to track sales unless you're doing an infomercial. Infomercials, by the way, are a totally different ball game. I'm talking about :30 and :60 second ads.

Coca Cola can afford television advertising. You can't.

Coca Cola is willing to spend millions of dollars every year on advertising intended to do nothing more that make people remember their name. Then, hopefully, when they get thirsty, that name recognition will translate into a 75¢ sale.

Television is an excellent medium for building name recognition. But you have to hammer people over and over again to get that recognition established. You've seen ads that become downright irritating because you've seen them so many times. Or, you've seen ads that were amusing ... the first three of four times.

If you have seen an ad so many times that you can sing along with the jingle, the advertiser has gotten his money's worth. He has hit you over the head so many times, that his message is now ingrained into your consciousness.

If you have seen an ad that many times, your television viewing habits are a good match for the model the advertiser has identified. You are exactly the kind of person they think is likely to buy their product. They already knew what shows you would watch before they ran the ads. Pretty scientific, huh?

Yeah, it's scientific. And science costs money. Can you afford the market research it would take to create a model matching your target customers' viewing habits? Most small businesses and professional practices can't even articulate who their target customer is yet, let alone figure out what TV shows they watch!

> **Lesson:** *Your television ad rep can clearly define the audience that watches each individual program. That means you have to place your ads only during the programs that your target audience watches. And you pay a premium price to do that.*

It makes sense, doesn't it? You want your ads to appear only during the programs your target customer watches. You pay more for that placement ... a lot more. But it's the only way to go if you're going to be on TV. It's the only way you reach a significant number of real prospects, and pay for a minimum of overflow.

The option is to pay for run-of-schedule placement. That means, they plug your ad in wherever there happens to be a spot nobody else paid for specifically. It's a lot cheaper, and therefore, very tempting. After all, you're on a budget, right?

Problem is, you may be on the 7:00 AM news, the Barney show, One Life To Live, Leave it to Beaver, and The Tonight Show. No one person sees your ad twice!

The key to name recognition and brand building is repetition. The individual must see you many times before the message creeps into their consciousness. If you're on a run-of-schedule rate, you might not hit anyone twice all week – let alone hope to hit someone in your target audience enough times to make an impact.

To be effective, television advertising has to hit your prospect many times in a short time frame. To do that without paying for a lot of "overflow," you have to be advertising entirely on shows that you know your prospect will be watching. And, you have to know that a large percentage of the audience that watches that program will be realistic prospects. You don't want to spend advertising dollars talking to a lot of people who will never buy, so this research is important.

Never mind the cost of the ads and the production. Can you even afford the research that should go into it before you ever write a script? Probably not. And if you're not doing the research, you're not making a good bet with your advertising dollars. You're better off investing the money in lottery tickets – the odds of success are about as good.

So, say you do have a budget like Coca Cola's. You spend millions to build name recognition.

Does that translate into sales? Coke's been talking to you for years. When's the last time you bought one?

I'm not demeaning Coca Cola here. I happen to drink Diet Coke, and as of this writing session, own stock in the company. It's a great company with a wonderful product line. But their advertising objectives are a lot different from yours. Just because you see their gorgeous, expensive ads on TV, and just because they're a profitable company, doesn't necessarily mean that advertising on TV will make you a profitable company.

It just took me a long time to make a simple point; You can't afford television. If you could, you wouldn't be reading this book. Don't be tempted.

What about local Cable TV?

Didn't you learn anything from the previous 1289 words? I just took a long time telling you that you can't afford television.

Yes, local cable is less expensive that network television … a LOT less expensive. Yes, it zeros in geographically on your local market area. And, yes, you can target programs you think your prospects will be watching. (You only "think" they will – you didn't invest in the market research you need to know they will.)

Plus, having been lured by the low price, you will now want to spend even less on creative and production. So, of course, the local cable station can provide all of the creative and production help you need at a very reasonable price.

About 562 words ago, I told you not to let a local TV station do your creative and production work. It will make you look stupid. The local cable station has creative and production capabilities about seventeen levels beneath those of the local network station. They will make you look stark raving mad. All at your expense!

I repeat: If you bought this book, you cannot afford television. If someone else bought you this book as a gift, they know you can't afford television. It's time for you to realize it, too.

Television is good for long term, repeated-contact name recognition and brand building. That's good for Coca Cola. You can't afford it.

Radio

Who wouldn't want hear their name and jingle on the same station as their favorite recording artist? You listen to KGYP every day, and you're sure your target customers do, too.

Radio is one media that is very good at defining their overall audience. I told you that in television, you have to pick each individual show to hit a specific audience.

Radio listeners tend to be loyal to specific stations. Think about the station set buttons on your car radio. There's one you listen to most of the time, then three or four others you go to as backups when your primary station is doing something stupid. But after a few tunes, you go back to your primary station.

But there are still different demographic groups listening at different times of the day. The people who listen during morning drive time aren't listening at 10:00 AM. You have to find out when your target customer listens, and pay to be on the air at that time.

Just like with television, you can buy run-of-schedule. It's cheaper, but you have no control over who will hear it. Odds are, too much of it will be overflow. Pay for the ideal times, or don't bother with radio.

Newspaper

Newspaper is the work horse of many advertising campaign.

If you're trying to reach a large percentage of your local community, newspaper is hard to beat.

Although the rates may seem expensive, consider the benefits of advertising in your paper.

>   1.) Newspaper reaches the majority of the (educated) population.
>   2.) Newspaper is there every day
>   3.) Newspaper allows the use of coupons
>   4.) Newspaper is great for lead generation advertising.

1.) Newspaper reaches the majority of the (educated) population.

You already know that most educated adults read the newspaper. If your *clearly defined target customer* is educated adults, this is where they come every day.

One of the challenges with newspaper, is making sure that your prospects actually notice and read your ad.

The ad design techniques in this manual will help considerably. But, you have to be in regularly enough to give them a chance to see you.

> **IMPORTANT LESSON:** *You must be in your daily local paper at least once every week, preferably more often. If you can't commit to doing that, don't use newspaper. You're not giving it a fair chance.*

Frequency is very important. People don't read the paper absolutely every day. They don't read every section or page every time they do read the paper. And, you'll be placed where you're hard to see at times.

Those are all opportunities for your prospect to miss your ad. It's got to be in over and over if anyone is going to see and read it.

And be consistent. I hammer and hammer on this. You must look the same every time you're in.

After seeing you peripherally on a weekly basis, they begin to recognize you. Eventually, they'll stop to learn more.

If you change your ad every week, you're a total stranger starting from scratch every time. The only way to get results in the newspaper is to be consistent, frequent … and patient.

Your audience is there. Give them time to find you.

2.) Newspaper is there every day

It's a great place to make timely offers. You can specify that your ad will be in on, say, Monday, to promote your Terrific Tuesday sale.

You can time the delivery of your message to arrive any day of the week, any day of the year.

That's one area where the newspaper actually has an advantage over direct mail. The audience isn't as qualified, but the timing is guaranteed. You have now way of guessing when our friends at the postal service will decide to deliver your direct mail.

3.) Newspaper allows the use of coupons

If you like to use coupon promotions, the newspaper is a great way to distribute your offer.

Whether you are doing so in space advertising or an insert, you can put your coupon into the hands of the majority of your city's educated, adult population.

And, with coupons, you can instantly measure your ad's response. When they start showing up, you know your ad was noticed ... and effective.

4.) Newspaper is great for lead generation advertising.

I don't like to pay for a lot of overflow advertising. And, newspaper is generally a lot of overflow – you pay to reach your whole city, even if only a small percentage of the population is likely to buy your product or service.

Lead generation advertising is the answer.

(It's also the answer if you can't afford big ads in your newspaper. Small, lead generation ads ... possibly even classifieds ... can be powerful marketing weapons.)

You can read about lead generation advertising in the chapter on One-Step and Two-Step promotions, so I won't go into it here.

Suffice it to say, lead generation advertising is the way to get that small percentage who are likely prospects to raise their hands and identify themselves. Then, you can work them one-on-one with direct mail – and without "overflow."

Free Community Papers

You may know them as the paper that arrives unsolicited in your driveway once a week.

Whether you read them or not, I can assure you that a good many people do. Don't turn your nose up because you don't use them to make your buying decisions.

If your prospects use these papers, you'd better consider being in them.

They're inexpensive. That's one of their big advantages.

Since they're inexpensive, they're a great place to test your direct response ads. You can tinker with your ad at minimal cost, fine tuning it until you start getting acceptable response. Then, you can roll it out to the local newspaper, or city magazine … whatever.

They also have a huge audience you may not be aware of. They land on everyone's driveway, just like they land on yours. Many people look forward to them.

Many now include local news, making them even more read.

Ask your community paper publisher about their readers. They know who picks it up and reads it. If they're a fit with your *clearly defined target customer*, by all means, get yourself in there.

Business Journals

All major cities have a local business journal. They are the newspaper local businesses look to for information and for sales leads.

If you market "business to business," in your home city, this is the place to be.

It's expensive. Sorry. It's expensive.

But, look at the audience you're getting. If you ask for the subscribed circulation, you'll find that these papers land in most local businesses. And they often land directly on the desk of the CEO, and other senior management.

Most copies land on the desks of business decision makers. That's access that is hard to match.

If you sell business to business, the business journal is probably worth the expense.

There are many more options out there.

There are city-specific magazines, association newsletters, church bulletins, restaurant placemats, little league fence panels. There's something for everyone. But you have to base your marketing and promotion investments on solid research.

Don't just take a flyer to see if something will work.

When you research potential media, don't base your decision on whether you read/watch/listen. What matters is whether your prospects do.

You have to first identify your *clearly defined target customer*. Then, you have to find media that they are likely to read. Ideally, you want media that ONLY they are likely to read. The more non-prospects read or listen to a specific media, the more overflow you're paying for.

Paying for a lot of overflow is inefficient use of your precious advertising dollars. If you have little choice but to media with heavy overflow, use lead generation advertising to get direct access to those in their audience who are real prospects. Then, use direct mail to speak directly to them in the future.

Whatever you do, be consistent, and be regular. Don't take breaks, don't advertise seasonally. Be there regularly all year. Your prospects need to be reminded of your presence.

And, if you're in regularly, people will see you as a solid, confident business. You've got to love that idea.

Chapter 13

Brochures

Does your brochure "sell?"

A brochure should be more that just information and pretty pictures. Like any other promo piece, your brochure should draw readers in ... make that draw the *right* readers in.

Then, it should take them step-by-step through the buying sequence, culminating ultimately in them taking a next step.

Draw them in ...

The cover panel of your brochure should be inviting to your clearly defined prospect.

I'm going to assume you're working with a color brochure. I believe in Shoestring Marketing(the title of my 1995 book, by the way!), but for this project I recommend that you spring for color. Of course, the techniques and sequence I'm talking about apply to a black-and-white brochure, too. But I'm generally talking about a four-color, glossy-stock piece.

Why? The brochure is often the primary collateral piece an organization offers. If there is only one piece that your prospective buyer would see, the brochure is the piece.

Hey you!

Nothing draws readers in like a good photograph.

And, nothing qualifies your audience like a good photograph.

When I say "qualifies," I mean that the photo will determines exactly who will pick your brochure up and read it.

People are most drawn to photos of other people. More specifically, people are drawn to photos of other people who are just like them. So your models should depict the kind of person who makes an ideal prospect for your offering.

Groups of models should be used to sell products or services that will either be purchased as a group, or used as a group.

If you're selling to families with young children, you'll have a mom, a dad, and a couple of kids(one boy, one girl … unless your offering is aimed at families with all boys or all girls).

Associations print thousands of brochures to promote their annual conventions. Many choose a photo of the destination for the cover. This can work if the destination is the biggest benefit of attending(and I've been to conventions where, sadly, that is the case!). But the biggest benefit is probably the networking and/or education. Maybe it's the trade show.

> **IMPORTANT LESSON:** *Your photograph should show people just like your prime prospect, enjoying the prime benefit you are promising in your piece.*

Your photograph will be the first visual focal point on the front cover panel. To be the first visual focal point, it will be the first graphic element at the top of the page. That's not to say it has to be all the way at the top of the paper, but that it just has to be the first element on the page. No titles, logos or headlines above it. You want them to see the photograph first.

Since the photo is so important to qualifying and drawing the right readers in, it should dominate the panel. I like to use 2/3 of the available space for a photo. You may be more frugal with your space, but consider the importance of the photo. If it determines whether people are drawn in or not, it deserves at least a dominant presence on the page.

Remember the formula ...

Your brochure should do a complete job of arousing interest, promising results, and proving that your organization can deliver.

The brochure will not, however, include a time-limited proposition like the other pieces do. You'll print up to a year's supply of your color brochure, so time-sensitive offers just won't fit. Plus, people will probably hold on to your brochure for future reference. Maybe they're not ready to buy when they first see the brochure. But, if they may be interested later on, and want to keep the brochure in a file so it's handy when the time comes.

A time-sensitive offer might alienate them when they reexamine the brochure after the expiration date.

The kind of proposition you want to make in your brochure is simply to take the next step. That step can be to set up an appointment, take a test drive, or talk with a sales person.

A Sales Person's Caveat

NEVER let someone take a brochure without recording who they are, when they took it, and any other observations that may help you close a sale later on. It's too easy to just offer the free information and hope they'll be so impressed by it that they beat a path back to your door to buy.

Don't assume that, just because they took a brochure, they're really interested. It's easy for them to say "we'll just take this home and think about it," when they know darned well the brochure is going in the next waste basket they pass.

You need to ask them when they'll be making a decision, and when would be a good time to follow up.

Your job is to make the sale, not wait for them to come back and buy. Be proactive every step of the way.

The Front Panel

The front panel is like the headline in an ad. It is the information upon which the reader will base their decision whether to open the brochure ... or toss it in the trash.

And the odds are against you ...

I hate to be the one to break it to you if you don't already realize this, but at least 80% of your expensive – gorgeous – full-color brochures go into a trash bin without ever being opened. For many, it's more like 95%-plus.

You can improve your odds considerably by displaying a benefit to the prospect predominantly on the front cover.

The ideal benefit display(I'll say it again!) is a good photo. People who look just like your prime prospects, enjoying the benefit your product or service promises, is the ideal attention-getter. If you can't afford a photograph, make it a benefit-laden headline that dominates the front panel.

Do not make the dominant element your company name.

Did you get that? <u>Do</u> <u>not</u> make the dominant element your company name.

People aren't looking for your promo package as they go through their mail, or the stack of brochures they've gotten from the hundreds of organizations that supply something similar to what you do.

They're looking for a reason to choose you over your competition. THAT is what should dominate the cover. Give them a reason to pick your brochure up first. (Need I tell you, that your company name is not a reason?)

The photo or the headline must be the first thing they see. If you use a photo, there should be a caption beneath it, emphasizing the benefit depicted above.

Look at your brochure now ...

Go ahead, pull one of your brochures out of the box. I know you have thousands, because they were cheaper to print that way ... at least, cheaper "per brochure." So, now you have a three-year supply of brochures that cost pennies each to print. Unfortunately, they may be costing you thousands in lost business, because they go straight into the trash.

I'm not trying to beat up on you. But I want you to think hard about how many copies to print next time. If you have thousands of your old brochure in boxes, I now you're not likely to toss them and start over now. (Although, it may well be your best move – if you're realizing that your brochure sucks, don't keep sending it out just because you've got a whole bunch of them!) But promise me you'll print a 12-month or smaller supply next time, please?

Q.) *What's the dominant visual element on the cover of your brochure?*

If you're like most organizations, your brochure screams your company name at the reader.

Or, you may have a picture of the company headquarters. Maybe its' a photo of one of your prize widgets. Please tell me it's not a picture of the company owner and/or staff.

Look at it from the eyes of a prospective buyer. Do they care what your building looks like? Do they care what you or your staff look like? They may not even care what the product looks like.

If you sell products whose physical appearance makes them superior to your competitors', then by all means, feature the product on the cover. But show a human being enjoying the benefit of owning one.

If you sell office furniture, put a comfortable, happy office worker in the chair. If you sell playground equipment, show happy/healthy children enjoying it. Get the idea?

The Sequence

And, remember *The Magic Formula*. Present your information in the proper sequence throughout the brochure.

Now, brochures should provide lots of solid information about your product or service. The cover letter that goes in the envelope with it … or the sales person who hands it to the prospect … will focus more on benefits.

The brochure will focus more on the "proof" step. But, before you go into "proof," you have to get their attention and promise a benefit. Those two steps happen right on the cover panel … and in that sequence.

An Example:

Here's a brochure from a golf center. It's directed at people who plan company meetings, inviting them to try a different kind of meeting venue. I must admit that, before I saw this brochure, it would never have occurred to me to hold a company meeting at a golf center. But, if you think about it, there are all kinds of things you can do to bond with your people, encourage team attitude, and just have a good time in a casual atmosphere.

So, here's the cover as it was first handed to me;

Westerville Golf Center

450 W Schrock Rd
Westerville, OH
614.794.2670

I felt there was a little confusion as to what the visual focal point was on this cover.

When your prospect picks up your brochure, their eye shouldn't have to work at where to go first.

Something ... one single graphic element, should draw the eye immediately. In most cases, a photograph will do that(Especially a photograph of people just like the prospect – We're all drawn to people just like ourselves.).

In this case, the photo competes with the company name for top billing, doesn't it?

The only element that hints at what the brochure is about, and who it's directed at, is at the very top in the smallest type in the space. The question: "WHERE DO YOU PLAN TO HOLD YOUR NEXT MEETING?" is probably going to be overlooked by most readers.

Why?

Once the eye is drawn to a spot down the page, the picture or the company name in this case, it does not go back up. So, the visual focal point (the photo or the company name for most readers) has drawn the eye past the most important information to the buyer.

To compound the situation, the question: "WHERE DO YOU PLAN TO HOLD YOUR NEXT MEETING?" is set in all capital letters. People are not used to seeing sentences(yes, a question is a sentence) set in all capital letters. So, they don't stop to read it – it doesn't register.

Natural Eye Patterns

Research has shown that, when most people pick up a page to read, their eye actually starts about one-third down the page, and two-thirds from the left. To show you graphically, the eye generally starts at the circled intersection in this diagram;

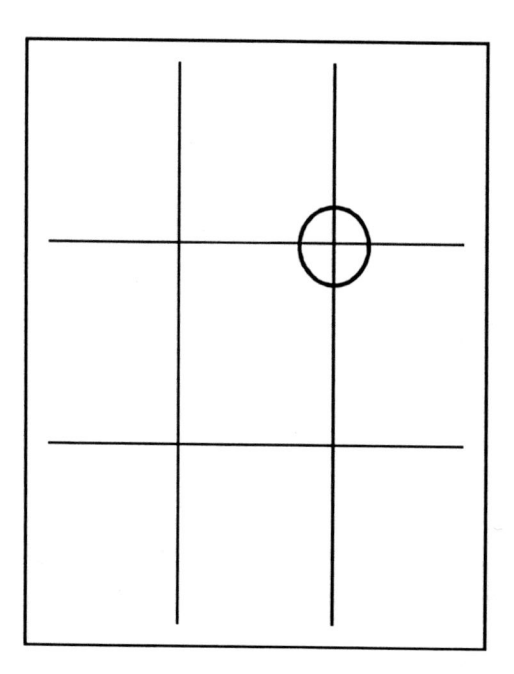

Why?

I don't know. Isn't honesty refreshing?

I'm serious, I don't know. I just read the research, and that's what they found.

And it doesn't really matter "why." What matters is, your reader is going to start at that point on the page.

If you engage them at that point, they will stay there, then continue in the natural reading pattern of left to right, top to bottom. They will not go back to the top of the page.

So, back to our example brochure ... the reader was probably engaged by the photograph. To some, the large logo and company name may have drawn their eye past the photo. Either way, they are down the page, and not likely to go back to the top. So, the important message ... the question "Where do you plan to hold your next meeting?", is not seen.

They see a picture, and the name of a golf center. If they don't golf, the brochure is in the trash. Even if they do golf, they probably see that the picture is of a miniature golf course. If they don't like miniature golf, the brochure goes strait to the trash.(Do you see a pattern emerging here?)

Even if they like golf, and even if they like miniature golf, they still haven't made the connection between the golf center and their next team-building event.

Since they're responsible corporate employees, and would never invest their time at the office thinking about their personal recreation(Yeah, right!), the brochure goes into the trash.

> **IMPORTANT LESSON:** *If you are creating a brochure to be mailed to businesses, the featured benefit must be something that will help the reader in the pursuit of their career. Notice, I didn't say it must necessarily help their business ... I said it must help that individual's career.*

Business to business advertising(which is what this brochure was designed for) usually talks about benefit to the buyer's organization. Here's another hot piece of information;

Never Forget: *The business buyer is not looking out for his/her organization. He/she is looking out for himself/herself.*

I don't mean they're irresponsible about their duty to company. Of course, they're not going to buy something that will be detrimental to the organization but beneficial to them. What they buy will be beneficial to themselves and to their organization.

But, given competitive products that are both beneficial to their organization ... with one more personally beneficial to the individual decision-maker ... the one that will help their career or life in the process will get the nod every time.

So, your brochure is in a stack with 50 competitors. All can make a good case for what the product or service does for the purchasing organization. But yours also tells the purchasing agent how you will make them look good, how they will be a champion for choosing you. Which one do you think they'll pick up first?

So, how about this for a makeover of the sample brochure;

Make your next meeting a truly Special Event...

(And you'll be the hero!)

WGC Westerville Golf Center

Unique Setting • Memorable Events
450 W Schrock Rd • 614 794-2670

I'm not wild about the photo, but I wanted to stick with as many elements of the original brochure as I could.

If you are going to use a photo, it should dominate the page. It will be the starting point for your reader's eye, so you want to put it at the top of the page. (Any copy above the photo will probably not be read, so don't be tempted to put type at the top of the page.)

Headline as a caption ...

Any time you see a photo in a printed publication, it's natural to look under it for a caption.

That's where you want the benefit headline. And this one tells the reader immediately that we're selling this facility as a meeting venue.

It promises a meeting that will become a "special event."

Then, it goes even further, to promise the meeting planner that he or she will be a hero! Too strong for you? Then promise it will be easy for him/her to handle the details. Promise their employees will thank them for coming up with a refreshing change of meeting pace.

But do something to tell the individual purchaser that you're going to make their life or career better.

> **IMPORTANT LESSON:** *Business buying decisions are made by individuals. Yes, they want to do what's right for the business or practice. But if you and a competitor are both good for the business, the one that does more for the purchasing agent will get the deal.*

I'm not suggesting anything unethical here. Don't try to buy the buyer. Don't promise benefits you can't actually deliver. Be honest and ethical all the way.

But recognize that an individual human being will make the decision to buy from you or from a competitor. If you are the only one to address their personal needs and desires, you will have their attention.

The benefit you use to grab their attention doesn't even have to be unique. If none of your competitors are presenting it, you become the leader.

Sequence

After promising the benefits, we tell them where they can get them.

The logo and business name are much smaller than they were on the original brochure. I don't want them to draw the eye away from the photo and benefit. I want the reader to take those in, in the proper sequence.

After they're excited about the possibilities, they find out where to go/who to call.

Then, I threw in a little tag line: "Unique Setting • Memorable Events"

This place is unique(If you're ever in Westerville, stop and hit a bucket of balls.), and an event held here will definitely stand out from the ones in hotel meeting rooms.

No outrageous claims, just the facts, Mam.

Then, the address and phone number. No more needed for the cover. We want them to go inside to get more information.

Inside the brochure ...

OK, you got them to open your brochure and look inside. You've made the first cut, because believe me, most of the brochures they received never got opened. So, congratulations!

Now what?

It's important to get the reader to receive all of your information, in sequence.

Now, your brochure may be a tri-fold. Or, it may open to two pages.

Either way, you want the reader to start at the top of the first page.

Knowing that their eye will naturally go to the upper/right 1/3rd of the open page, you need to put something at the top of page one to draw the eye.

Now, what draws the eye better than anything else? Yes, a photo. A photo of people enjoying the benefit you have promised on the cover.

So, we want a photo of a group of business people letting their hair down, enjoying a very special event. It should show off the facility from the point of view of a meeting planner. People having fun, working as a team, eating good food, enjoying cold libations ...

The photo has to be specific to the buyer you're talking to. This brochure is for meeting planners, so we don't want pictures of young kids cutting up on the miniature golf course. We don't want photos of obviously serious golfers working hard on the driving range. Those images are for other media.

The first photo is the strongest – we don't want the eye to wonder where to wander. We want them to start at the top, left.

Then, we want to lead them graphically into the text.

Give them lots of information. How many people you can handle for one event has to come early. If their meeting is for 500, and you only accommodate 100, they need to know that early. In fact, if you don't tell them early, they'll wander around the page looking for it. If they find it on the last panel, even if it's the right number for them, they've skipped all of that other information to find it.

Do you think they'll go back to the beginning, then? Don't bet on it.

> **IMPORTANT LESSON:** *You have to present the information in the sequence in which they need it. So, you have to know your buyer and what matters to them.*

This is a big difference about the brochure vs. the flyer or ad. They expect more facts and details in the brochure, and they expect to find them easily. Charts and graphs that communicate important numbers simply are extremely valuable in brochures. Give them the information they need at a glance.

Use the graphics and photos to keep the eye flowing through the proper sequence. Don't distract the eye with a lot of pictures that don't tell your story.

By "tell your story," I mean that you should be walking them through your information, using photos and graphics along the way. Each graphic or photo supports the information it appears with.

So, that first panel is talking about what size groups we can handle. The first photo will be of a group(the largest size we can handle.) Then, maybe we talk about the serving capabilities of our kitchen and wait staff. The photo will be people seated at table, enjoying a terrific meal. Or, if we don't offer seated dining, we see people standing around the grill eating hot dogs and drinking beer.

You get the idea. The "story" has a sequence, and each photo or graphic supports the particular step in the sequence that it appears with.

Contact Information

Across the bottom of each page, you should place contact information; Your organization's name, telephone number and web site address. Make it small – it should not distract the eye. It should simply be there any time they might need it.

Contact information should never dominate a page – benefits should always dominate. But contact information should always be close at hand. Imagine if the prospect was sold on your product or service, then couldn't find how to get in touch with you!

And include it on every page. You never know how the prospect my tear or cut your brochure up. If there is a reply/order form in the brochure, make sure there is contact information on the actual reply/order form, and that it will still be easy to find on what's left of the brochure after it's been cut or torn out(in case it gets separated from the rest of the brochure and package).

Keep Holy The Magic Formula

From front panel to back, you have to take your prospect through the whole selling sequence. Even though there will be a sales letter in the package you mail it in, it will probably get separated from it, and have to stand on its own.

Make sure your brochure makes the whole sale, taking the prospect from "total stranger" to "ready to write a check."

Chapter 14

Email and Ezines

As I say in the chapter on web pages, what you're getting in this book is not the best hi-tech info available.

In fact, I'm woefully low tech.

That said, I do have some tremendously useful information for you. I just wouldn't recommend that you make this manual the only one you use to design and write web pages, Email campaigns, and Ezines.

Why do I say that? I don't like email. I like two ezines, and find the other 18 I've subscribed to (in moments of weakness) to be a total waste of my time.

The difference between the two;

For the purpose of this chapter, let me tell you what I am referring to with the terms "Email" and "Ezine."

Email

Email is the equivalent to a letter in direct mail. It is written as though it were being sent to one individual, just as you would a letter. It may be used to inform, to sell, or simply to keep in touch.

Generally, an email will be about one topic, product or service. It may be sent at any time, with or without a normal pattern.

There is a certain political correctness the self-appointed web police want you to follow with email. There are no actual rules out there. But those who consider themselves the keepers of the Internet's virtue seem to think it is rude to send a sales email without getting the recipient's permission first.

These people call email that they did not specifically ask for "Spam."

Although I must admit that I receive a lot of email that I don't want, it's a small chore to block email from any sender from whom I prefer not to hear. The Internet Virtue Police(IVP) will quickly point out that the Spammers can easily change email addresses to end run around your block, and hound you incessantly until the day you die.

So, now there are Spam Filters. You can list key words that, if they appear in the subject line or in the body of the email, will trigger the filter and the email will go into a bin, never to be seen unless you go looking for it specifically.

The problem with spam filters, is that your best friend may innocently refer to "porn," or accidently misspell "born," and her message is filtered to your email dungeon. When her new baby is porn, you may miss the birth announcement.

If you are sending email sales letters, you have to be careful not to use the words that so many Spam Filters trigger on many words you may use in normal conversation. Words like "Free," "Sale," and many other four letter words will cause Spam Filters to reject your sales letter ... even when you have been careful only to address it to people who want and need your products or services. Before you hit the "send" button, go through the text and change any words that may even remotely hint at spam.

My opinion: I can't filter what lands in my postal mailbox. Why should I hope to filter what lands in my email inbox? I know, it doesn't cost people much to send email over and over again. But, it doesn't take me long to delete them, either.

Typically, I read about one out of every 10 or 15 emails in my inbox. I decide in about two seconds whether an email gets opened or deleted. In the inbox, you can see who it's from, and the subject line. If it's not from someone I know, the subject line has to be extremely compelling. And I'm not easily compelled. Hey, I'm a copy writer myself – my BS-sensor is pretty strong.

Here are just a few that showed up in my inbox this morning.

FROM	SUBJECT
FREE	7 day free supply of heartburn medication
Grow Larger	Increase your male size
No More Debt	How much do you owe?

I could go on, but it doesn't get much better.

Who on earth would ever open any one of these emails? I have no idea who they are. They're making uninteresting or unbelievable promises/offers. They apparently bought lists of random names, and sent all 100,000 of us the same email, hoping someone out there would be stupid enough to bite.

I rarely open an email from a total stranger.

I never, EVER open an email that came from a free email provider. I'm sure there are a handful of legitimate businesses that actually use Hotmail.com as their email provider. Well, no … I'm not sure there are. If you use a free email service, I assume you've been kicked out of every legitimate paid service by now. I'm not opening your Spam.

Another piece of information that shows up in the inbox list, is the size of the message. A large file from an unknown sender is an instant delete. So, if you're sending a sales message, make it a short text message, including a hyperlink to the site where I can get more information if I'm interested. A compelling headline on a very short text message might get me to at least see what it's about.

By the way, I never EVER open an attached file from a stranger. It's just not safe. So, don't send the additional information in the form of an attached file. First of all, that will make the file size on the inbox listing large … meaning it will get deleted. Secondly, if you don't have a web site to refer me to, you can't be much of a business. If you're not serious enough about being in business to at least have a web site, I'm not buying anything from you anyway.

The IVP feel very strongly that Spam should be somehow controlled. I hate Spam as much as the next guy. But there's no practical way to control it, except to block, filter, or delete the bad stuff at your own inbox. These same intellectuals think "junk mail" shouldn't be delivered to their homes. They probably think advertising is ruining newspapers and TV.

Advertising, be it via email, postal mail, or media, is what makes the world go 'round, my friend. (It's certainly what makes MY world go 'round.) Without advertising, your new product or service doesn't have a chance. When you get a blistering email from a member of the IVP, sympathize with them … only for a moment. Don't reply, that puts you on their level. Delete their little diatribe and move on.

They have as much right to send you unsolicited email as you do to send it to them. Remove them from your mailing list, and be done with it. Life's too short to get all upset (like they did!).

> **IMPORTANT LESSON:** *Don't build your business around email marketing. Show that business plan to investors, and they'll laugh in your face.*

If you want to test any business idea, go try to find people to invest in it. You may be foolish enough to put your own money on the line, but when you find that nobody else is willing to bet on your idea, you should get the message that it's flawed.

There was an era when email marketing was promising. That era ended at about the turn of the century … Yes, this century – the 2,000s. People are sick of having to delete 80% or 90% of the messages in their inbox before they can get down to business. And, try it with your customers, and you'll probably lose some of them.

I used to buy client gifts regularly from a company in the Midwest that packaged and shipped steaks. I ordered online regularly. But not, apparently, regularly enough for them. They inundated me with email plus telemarketing. My last communique with them was to tell them to put me on their "do not call" list, and to remove my email address from their database. I still buy the gift of fine steaks, but now I buy them from a different company; Dodge City Steaks.

Push people too much, and you'll start losing what used to be good customers. A lesson to be learned by the steak folks in Nebraska's largest city.

So, you use email as you would a sales letter or post card mailing, and you use and ezine as you would a newsletter.

Ezine

An **Ezine** is the equivalent to a magazine (hence the "zine") or newsletter. It is written as a journalistic piece. It may include news, information, sales messages, or all of the above.

An ezine may talk about any number of topics, products or services. It is sent on a periodic basis, the idea being that the recipient is expecting (and looking forward to) it. And that is what makes it an effective marketing tool … if it's done well. People look forward to it, and are a ready audience for the low-pressure sales messages imbedded in it.

It should always provide useful information. If it's nothing more than a weekly sales letter, it's going to alienate more than sell.

That doesn't mean you can't do some selling in your ezine. Hey, a newsletter or magazine would have advertising interspersed with the editorial content. Certainly, an ezine can too. But make it about 20% of the ezine maximum. In fact, if you make it more like 5% or 10%, it will be more subtle.

But the most important thing, is to make the ezine rich with valuable information. By that, I mean information that is valuable to *your clearly defined target customer* specifically.

If you're in the antique business, it makes sense that your web site must be about antiques. Only people who are interested in antiques are likely to be drawn there. If someone finds their way to your site accidentally (because your company name happens to be Kornikova), they will leave the site. But, the real prospect will spend time on your site, and will possibly sign up for your ezine. Now, everything in your ezine will be of interest to antique lovers.

You want the information in your ezine to be so valuable to that individual, that they look forward to receiving it every month.

I have subscribed to dozens of ezines in my day. Many, I regret ever having given my email address to. They've sold it to others, they've filled my inbox with crap. But their biggest sin is pretending to have real information for me, when all they wanted to do was send me a monthly sales letter. (I'm tempted to turn them over to the IVP.)

Building your Email list

There are a number of ways to capture email addresses for your ezine and email lists. Notice, I said "lists" plural.

Email is your equivalent to direct mail. Direct mail sends offers of useful products and services to people who would benefit from owning them. It would be nice to have a list of names who have given you permission to send them sales letters ... but that ain't gonna' happen.

If you only promote useful products and services to people who can really benefit from them, you are not "spamming" in my opinion. Now, some of the people who receive those promos might not agree with me ... IVP especially. But, they can block or filter you if they don't like it. Sorry.

So, your email sales prospect list should include only highly qualified prospects. Don't rent 400,000 names to send your offer to. You're wasting 399.000 people's time. Segment your list just as you would if you had to pay postage to mail to them. Target your offers carefully, and your click-through and click-to-sale rates can be very high.

A great way to add names of people who will be expecting to hear from you, is by offering a "hot buys" and "last minute specials" information service. This works with fax blasts, too.

I do a lot of work with the travel industry – this works great for them. The cruise lines drop prices drastically a week or two before a ship is about to sail half empty. They email their travel agents, who can in turn email their list. (If your schedule is flexible, this is a great way to get a cruise at a deep discount. Ask your travel agent to be on their last minute specials list.) Any distressed merchandise can be moved this way. If you do this, the return address should be the clever name you've given the service. "Bob's travel rush deals" or whatever ... so they recognize immediately that this is the information they signed up to receive.

Giving your "preferred customers" the first shot at new merchandise or special pricing will get them looking forward to your emails. The return address on those should be some name you give your preferred customer program. Continental Airlines sends me offers "For our Elite One-Pass members only."

The Ezine list

Your ezine is only for people who asked for it. Since it will come out on a regular schedule, like any other periodical publication, people should be looking forward to it.

Don't send your ezine to your whole customer list, and certainly not to your whole prospect list. It should only go to those you ask for it.

But be sure to make it easy for them to ask for it, and encourage them to do so.

Actively promote your ezine, in the tag line of any article you write. Any time you speak to a group invite them to sign up on the spot. Of course, promote the ezine on your web site, and make it easy to sign up for it. And, offer a "free subscription" on your order forms, both printed and online.

How NOT to build your list …

If you just want a whole lot of names, run a sweepstakes. You'll get a whole lot of names. A whole lot of useless names.

Here's another one; Offer virtual greeting cards. You'll get a long list of unimaginative freeloaders.

And, a favorite of many marketers: Surf web sites and grab addresses from the "contact us" page.

There are few things less valuable than a long list of names who either a.) Came to you for something free, or b.) You picked out of the air without them knowing it.

Opt In

There should be a place on your web site where they are invited to "opt in," meaning to sign up for your ezine. Having done that, they should recognize your name or the name of the ezine when it arrives.

Remember that all of your printed promotional materials should include a web site address. You should be spending some of your marketing budget to drive traffic to your site, assuming your web site is a strong sales vehicle for you.

When people get to your site, you want to do something to keep in touch, invite them back, promote products and services to them. The ezine is the perfect vehicle. So, you want to promote the ezine on your site, and invite them to sign up for it.

Opt Out

Unless people have asked to be on your ezine list, they should not receive it. It's clutter in their inbox. They'll either block your future email to get off the list (eliminating your opportunity to ever communicate via email), or send you a blistering email asking to be removed.

Some people will subscribe to your ezine, and immediately forget that they have. Or, they may receive it and decide they really don't want to receive it after all. You don't want them to simply block your address, barring you from ever sending them an email again. You want them to be able to "Opt Out" of your newsletter list.

Each copy of your ezine should include a statement to the effect of;

> *You are receiving this ezine because you asked to be on our list. If you wish to unsubscribe (opt out), please click on getmeoffyourfrickinlist.com and you will be removed.*

Of course, you could send your ezine from a different email address than you send your email sales letters, thereby attempting to end run around the ezine blocks. But, I think you should use your good name as the return address on everything that goes out. Remember, the recognition-building process calls for repetition, repetition, repetition. If you keep sending things with different return addresses, you're not getting those repetitions.

And, any attempt to bypass the recipient's blocks and filters will simple piss them off. If they don't want to hear from you, stop sending to them.

The Subject Line

The Magic Formula applies to web based communications, too.

The "Subject" line (coupled with your return address) of your email is the attention step in *The Magic Formula*. If it doesn't make the reader stop and open the email or ezine, all of your effort was wasted.

The Subject line must be short, to the point, and worded so that it doesn't trip the spam filter. Be careful to avoid wild claims. Don't put words in all capital letters – that spells s-p-a-m immediately. No exclamation points. No quotation marks. No weird punctuation. Don't say "Hi," or "How are you?" Make it straight-forward, to the point.

And make it specific to the self-interests of your *clearly defined target customer*.

There's a whole chapter in this manual on how to write good headlines. The only thing different here, is that you know your prospect will at least see the headline. You don't have to do anything cute to draw their attention.

And, you are limited to a handful of words. Keep your subject line short – absolute maximum 40 characters. Less is better.

The body

Once they're in, you'd better give them something important immediately, or they're gone.

We're trained by the spammers to screen our emails carefully. If we are tricked into opening something with no import to our world, we're downright mad. (The IVP people get so mad, they write you a nasty reply.)

Whether you're sending a sales email you'd better get to the point fast, and in a minimal number of words. This is not the time to go into great detail. If you get the reader interested, they can click on your web site link to get the rest of the story.

So, the email is just the teaser. The real info is accessed through the hyperlink you included in the email. It should go directly to the page containing the right information. Don't send them to your home page, and make them navigate their way to the right page.

Remember, people are lazy. If you ask them to do all the work, they'll be gone in a mouse-click.

Ezines should also dive straight into useful information. Don't ever start with advertising – they'll be looking for the "Opt Out" link immediately. Give them solid information that will help them with whatever it is you help people with.

Ezines can be long, but each piece of information should be a reasonable bite. Don't prattle on in the ezine. Provide links to more in-depth information for those who want it. Run a few paragraphs from a full-length article, then provide a link to the complete story. Again, take them directly to it ... not to your home page, left to find their way around.

> **IMPORTANT LESSON:** *Any time you provide a hyperlink, set it up so it opens a new window. If you just transport them reader somewhere else, they may forget where they came from ... and never come back.*

My favorite ezine is Speaker Net News. If you're not a professional speaker, the content won't be of interest to you. But the model for how they did it will.

Each item in the ezine is contributed by one of their subscribers.

> *They're not story exchanges like the cheesy ezines do. I was once advised to exchange stories and links with people who write ezines for similar audiences. It sounds good, but what really happens is, their newsletters are a bunch of poorly-written, unfocused drivel. Nobody wants to read three screens of unfocused drivel.*

In this one, the people who started the newsletter edit each contribution down to a paragraph or two. If your contribution is of questionable value, it won't show up.

They show the name and email address of the contributor, so you can send your comments or answer to their dilemma directly to them.

And none of the contributions are sales messages. Oh, there are a few suppliers to the trade that give advice ... hoping to draw attention to themselves. But if it's salesy at all, it doesn't make it to the ezine.

The other ezine model is to write everything yourself. If the purpose of the ezine is to demonstrate your mastery of your trade, this is the only model that makes sense to me. You can include links to articles by others, but I wouldn't reprint them in my ezine.

The idea isn't to see how long you can make the thing. I think the people who include articles by others feel that length is more important than quality. If your readers have to wade through a bunch of unrelated, uninteresting stuff to get a little bit of meat, they're gone.

Cut to the chase, already.

Open Rates

One of the measurements of email and ezine effectiveness is the "Open Rate," meaning the percentage of sent messages that are actually opened by the recipient.

Of course, that doesn't necessarily equate to sales, but it does tell you whether your messages are being read.

A much more important measurement is click-through, or how many people go to the links you provide. Although still not equating to sales, this number at least tells you whether you are arousing any interest or not.

The most important number is click-to-sale rate. How many people went to the link, and ended up ordering your product or service.

Tracking that kind of information is all done magically by software. If you're serious about making your sales letters and ezines actually sell, you must track those rates.

Just like direct mail, you have to test, test, test. Strive to get better results every campaign. More click-throughs, and more click-to-sales.

Economy of scale

The fact that you can send 10,000 emails or ezines as cheaply as one, makes this kind of marketing extremely tempting.

You can buy a list of 400,000 email addresses for a song. Many marketers think, if they only get a one-hundredth-of-one-percent conversion to sale rate, it was well worth it. But even one-hundredth-of-one-percent is difficult today, and getting more so every day.

Most people now have internet access, and almost all of those people have email. It doesn't take long for them to realize that most of the email in their inbox is a waste of time. Sure, some people are suckers, and fall for anything. But, is that who you want to be selling to anyway – ignoramuses you can flim flam out of a few dollars? (If so, shame on you … and don't tell anyone you learned about advertising from me. That's not what this book is for.)

But remember; *As with any promo piece, your challenge is to stand*

How to create your own POWERFUL Ads and Promo Pieces, by Larry Mersereau, CTC *out in the crowd, get noticed, get read, and get response. Trying to get noticed among the millions of email messages – most of which the recipient will immediately delete – is not easy.*

If you want your emails and ezines to be opened and read, you have to establish brand recognition with your audience first. Your return address had better be something your prospects who receive you email recognize, or the odds of them opening it are slim to none.

Chapter 15

Flyers, Fax Blasts and Inserts

> *You can stick 'em on your window, stick 'em on your door*
> *Put 'em under windshield wipers, fax them out and more*

OK, poetry isn't my strength! You didn't buy this manual for the poetry anyway.

Flyers

When it comes to low cost/high return promotion, you can't beat the lowly flyer.

For the cost of photocopies, you can produce as many copies of a basic marketing piece as you want. And you don't have to spring for color(although color gets less and less expensive every day). You may want to use colored paper, but that's a minimal expense to dress up your flyers.

Where to use them ...

Flyers can be used any time you want to put an actual piece of paper directly into the hands of a total stranger. The idea is, you place it somewhere where they can't miss it. In fact, you'll probably put it where they can't avoid it, like under their windshield wiper blade or hanging from their doorknob. You can hand them out on street corners, drop them from a helicopter.

When I say a total stranger, I mean TOTAL. You don't know who they are, what their mailing address is ... you know squat about this individual you're trying to contact.

You have little control over who actually receives your communique.

What you do know is that they park in your parking lot, or they live in a neighborhood you want to target. Maybe they pass a specific street corner at a specific time of day. In other words, your distribution is not targeted by who the person is, it's targeted by where they are.

Since they are targeted geographically, you will be distributing copies to lots of unqualified buyers. Your cost per copy may only be a penny or two, you will probably hand out hundreds of copies to reach one good prospect.

So, plan on big numbers for distribution. If you're putting them under windshield wiper blades, go out several times through the day as the cars in your lot turn over. Plan on putting out a lot of "overflow" copies – copies that were a waste of paper and effort. That's the nature of the flyer.

Of course, you could only put them under the windshield wipers on BMWs and Cadillacs. Or, you could only hang them on the doorknobs of houses with kids' bikes and swing sets in the yard. But, for the most part, you're targeting people who are in a specific place at a specific time.

If traffic *right now* is what you're looking for, flyers are a good way to reach it.

What to use them for ...

Flyers are an inexpensive way to get the word out about a short-term special offer ... *FAST*.

If you're a retailer, and you want to move some merchandise today, this afternoon ... you can walk outside your front doors and quickly tell everyone who is currently visiting other merchants in your block or mall.

IMPORTANT LESSON: *Put a larger copy(have it blown up to poster size at your local copy shop) in your front door, so they can* *see from a distance which merchant the flyer came from.*

Maybe you've got a restaurant, and want to catch the lunch-hour traffic in your neighborhood. Start handing them out on the street at about 11:00 AM. Offer a free dessert or cup of soup with lunch. How about half price for the second party at the table with a full-price meal. Make it a compelling offer – this is your one shot at getting an individual to change their lunch plans.

Your flyer offer should be good for a very short time period. It should demand that the buyer walk in *right now* with the flyer to get the deal. Use words like "Today Only" and "You must act NOW!" in your copy.

Why? They will only look at your flyer for a few seconds at most. If they are not motivated to take advantage of the offer immediately, it will go into the trash, never to be seen again.

People are not likely to save your flyer for future reference.

(And put a date on it. "Today Only" isn't very compelling if today's date isn't there.)

Your proposition has to offer something very special if it is going to generate any response. The decision to act on your offer or throw it away is a very fast one, so the offer has to grab their attention.

This is no time for "10% off." This is where you run your "Half Price Today Only" promotion.

FAX Blasts

If you have a list of fax numbers, whose owners have given you permission to advise them of special offers via facsimile, you can use the same design for your fax blast. Print it on a piece of white paper, and fax it to your list.

"But Larry," you might say. "It will look like blatant advertising in their stack of fax messages."

Of course it will! What did you think, that you'd disguise your piece as some important business correspondence? Try to slip it in, and they'll get mad at you. You'll get angry calls, revoking the permission you have to send faxes.

Don't try to fool people. Advertising is advertising. If they don't want to read an ad, they'll throw it away. If your fax comes disguised as some important message, then it turns out to be advertising, they'll curse you and vow never to do business with someone who would try to dupe them.

The flyer, designed as I've outlined, will make a perfect fax sheet. Yes, it will stand out in the stack of business correspondence. You want it to! "Stand out in the crowd" is the best thing you can hope for with your advertising and promotion. Embrace it!

Again, faxes go to people who have given permission. Never fax people who have not indicated that they want to receive your special offers. Not only will you alienate people, you could get yourself into legal trouble.

Life's too short to have to deal with lawyers any more than absolutely necessary.

The down side ...

Some people don't appreciate pieces of paper being virtually pushed in their face. Until, that is, it includes a spectacular offer for something they really want.

Don't lose sleep over the people who don't like your marketing strategy. If you're trying to move merchandise fast, you have to pull out all stops.

> **IMPORTANT LESSON:** *Don't distribute pieces of paper on windy or rainy days. Wind turns them into mobile trash(which may earn you a cleanup bill!), and rain renders them unreadable.*

And, have a little environmental conscience. People notice if you're a trash generator. They don't necessarily recognize environmental responsibility, so don't look for a gold star for good behavior. But your flyers look bad lining the ditches or curbs around your business.

Inserts

This is like distributing flyers on a large scale.

An insert is basically the same as a flyer, but it is distributed as a "ride along" with a newspaper or magazine.

You can put them in your local newspaper, a business paper, or a pennypincher. In some cities, magazines are delivered by local companies that can place your insert in the shrink wrap.

Here's where most businesses and practices go wrong; The publication comes to them with a grandiose plan for using inserts. The cost is pennies per household. They've put together a speculative design for you. It's a beautiful, full-color thing. And, they'll even give you a great deal if you try just once.

So, what's not to love about that?

It's not part of your marketing plan (you do have one, don't you?), that's what. If you didn't have this in your plans, don't add it because the sales person impressed you.

Only do it if it fits into the rest of your plans.

And, if you do decide to do it, design your own insert. The creative people at the publication have no sense of branding and recognition building. Oh, they know repetition is important. But they only know it's important because it brings them revenue over and over.

Repetition is only valuable to you … the advertiser … if every exposure reinforces your brand. You do that by making everything you put out there look the same.

Repetitions only build up if the public sees the same "face" from you every time.

So, don't buy an insert plan unless it was part of your own marketing plan. Don't let somebody who hasn't been involved in your brand building efforts lead you astray.

And, it only belongs in your marketing plan if talking to everyone in that particular publication fits your overall goals. It's just like running space ads in the same publication. You're paying to address every single subscriber and newstand buyer. If most of them do not fit your *clearly defined target customer's* profile, you're paying for a lot of overflow.

Designing your piece …

You want easy? Here it is:

Your piece (flyer, fax blast, or insert) should look just like your display advertisements.

In fact, if you're using display advertising in local publications, flyers and fax blasts that look just like the ads will help build those valuable repetitions. They have to see you half a dozen times before you get into their head.

If they see you in the paper (how about a space ad in the same paper you insert with?), on their fax machine, on their windshield, your people handed them the flyer when they walked buy, they saw it blown up to poster size in your front window, on table tents in your office ... get the picture?

> **IMPORTANT LESSON:** *Come up with just one ad layout, and use it everywhere that you appear in print.*

Isn't that a relief? Once you've come up with a sensible design, you don't have to do any more designing! All you have to do is insert different products, services, or promotions in the same layout. Since it's familiar after they've seen it a few times, it will get attention.

People are drawn to the familiar, not to the obtuse.

They have to see you over and over. If you don't look the same every time, they don't recognize that it's the same business or practice, so the repetitions don't accrue.

Use the same techniques you've read throughout this manual; Simple border, bold attention headline. Start them at the beginning and lead them step by step through your promise, proof and proposition. Then make it easy to respond.

Don't expect them to read a Magna Charta.

I've already said it many times: "Give them all the information they need to make an intelligent decision on the action you're asking them to take." But, in this case, the action you're asking them to take should be a no-brainer. The offer should be so good, that they'd have to feel like a schmuck if they pass it up.

It should be simple, easy to understand, and demand that they act *right now*.

You'll only have their attention for a few seconds at most. Don't give them complex offers and perplexing explanations. Cut to the chase and make it an easy decision for them to take action.

Chapter 16

On-Hold and Voice Mail Messages

I've put these two in the same chapter, because … well, they're both telephone tools.

Both are situations where your prospect will be listening to a voice coming from a person they cannot see. Since they can't see the person who is talking to them, their impression of that person(and, thereby, your organization) will be drawn from their words and their speech.

That's an important issue … more important than many people seem to realize.

If the voice is not pleasant, articulate, and sincere … it doesn't matter much what the actual words are. What you say is not nearly as important as how you say it.

Of course, the words are important. But I want to make the point very clearly that the voice that delivers them can bring them to life or destroy their impact.

On-Hold Messages

In case you're not familiar with "on-hold messages" – They're a loop that is played constantly on an audio player that is connected to the telephone system. Any time a caller is put on hold (hence, the title), they hear the message.

They don't hear the whole message. They join the message in progress at whatever point it happens to be when they're put on hold.

That makes for a n interesting scripting challenge.

One of your business goals should be to limit the amount of time anyone is on hold to :30 seconds or less. :60 seconds is an eternity when you're waiting to see if you've been forgotten, or if someone really is coming to help you.

If you are limiting hold time to :30 seconds or less, people are getting small chunks of your total on-hold message.

The mistake most on-hold messages make, is to try to deliver long, convoluted messages. If people are only there for :30 seconds or less, they don't get any more than a tease. Now, that tease may be designed to make them ask for more information when they are connected, but that doesn't happen very often. Hey, they called to talk to someone. When that someone picks up the call, they want to get down to business.

So, what's a business or practice to do?

I believe in :15 second messages. I would alternate them with :15 second music spots. Stock music in any style is available in :15 second spots, so that's easy.

The hard part is writing :15 second scripts that bring home a complete message.

This is not a hard sell opportunity. It's a chance to share a little information, and demonstrate your expertise. These should be similar to the "Tip of the Month" post cards. Short, sweet, informative, interesting.

If people are good enough to wait on hold, they deserve something fairly interesting and entertaining. A hard sales pitch to this captive audience can be downright offensive.

Of course, you can't just repeat the same :15 second message and :15 second music spot over and over. You need several in case, Heaven forbid, the caller gets left on hold for a minute or two.

Back to the importance of the voice; Don't do this yourself. This should be done by professionals, including a professional "voice over." You're going to produce this thing once, and probably use it for months ... possibly years.

The voice should reflect your organization's personality. Are you an upbeat group? Terminally business-like? Fun? Somber? Hey, you should know this. If you're a funeral home operator, I would expect a different kind of voice than I would expect from a balloon-bouquet store.

Spend the money up front to produce something you can be proud to play for everyone that calls in. Do a half fast job on this, and you'll embarrass yourself daily for a long, long time.

Voice Mail - Inbound

I'm a one-man band. My business is me. I am my business. No assistant, no staff.

That means that if you call, and I'm not in the office ... even if I'm just on another line ... you're going to get my voice mail.

I appreciate your call. I truly do. Not like the big company's, whose recording says; "Your call is very important to us." Hey, somebody there could answer the phone, couldn't they? If my call really was important, they'd have enough people to handle it. I digress(again).

So, you have to get the message that I appreciate your call (that I TRULY do). That means my voice has to be sincere and enthusiastic. My voice has to reflect my business personality. I'm enthusiastic, and I think business should be fun.

The first words should confirm that they reached the party they called; "You've reached ..." If you're an individual, that would be your name. If it's a company, it would be the company name. If it's an individual at a company, it would be "Bob at XYZ."

Then, I like to add your tag line, if you have one ... and if it's short and sweet. This whole thing has to take less than :15 seconds. They didn't call to listen to an infomercial. They called to talk to you.

You don't have to say "I'm away from the phone or on another call." (Well, no kidding? I think you're sitting there, refusing to answer because you think it might be me.)

What they need to know:

It would be nice if you could have two different inbound messages; One for calls that come in during business hours – you're there but can't answer the phone right now, the other for calls that come in after hours.

During business hours, you have to apologize. I mean, face it; Some nice person called, wanting to do business with you, and you don't have enough people to take care of them immediately.

I know, you've tightened your belt, you've got people on vacation, somebody's out sick … blah, blah, blah. The customer doesn't care. They've gone to the effort of calling, and you're not ready for them. So apologize already.

And, you're not going to love this suggestion: Why not say: I'm really sorry we're not able to pick up the phone right now, so I want to offer you a free gift. When we pick up the phone, ask for a free copy of …(something valuable)".

That would accomplish two things; 1.) It would somewhat placate the customer who has been treated rather shabbily, and 2.) It might cost you more than it would to go ahead and hire more help – so you would. Then your customers would get the immediate attention of a human being in stead of an apology from a recorded voice.

(Can you tell I feel strongly about handling inbound calls?)

The second message should be for after hours callers. It should tell them when you are open, and other options available to them in the mean time.

If they can leave a message, tell them when you'll be returning their call. If it's going to be a while, give them another option. Mine says "for immediate information, visit my web site MagicFormula.com."

The drawback with having two recordings, is that someone has to switch messages every morning and evening. But your customers get better information.

But in any event, keep it short. Again, they didn't call to hear a sales pitch. Show them the courtesy of respecting their time.

Voice Mail - Outbound

What percentage of your outbound calls are actually answered by the human you're trying to call?

It's probably safe to say that you'll reach a voice mail recording more often than you'll reach a human, at least on calls to businesses during business hours.

So, it just makes sense to be prepared to leave a message. And the message should be scripted before you dial.

In fact, it should even be rehearsed before you dial. You'll sound more confident, you won't stumble on words. You won't leave out anything important, and you won't rush – because you wrote a short script. SHORT, to the point.

Another good reason to be scripted: When the prospect's inbound voice mail message plays, you can listen to it carefully. You want to use any information they give you, and use it next time you call. If they're out due to illness, your next call can include "I hope you're feeling better."

If you aren't scripted, you'll be thinking about what you're going to say in stead of listening to their message – and you may well miss some information that could be valuable in the future.

If you're calling to sell someone something, your voice mail message has to convince them that it's in their best interest to listen to the whole message, and return the call … or, be prepared for the next step.

You will have different scripts for different situations; One for a cold call to a total stranger, a different one for a follow-up call to someone who already has your proposal.

Most people go in totally unprepared. At least give some thought to what you're going to say.

> **IMPORTANT LESSON:** *Start with your name and phone number, then end with the same information. Say them slowly, articulately, so the listener has plenty of time to write the number as you speak.*

Don't make people listen to the whole message if they don't have to. Give them your name and number up front in case they want to dispense with the rest and call right now(wouldn't that be nice?).

The Magic Formula

The opening line is the attention step in *The Magic Formula*. After identifying yourself, you want to grab their attention and make them stick around for the rest of the message.

I call a lot of people who hire professional speakers, but who have never heard of me. (I don't know, they must live under a rock or something – shocking as it is that there are meeting planners who have never heard of me, I have to assume the worst and make some kind of introduction.) If I start with "I'm a professional speaker," they'll hang up immediately. They hear from a hundred professional speakers a day. They don't need another one ... and they're sure as Hell not about to return the call to one.

So, I have to start with a promise of a benefit. What I promise varies, depending on the prospect. An association meeting planner might get "If boosting sales is a topic your members might like to see on your convention agenda ..." It promises a benefit, and tells them what I do all at once.

> **IMPORTANT LESSON:** *Be ready to tell them the answer to the question; "What do you do?"*

You've been asked on airplanes and in elevators. What do you say? If you're like most of us, you kind of stumble through it.

You should be able to say who you are and what you do in :15 seconds. And any idiot should be able to understand it.

At the very least, say "This is Bob Jones with XYZ Company. We specialize in ...", or "Our clients enjoy ... (benefit)".

Go ahead, write your script. Use it in the elevator, on the golf course, and in your outbound voice mail messages. If they don't find out anything else about you, they should at least know what you do in terms of benefit to them.

Remember to make it about them – 'cause that's who they care about.

In messages to cold-call prospects, I never ask them to return my call. They're not going to, and it's a waste of their time to put it in the message.

So, I have to prepare them for the next step. "I am emailing you right now ...", or "I'm dropping something in the mail, I'll call again Tuesday when you can have it in front of you ...". Then, I repeat the benefit: "If boosting sales would be of interest to your members, I hope you'll take a look at the material I'm sending. Talk to ya' Tuesday."

Benefit, Action, Benefit, Reminder of the action. All in :10 - :15 seconds.

Scripting

The most important thing is to go in prepared. And it's true for both inbound and outbound voice mail messages.

I call people every day who obviously gave not thought whatsoever to their inbound message; "This is Bob. I'm either out of the office or away from my desk right now. Leave a message and I'll get back to you as soon as I can." Have you heard that one before? Like, a thousand times?

Before you start recording, write out what you're going to say. Read through it a couple of times. Time it, so you know if you're killing too much time. If it's long, don't speed up – cut out some words.

You know, the odds are, you'll be talking to voice mail more than not when you make outbound calls. So, don't sound surprised. Be prepared to say what you need to say: Speak slowly and clearly. Any time the other party has to write down a phone number, S-L-O-W D-O-W-N. Give them time to write each number as you say it.

Use the right words, at the right speed, in the right tone of voice. The only way to be sure, is to write it down and rehearse it before you pick up the phone.

Don't just open your mouth and hope something good falls out.

Chapter 17

Trade Show Exhibits & Point-of-Purchase Displays

I know, these two items are totally different animals.

That said, I want to talk about their similarities, and the mistakes I see most often in both. Because most businesses and practices make the same mistakes.

What's In It For Me?

That's the only thing your prospect wants to know. And they're not willing to work very hard to find it out.

I go to more trade shows than the average person. In my work as a professional speaker, many of the events I work at include trade shows.

And, I always walk through the trade show. I think it's a courtesy to the event planner and to the exhibitors. Hey, they want traffic in their show – if I'm nothing else, I'm at least more traffic!

Plus, I find that wandering through the trade show aisles can be a real education. I can't know everything about every industry I talk to. But, I should at least have an idea of what kinds of exhibitors are supporting the event. Heck, it's often one of the exhibitors that sponsors(meaning: puts up the money) my presentation. I have to at least stop by their exhibit and say "thank you."

So, I've not only been to more trade shows than the average guy. I've been to shows in a broad varieties of industries. In the past few months I've been to a Bowling Center Proprietors' show, Specialty Tools & Fasteners, Dive Marketers, Travel Agents, Farm Equipment Dealers, Bankers, Chimney Sweeps … you get the idea. A broad range of interests.

And they all make the same mistake. Not all exhibitors make the same mistake, but the majority of exhibitors in every industry do.

What is the big mistake?

Almost every exhibit makes their company name the dominant graphic element of their display.

Coming in a close second, is their product name.

Then, you see a whole lot of features. Weight, PSI, BTUs, Tensile Strength, Capacity …

"But Larry," you might say, "That's important information." Yes, it is … once the prospect is interested enough to delve into it.

It's not important until the prospect asks about it.

What you need in your trade show display(and bear with me P.O.P. people, yours need the same thing) is a benefit-laden, attention-grabbing graphic or display.

If you sell lawn mowers, lay down a gorgeous spread of perfectly-cut sod. If you sell Pizza Ovens, of course you want to give samples … but you also want to show why your oven is better than your competitors'. (Does it turn out more pizzas per hour? Demonstrate with a with a pizza eating contest that only your oven can keep up with.) If you sell women's bathing suits … invite me to your show, please!

Differentiation

You should know what makes your product better than your competitors'. (And it's not service, I can tell you that one right now.)

Here are some of the areas where you might try to stand apart from your competitors;

PRICE – SERVICE – CONVENIENCE – SELECTION
DEPENDABILITY – QUALITY – UNIQUENESS

Service is in there …but here's a very important piece of information;

> **IMPORTANT LESSON:** *It's not enough to outdo our competition in just one area. "Service" by itself is not an advantage. You have to outdo your competition in at least two significant areas. "Service" plus "Convenience" can make you pretty irresistible, and make price less of an issue.*

That last point is important. Too many businesses compete largely on price.

The last "real job" I had was working for a travel agency franchise company. The president of the company had been a banker in his past life, not a travel agent. But he had bought from a travel agent before, and actually been in an agency, so I guess he thought he was qualified to run a travel company!

He was good at selling franchises. People sunk their life's savings into owning a little business. The pitch was that they'd travel for free or next to nothing. Most of them lost more money every year than the travel could ever be worth, but it sounded good at contract time!

And it gets worse. He would encourage them to put this headline in the Yellow Pages: "Lowest Air Fare, GUARANTEED" – a twelve month commitment to squeezed(if any) profits! (There was an ulterior motive in having them put it in the Yellow Pages: It did make the phone ring. He wanted them to think that they would be automatically busy when they hang up the franchise name. And, busy they would be. Broke, but busy!)

I can tell the story, because the company no longer exists(no surprise there!).

Anyway, what that has to do with competitive advantage;

His mindset was that people buy totally based on price. So, the ad he pushed for all new franchisees carried the dreaded headline "Lowest Air Fare, Guaranteed."

Now, you can read, or you wouldn't be reading this manual. If you can read, you're reasonably intelligent. I pray that you're intelligent enough to see that this headline is INSANE.

Don't ever, <u>ever</u> promote your business based on "Lowest Price Guaranteed."

You know somebody is going to beat your price some day. Then, you'll have no choice but to match it, whether it's profitable or not. In today's litigious society, you could even get sued.

Have you ever heard of "predatory pricing?" That's when a competitor comes in an prices below profitable levels, forcing you to match. A bigger, stronger competitor may be able to withstand the losses long enough to put you out of business. The major airlines used to me famous for doing this to low-fare airlines when they entered a city. They'd one-up the low-fare carrier with even lower prices to hold on to their market share. The start-up carrier gets no business, and eventually goes broke or pulls out of the market.

The big "box stores" compete at this level. Price is their primary competitive advantage. But, do they offer good service? Are they convenient? Is there anything "different" about their products? OK, they have "Selection." So, those are their two; Price and Selection. If that's what you want, go to a box store. If you'd like to talk to a human being that cares whether you're happy after you buy, go somewhere else.

Larry, What's the Point, man?

You have to know what your competitive advantages are, and reflect them dominantly in your trade show or P.O.P. displays.

When people walk buy, the benefit of buying from you in stead of from your competitor should absolutely jump out at them. When it does, they will stop to read your features, and your company name.

But your company name or product name alone won't stop them for even a second.

Time!

It's about time. People are in a hurry. At the grocery store, on the trade show floor.

If you work a trade show exhibit, you'll see them walking by. Some look like they have blinders on, don't they? They're walking a straight line down the center of the aisle ... *fast* ... with their eyes focused forward. Heaven forbid they should make eye contact with an exhibitor!

They're actually looking several booths down the aisle. They wouldn't be in the trade show if there wasn't something they're looking for. They just want to find it without having to waste a lot of precious time talking to people who don't have it.

You may be the one that has it. But would they ever know by looking at your booth from twenty feet away? They will be checking you out from beyond-eye-contact-range.

> *Will they see your competitive advantage? Will they be able to tell at a glance what you do and what makes you better than the others who do basically the same thing?*

There are other trade show attendees who stroll the aisles slowly, taking time to look into each booth. This is what I do. I want to know what products and services are available. I want to know what it is about each one that appeals to the trade show attendees.

Needless to say, you should not waste time and money exhibiting at a trade show that has nothing to do with your product.

For some reason, lots of MLMers think EVERYONE should be buying their product. It's especially true of the health care products. Vitamins, back massagers, weight-loss products ... I've seen them buy booths at trade shows of all kinds. OK, I can see why scuba enthusiasts need vitamins ... but I don't think a dive marketing conference is where they'll be looking for them.

Maybe I'm wrong ... if you're an MLMer who's had great success selling at non-related shows, email me with your results. Don't just say "we did great," tell me how many dollars per attendee you took in. Tell me you had measurable, positive results, and I'll recant this whole thing in my next revision of this book.

P.O.P.

Point of Purchase, or "Point of Sale" ((depending on where you come from(like "soda" or "pop")) displays face the same challenge.

People are speeding through the store aisles, seeking specific items. In the grocery store, they even have a written list of items they plan to buy, possibly by brand name. Kleenex, Saran Wrap, Coke, Reynolds Wrap are common on my list. When I buy milk, it will be Borden's. My spaghetti sauce is Classico.

The mixed nuts will be Planters. The potato chips will be Lays ... and I'll only buy the items that I put on my list before I walked into the store ... unless your point of purchase display can seduce me into picking up your product right then and there.

How can you change my mind?

Tell me(at a glance) why your chips are better. And tell me in terms of how I will experience your chips. Oh yea, I said it: Experience. I don't just eat food, I experience it.

CRUNCH

Got a product that will clean my kitchen sink faster?

FAST

That pretty much says it, doesn't it?

Compare that to what most exhibits and displays do;

Bob's Company Inc.

What does Bob's do? What do they make? I don't have time for this, I'm looking for my Mrs. Baird's 7-Grain Bread. Out of my way, Bob.

Bottom Line

Trade show exhibits and point-of-purchase displays are just like any other promo piece. The first thing you have to accomplish is; get the prospect's attention. You have to promise a benefit – something that will make the prospect's life better if they buy.

Save me time, give me a flavor explosion, make cleaning the stove easier. If you promise a benefit that matters to me … to me, not to you … I will stop and take the time to find out who you are, because I want to buy from you.

Lead with a benefit that makes it worth my while to stop and learn more.

OK, you got me to stop. Now what?

Your display or exhibit got people to stop in their tracks to learn more.

How much time do you think you have? You've got a few seconds at best to get me to pick something up or walk away.

You want to put something in your prospect's hands. A sample, a free pen, the joystick on your demo, some popcorn … something.

Here's the deal: You have to get the prospect physically involved or they're bored. When they're bored, they're gone. If they don't leave physically, they're polite. But they're still gone – unengaged.

Make them pick something up, or put something in their hands.

> **IMPORTANT LESSON:** *Once they are physically involved, they are likely to stick around longer. And, the longer they stick around, the more likely they are to buy.*

You've interrupted their pattern. You've broken through that fog they're in.

They were walking the aisles, trade show floor or store, probably on the lookout for something specific. You may or may not be the specific thing they were looking for. But you have now pulled them away from their standard pattern.

Now that you've pulled them in, you have to entertain them. Get them reading, playing a game, working your sample machine, reading your package, tasting your sample.

Make a Proposition

As with any promotional medium or piece, you must keep Holy *The Magic Formula*.

If you fail to make some kind of a proposition, you pretty much eliminate any chance to getting the prospect to respond.

Have them pick your product up. In a trade show, make sure a human being talks to them, and captures their contact information for future promotions.

The proposition doesn't always have to be a sale. And it may be unrealistic to expect a sale in some cases.

But at least send them away with a coupon, or get an email address … don't let that brief encounter in the store or trade show aisle be the last.

Chapter 18

Classifieds & Small Space Ads

Don't turn your nose up … yet.

It's interesting to look a the morning paper, and see what's being sold in the classifieds vs space advertising.

I'm looking at a full-page, color ad promoting turkeys at 14¢ a pound(it's Thanksgiving time as I write this). Another has underwear on sale. Then I see one promoting cotton turtlenecks – $18 just in time for the cooler weather ahead.

Now, let's turn to the classifieds. What are they selling there? Cars for tens of thousands of dollars. Houses for hundreds of thousands. "Careers" that seem to promise $millions!

Yes, the cheapest advertising in the newspaper is being used to sell the most expensive items. What's wrong with this picture? I mean, how many turkeys do you have to sell to pay for a full-page, color ad? (Don't fire off an email to tell me. I know it's a "loss leader" designed to draw traffic to the store. But still …)

The point is, don't turn your nose up at classified advertising. Lots of people read them, and millions of dollars are made from them every day in America.

Classified sections appear in most magazines, newsletters, and of course, newspapers. You can target your classifieds just as you would space advertising, buy placing them in publications that appeal to your *clearly defined target customer*.

Of course, you have to be selling to a market that would read the classifieds in the publication you place them in, and your product or service must fit one of their classifications. If that is your situation, they classifieds give you unique access to people who are going to that classification looking for what you offer!

Most business trade magazines have classified sections that are very well read. You may belong to an industry association whose newsletter runs a classified section. Your religious organization may have a classified section in the weekly bulletin.

Small Space Ads

Business newspapers, and business sections of community newspapers, often have either classifieds or "business card" pages. There are two challenges with these small space ads;

1. Your market must read the publication, and especially, its classifieds. And
2. You have to present your message in a very few words.

Once you've found a publication that's right for your offer and that your prospects are likely to read, you have to put your message into as few words as possible.

Unlike display advertising, where you pay by the column-inch, you pay by the word for classifieds.

That means every word counts ... because every word <u>costs</u>.

Economy of verbiage is the challenge.

Here's an example. I recently ran some lead-generating classifieds for a marketing plan book. My message was; You will be more profitable next year (and the next) if you take the time to write a well thought-out marketing plan. To do that, you'll need help. This book is the answer.

The problem is, nobody wants to write a marketing plan! Everyone thinks they can get by with a plan "in their head". If I had said "How to write an effective marketing plan" nobody would read it. Now, the marketing plan is what they need, but it's not what they want.

> **IMPORTANT LESSON:** *People buy what they want, not what they need. So, you have to talk to them about what they want.*

Plus, "How to write an effective marketing plan" is too wordy. Long headlines are fine if you're writing for a large space add. But in the classifieds, you pay by the word. Plus, people who read the classifieds expect to get your whole message in one or two lines. Throw in a long, wordy ad and you'll lose them.

So I really had to sell the benefit, and get the prospect to call me to find out how to get it. So my ad simply said;

Boost Your 2002 Profits
Free Info Call 888 224-0236

The Free info was a six-page letter explaining the concept and the product, with an order form.

You can see the whole letter I used in this promotion in the chapter on sales letters. This promotion was a learning experience for me ... I think you'll get a kick out of the "whole story" in the sales letter chapter. Some lessons are learned the hard(read that: expensive) way!

In a nutshell; This two-step promotion sold like Hell ... but I lost money on it. Read the story, and see if you've ever done something this stupid in your business!

Pain-Free Response

One of your challenges in a classified, is to make it painless for people to respond.

It must carry zero risk. None, zip, nada.

They have to be totally comfortable picking up the phone to call, meaning they don't have to brace themselves for a sales pitch. People are terrified of sales folk. Personally, I'm pretty good at just saying "no thank you" as I hang up. But not everyone is comfortable with that.

So, they don't want to respond if they think they're going to be accosted with a verbal "arm twisting."

So, a great response-builder is to offer "FREE Recorded Message." Then they know they won't have to talk to a sales person, and can hang up when they want to.

The recording has to walk them to the next step in the sales process: "Leave your name and address, and we'll send ..."

Your recording should be businesslike, to the point, and not sound like a pep rally. A shouting voice, a fast talker ... any of those things you hear on the automobile dealership ads on TV (I just heard one today that actually shouted at the camera: "DON'T BRING A LOT OF MONEY, YOU WON'T NEED IT!" Who writes this crap?).

A calm, trustworthy voice should start right at the beginning of *The Magic Formula*.

The attention step is simple – hey, they called you, right? So, introduce yourself and thank them for calling. Promise a benefit, then back it with some proof. Make a proposition that motivates them to take the next step in the sales process. Then, make the next step as painless as this call was. "Press '1' at any time to leave your name and mailing address. We'll rush your free, special report ..." That action step has to be easy, painless, risk-free.

Or, the "next step" after your recorded message could be to "order now - log on to www.yoursite.com and use our secure order form.

But, if your next step is to order and transfer money from their pocket to yours, make sure you have abided by the cardinal rule of advertising:

> **IMPORTANT LESSON:** *You must give your prospect all of the information they need to make an intelligent decision on the action you are asking them to take.*

So, if you're asking them to hand over their hard-earned money, you'd better be sure that a classified plus a telephone recording told them all they need to know to make an informed decision. If not, you have spent the money for the ad, sunk a hook, and you've reeled in a live prospect. Then you "threw them back into the ocean."

They won't leave a message asking for more information if you tried to close the sale. They will only respond to your proposition. If your proposition was "buy now," and they weren't ready yet, their answer will simply be "no." They hang up the phone, they're gone forever.

So, in the telephone recording, you should offer another piece of information that is valuable enough to make them comfortable with the idea of leaving their mailing address or email address. So, at least now, you have generated a "lead." If all they did was call and hang up, you generated a response ... but it dead-ended.

Even if they don't buy the product or service you're promoting right now, you can include them in your mailings or emails for future promotions. In fact, another mailing about this same product or service may score with them the second time around. Very often, the second push for the same product or service ... directed at the same audience as before ... will draw half or more as many sales again as the first push.

Graphic Design

Graphic design does come into play with classifieds. But you only have typography to work with, and probably a limited number of possibilities.

The classified I showed in the example above used two different type sizes. The headline was larger than the subhead, just as you would do in a space ad. The headline was bold, as well.

There's a whole chapter on typography in this manual. You can do a lot visually, just with type faces and styles. Classifieds probably won't let you do much more than add bold style to the first few words. Those, of course, will be your headline.

Small Space Ads

I included Small Space Ads in the same chapter as classifieds, because the same rules and limitations apply.

You have limited space, so you have to make every word or illustration work hard for you.

You have to use graphic design carefully, because your small ad can easily get lost in the clutter of larger ads surrounding it on the page. Although you design your ad all by itself on a white page or screen, your reader has to be drawn to your island or calm in a field of clutter.

"Business Cards"

Many publications, particularly Business Journal-types, offer a reasonably-priced "business card" advertising opportunity.

It's called a "business card" ad, because that's the general size and shape: about the same as a typical business card. Most business cards are 2" x 3", but the ad sizes aren't always exactly that size. But they are the same general shape.

Your ad will be one of a dozen or two on one page. All are the exact same size, so you can't blame that if your's doesn't work. In most cases, all are in black and white, so you can't blame someone else's color for stealing your thunder.

What do most people put in these ads? A reproduction of their business card, of course!

How interesting is a full tabloid-size page of business cards? Company name and logo after company name and logo.

Take a look at any publication that sells these ads, and you'll see what I'm talking about. Many ads don't even make it clear what the company does. I can't imagine spending advertising dollars on something that doesn't even tell the reader what you do or sell!

You already know I don't believe in spending promotional dollars on anything that doesn't scream out for *RESPONSE*. It's the only way you can know whether anybody is reading your ad or not.

The typical "business card" ad says "We're XYZ Company. Please remember our name." Many stop there ... don't even say why you would ever have a use for their name! They just want you to know who they are.

Some go a little farther, and say "We're XYZ Company. Please remember our name if you ever need _____ (product/service)."

Do they think people are going to tear out their ad, and stick it to the refrigerator door with a magnet? Do they think people have some filing system where they keep the names of people who provide various products and services? I hope not!

So, what do you put in your "business card" ad?

Here's where you're going to really stand out in the crowd;

First, realize that you have to stand out on the page graphically first. If you want people to read your ad, you have to stand out in the crowd. So, your ad has to look a lot different from the others.

In fact, you should understand that nobody goes through that page and reads every ad. In fact, I don't think most people read that page AT ALL. So, you don't just have to stand out on the page, you have to grab the people who are just flipping the page with no intention of stopping at the page.

So, your headline ... which will dominate the limited space that you have to work with ... will shout:

"Hey _____(type of person). Stop and read this!"

OK, you're not going to use those words exactly(although, they would certainly stand out on a page full of business cards!).

Here's an example that illustrates exactly what I'm talking about. This was an ad that was submitted to me for use in one of my ***Marketing Makeover*** workshops. As the name implies, I get ads and promo pieces from people who are going to be in my programs. As I teach step by step copy writing and design skills, I whip out sample pieces for the audience to rework as part of the program.

This ad came out when I was teaching people how to A.) Write powerful headlines that draw a specific kind of prospect in, and B.) Use graphic design skills in a small space ad to get that headline noticed so people will stop and read the rest of the ad.

I've said it elsewhere in this manual, but here it is again(he preached);

> **IMPORTANT LESSON:** *Your headline is 80% responsible for the success (or failure) of your ad. If it doesn't make the right kind of prospect stop in their tracks, it doesn't matter what else you put in there ... because they'll never see it!*

What's the most common "headline" in the business card page? Company name.

Everybody wants you to know their company name. So, IF some intrepid readers wades into this page full of totally BORING stuff, they will be instantly drawn to anything other than a company name.

How hard is that? Your headline is going to say:

"Hey _____(type of person). Stop and read this!"

Here's how you do it;

Back to the ad I told you I got from a workshop participant for a makeover. Here is the origianal ad;

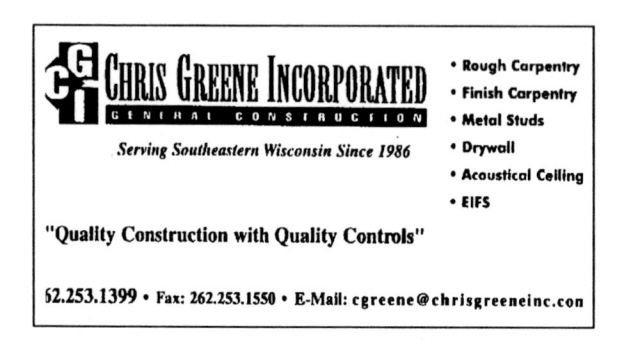

Chris Greene Incorporated
GENERAL CONSTRUCTION
Serving Southeastern Wisconsin Since 1986

- Rough Carpentry
- Finish Carpentry
- Metal Studs
- Drywall
- Acoustical Ceiling
- EIFS

"Quality Construction with Quality Controls"

62.253.1399 • Fax: 262.253.1550 • E-Mail: cgreene@chrisgreeneinc.con

If you know Chris, don't give him a hard time. He made the same mistake that most business owners and professionals make in all of their advertising, not just on the "business card" page. Read the newspaper – you'll see most businesses make their company name their headline.

This ad is just like the rest of the ads on this page. It's a business card.

At least Chris told the readers what he does. But it's unlikely very many people will ever see this ad. It's one of many that look the same on this page.

And, it's even more unlikely that he'll get any response.

Somebody would have to just happen to be in the position of looking for someone who can handle the rough carpentry (or one of his other talents) for their upcoming projects.

Now, Chris does a lot of work for developers. Most subcontract a lot of the work on their projects to people just like Chris. And there are dozens of people like Chris for them to choose from.

Do you think more developers would become aware of Chris if he ran this ad?

> **Attention: Developer**
>
> **FREE Booklet**
>
> *12 Questions you MUST ask your contractor before you let him or her set foot on your property!*
>
> **No obligation - Call NOW**
>
> CHRIS GREENE, INC. (262) 253-1399
> GENERAL CONSTRUCTION www.ChrisGreeneInc.com

The headline talks directly to a specific kind of reader. They may be flipping through this paper, and may have no intention of stopping to read a bunch of business cards(Who would?). But this would catch their eye if they even give the page a glance.

And, it goes to the point of offering some valuable information … for FREE. Who can ignore that?

And remember, there must be NO RISK.

This ad says "No Obligation." In your business, it might be worth saying "No salesperson will call" if that's the truth. But do whatever you can to make it easy, painless, and risk-free for the prospect to respond.

Here's another ad that uses the same technique with a different market;

Lower your Golf Scores

FREE Booklet: 10 Practice Tips To Improve Your Golf Game...*FAST*

PGA pro Doug Hendricks shows you how to get maximum results. No obligation - call NOW!

Tee It Up Golf

Driving Range • Par 3 Course • Instruction

21 Hagerty Blvd West Chester

www.TeeItUpGolf.net 610 436-4469

Rt 202 to Matlack, South to Hagerty Blvd, Left 3 blocks

This is a larger ad, but still only 2 columns x 3". It appears in the community newspaper. It's there to find the estimated 16% of the market who plays golf. It asks them to raise their hands, so we can now address them directly by mail in the future.

Again, it talks to a very specific audience. Yes, they're only 16% of the people we're paying to reach with this publication. But we're using a small space ad there to ask them to raise their hands.

Small space ads can make a big impact. But you have to be bold enough to narrow down the field of people you're talking to.

The more you address a specific kind of person, and offer something that is of particular interest to them, the more response you can expect.

The more broad your appeal, the fewer people will read it. That's a paradox of advertising that doesn't seem to make sense on the surface. But the more people you try to address, the more you have to dilute your message. The more diluted the message, the fewer people are going to be drawn in by it.

We could have talked to anyone who will ever build or remodel anything. Then, the title of our booklet would probably have to have a broader appeal: 12 things you must ask anyone who will work on your construction or remodeling project before you ever let them set foot on your property." See what I'm saying? That's just not as powerful, because it's not as focused.

A strong focus narrows your audience, but does more to draw and interest the specific prospect.

This is step one in the establishment of a long and profitable relationship with the respondents. Chris has to deliver a useful booklet, that tells them things they might not otherwise learn. It gives him an opportunity to demonstrate his mastery of the subject, but the information must NOT be a sales pitch.

There can be a sales pitch included with the information. There's nothing wrong with including a sales letter and a brochure. And, of course, you would make some kind of proposition "just to thank you for responding." But the booklet itself must be what he promised; useful information, not a sales pitch.

And, he has to follow up after sending the information.

A knowledgeable sales person … preferably Chris himself … should call a couple of weeks after the booklet was sent. He should ask if it was helpful to the types of projects this person works with. That should open a dialog about what kind of projects they do, and what kinds of problems they may be having with sub-contractors now.

Then, he would answer with more valuable information – not just a sales pitch. Although, now he can say "let me tell you our philosophy on that aspect of building …"

Valuable information for FREE. Dialog that will help the respondent handle future projects more effectively. "Here's how our way of doing it will help your projects succeed."

Who wouldn't want to take that relationship to the next stage?

Classifieds and small space ads are great for lead generation activities.

They can also be effective for one-step sales. But to do that, you have to be in the right publication – where real buyers go to the classifieds to buy – and you must fit one of their classifications.

It's ironic that cars and real estate … the two most expensive things most people ever buy … are sold every day through the classifieds.

Don't assume your product or service can't benefit, too. The only way to be sure is to test. At least you can test inexpensively in the classifieds.

Tested Advertising Methods
by John Caples
Prentice Hall ISBN 0-13-095701-1

Chapter 19

Web Pages

Why do you have a web site?

Think for a minute, and write it in the margin notes now. Not a long dissertation, just a few words.

If that was difficult, don't feel bad. A lot of us have web sites with no clear mission. Maybe you sell some product, maybe it's just an electronic brochure.

Most smaller businesses (and a lot of really big businesses!) don't really think through what their web site should accomplish for them. So, like their other advertising and promotional expenses, the money goes out every month but nobody's really sure it does any good.

A web site is like every other business investment: You should demand measurable return on the money you shell out every month for web hosting and site development. If you're not getting it, you must either make some changes in the site or some changes in the site's mission.

Who are your prospects?

It should go without saying that the Internet won't reach non-web-savvy prospects. Basic as that may sound, there are thousands of businesses paying for web sites whose prospective customers will never see it. If your buyers don't use computers, stop reading this chapter. If you have a web site, close it down and use the $50 a month to beef up your mail list.

If you're sure your prospects do use computers ... and the overwhelming majority of educated people do ... then a web site is an excellent way to make your products and information easily available to them.

You're literally at their fingertips. That is, IF they know where to find you.

Promoting Your Web Site

It should go without saying that your web site address should appear on every piece of paper, advertising specialty or broadcast media spot you put in front of your prospects. But the web address alone doesn't give anyone a reason to visit your site.

You must promote the benefit they will receive when they do visit. Adding a simple line like: "Free marketing info at MagicFormula.com" will make a big difference.

If you are using a web address as the response medium for a specific promotion, the first thing the prospect sees when they go to that address should be that specific promotion. If you have to buy another domain name to do it, so be it. Don't send them to a general home page unless the product in the promotion dominates the page.

Remember, people are lazy. They won't scour your menu to find the promo du jour. When they type in the address and click on "go," the promotion they're responding to should hit them right in the face. And the copy on the page should immediately take them to the next step in the buying process.

Two pages for each product

Some people want a little information, some people need a lot.

The first page of information about a product should have a photo of the product ... in use by a "typical" buyer if possible. Then a benefit-centered headline. Then a paragraph or two of benefit-centered copy. For many people, that's enough to click to the shopping cart.

By the way, make it easy to "add to shopping cart," and give the prospect numerous opportunities to do so. Let them click on the product photo, click on a highlighted word in each paragraph, on a separate "add this item to your shopping cart" line underneath the copy.

You are selling here – close early and often.

The reader should also see the opportunity to "click here for more information." That should take them to the second page, which will actually be a long sales letter. Don't forget, you should provide all the information your prospect needs to make an intelligent decision on the action you're asking them to take. If you want them to buy, you have to tell them everything they could possibly want to know about the product. Write benefits first, then back them up with proof. Use *The Magic Formula* just as you would in an advertorial.

"But Larry," you might say, "Isn't long copy going to bore people?"

As long as you write about your prospect's favorite topic, they'll eat up every word. What's their favorite topic? You know by now: It's themselves. Write in "you" copy, and they'll be riveted to your compelling communiqué.

And, that's why there's a long and a short version for each product. Some people are ready to buy when they come to your site. Don't make them sort through a long description to find how to order.

> **IMPORTANT LESSON:** *Make it easy to order – pepper hyperlinks to the order form throughout the descriptive copy. Put a link under the picture of the product, and next to the price. Don't make them search for "order now."*

Get focused

Get focused on a specific audience. In marketspeak that's getting "Niched."

Since the Internet reaches so many people, in such a broad range of demographic and geographic descriptions, you have to zero in on a small percentage of them.

Why?

If you try to be "all things to all people" by trying to design a site for everyone, you will be competing with literally thousands of other sites for each prospect.

If you're niched, reaching out to and designing your site for a very specific kind of prospect, those prospects will see you early in their search because you have fewer competitors going after that same prospect.

For instance, my own site. It's nothing fancy. But it's focused. I provide marketing and advertising support for small businesses and professional practices. Even being that focused, I have a lot of other sites to compete with.

But think how many more I would have to compete with if I just said marketing and advertising. Or, if I just said small business. Or, it like many web sites, just said nothing at all to narrow things down.

I don't look to the search engines to provide my traffic. And, I don't recommend that you do, either. Promote your site relentlessly and drive your own traffic. Then, you can speak only to people who are likely to buy from your site, and stop beating your head against the wall trying to stand out among millions of web sites.

My rule of advertising media selection is: "Go where your prospects are … and only where your prospects are."

You don't want to spend money talking to people who will never do business with you. Now, the argument you may give for your web site is; "It doesn't cost any more to reach the whole universe – my monthly cost is the same." True. But how do your real prospects find you?

Local Hosting

There are local web site hosts in your geographic market area that spend a lot of money generating traffic to their "mall." They concentrate on the local community, or people coming in to visit the local community.

If your business is one that deals primarily with people in your town, one of these local "mall" sites is ideal. Just as part of your rent in a physical shopping mall goes to traffic-building advertising and promotion, part of your hosting charge goes to promotion of the mall site.

> **An Alternative:** *At least pay to have your site linked to your Chamber of Commerce's home page. Expensive? Probably. But it you do business with the local community, it's probably a better investment than a large yellow pages ad.*

Of course, you want to stay on top of the promotion your host is putting out. Good ones advertise in the local paper, on radio, possibly on television. If they're not, then there's really no benefit to hosting there. And there's certainly no reason to pay more for hosting.

There are hosts that specialize in certain types of businesses. Want to see an interesting example? Check out http://www.metaphysical-mall.com/. You may not have found that one on your own! It's a group of businesses that all cater to a specific type of prospect.

The mall's job is to generate the right kind of traffic for the merchants they host.

> **The Point:** *Host your site where all of the incoming hits are qualified, target prospects.*

Have a look at http://www.cowboys.com/. You'll find everything Western.

A lot of web sites are getting thousands of hits. They're probably spending thousands of dollars a year to generate that traffic. But how many of those surfers are realistic prospects for what they're promoting?

Heavy traffic is worthless if few of the browsers are potential buyers.

A good mall site spends the dollars to generate thousands of hits. Their advertising is directed at a specific kind of prospect – they're focused. Their resident merchants are assured almost 100% qualified traffic.

You may spend more for hosting, but the quality of your hits is much higher. And consider how much you would have to spend on your own advertising to generate the amount of traffic the mall generates. The hosting is probably a bargain.

If you belong to an association that people might visit to find people like you, it may be worth linking to them. If you go to the National Speakers Association web site, you can quickly find me … under marketing … with a link.

I believe the hardest part of success on the web is drawing traffic … make that <u>qualified</u> traffic. If there is a specialty mall that already draws the kind of people you need, consider paying a little more for instant access to a qualified audience.

By the way, the malls can usually help with site design, too. Many have their own secure shopping cart where buyers can order from all of the merchants in the mall in one form. Since they host related sites, they have experience with either your business type or your locale. Their expertise can save you a lot of trial and error.

Mission

There are several different reasons why you might have a web site.

1.) Online Sales
2.) Electronic Brochure
3.) Because your competitors do
4.) Because everyone in the world does

Let's look at them David Letterman style: in reverse order;

4.) Everyone in the world has a web site

Well, it's really not everyone. And not everyone can or will use the Internet. If your target prospects are not the kind of people who can or will use the Internet, save your money. If your market does not lend itself to marketing online, save your money.

3.) Your competitors have sites

Don't do this just to "keep up with the Joneses." Reactive marketing is almost always a bad idea. Don't respond to everything your competitors do by doing the same thing.

In fact, you may be able to end run around them by doing what they're not. If they're putting lots of effort and money into web promotion, they may be leaving other areas wide open for you.

Have a site because it's good for business. There's no other good reason.

2.) The Electronic Brochure

Many web sites are little more than a company brochure in electronic format. There's nothing wrong with that.

The copy and design of an electronic brochure should follow the same rules as a print brochure, with a couple of exceptions;

First, don't get carried away with graphics. High resolution photos can make for slow loading when the prospect gets to your site. People are lazy ... and impatient! They won't wait long for your page to load.

Make your home page a clean, simple welcome. Give it a headline just like any other promo piece. Tell the visitor your number one overall benefit. Then give them very simple and easily-executable choices on where to go in your site. Keep it clean and simple. Make it easy to go to the next step.

The first page may not even have any promotional copy. It may be as simple as two or three menu choices, each addressing a specific product or department. Or, each may address a specific kind of prospect. My site offers consulting, speaking and writing. Three different products, three different types of prospects. Meeting planners don't care about my writing, and magazine editors don't care about my consulting.

Second, realize that you have powers available to you online that you don't have in print. Use them, but use them wisely. Audio, animation, streaming video ... all can be used to your advantage or detriment.

A video demonstrating your product can be a tremendous sales tool. But it should only come on screen when the prospect requests it. I've visited many sites that start with some dazzling audio/visual display right on the home page. Some go on for several minutes while you try to figure out how to shut them off or move to another page. I usually move to another site. I'm gone.

Respect your visitors. Respect their time, and their intelligence. Don't insult them with comic-book animation that has nothing to do with your product. Don't make them sit through a multi-media presentation they didn't ask for. And don't make it difficult for them to find exactly what they're looking for.

That all sounds down to earth and basic to me. Why do so many web designers use such capabilities to their own detriment?

Because most web sites are designed by technicians, not marketing people. Technicians love to show off their capabilities. You've seen the sites that show off the computer more than the product they're supposed to sell. What a waste! They managed to get me to their site, then turned me away when I got there.

LESSON: *Unless you sell video games, don't make your site look and act like one!*

Animation

If you design web sites, I know this word is on your mind.

In short: DON'T.

Don't do it. Moving pictures are for cartoons. They're a distraction from what you want your prospect to do, which is BUY.

Always remember that you're not in the entertainment business. Tempting as it may be to use all of those hip tools you have at your disposal, they don't do anything to help your site sell.

Web Page Design

Restraint. That's the word I want you to remember: Restraint.

In a world where graphics, color, sound, even animation are affordable, it's tempting to use everything in your web site. Don't do it!

OK, I know I just lost a few people. Some people just can't resist, and can't fathom a reason for resisting the temptation of making their web site look like a carnival. When a kid walks into a carnival, they're overwhelmed by the environment and the choices. What to do, where to go first?

If you bought this book hoping to learn the secrets of HTML code, now is a good time to return it for a refund! I really don't know squat about creating web sites … but I've got a lot to share with you about the non-technical side of web page design and copy writing.

Several years ago, I bought a copy of Microsoft® Front Page, thinking I could design my own site. After all, I can design and write print media ads and promo pieces. Why not do my own web site? Besides, I'm a believer in frugality wherever possible. Designing my own site would save hundreds of dollars.

Well, I've learned my lesson … the hard way. Trying to create my own web site was one of the biggest disasters of my career. I'll never get back the wasted hours. The people who visited the site I put up will never be back.

IMPORTANT LESSON: *If you're not highly qualified to create web sites, go hire someone who is. Functionality is as important as* *content. I can help you with content, but I recommend you spend the money for a good consultant to get the functionality right.*

That said, let me tell you what I think is important in a web site;

Simplicity ...

Too many web sites are like a carnival midway. Remember when you were a little kid, and your parents took you to the state fair? It was overwhelming! So much excitement. So much movement. Some many lights, sights and sounds. What to do, what to do?

That's the way it feels when you land on half the web sites out there. Unless your market is 15 year old attention deficit disorder sufferers, you don't need a bunch of whistles and bells. Leave the flash and glitter to the people who think they have to have it to impress their prospective customers.

Fact is, all that BS confuses and offends most people.

For one thing, most people still access the web via dial-up modems(writing this in February of 2003). That's changing little by little, but it's not wise to assume your prospects all have broadband access.

If your site takes more than a few seconds to load, people are clicking to the next site on their surfing itinerary before they even see your little animated song and dance.

And, they have to be able to tell a number of things at a glance;

      1.) What you do
      2.) What is available on the site
      3.) What value it has to them
      4.) How to get the answer to their question immediately

That doesn't sound so difficult, now does it? Let's look at each one;

1.) What you do ...

Get online sometime soon, and surf around a bit. As you go, look at just home pages to see if you can tell at a glance what the organization does.

You'll find a lot of people are real proud of their name. In fact, the home page is often little more than the organization's name, a photo of its building or founders, and a menu of what's on the site: Things like "about us," and "contact us." Because to "them," "they" are what's important.

What's wrong with this picture?

As in all of your promotional materials, the one that really matters is your prospect. It's not you.

So, starting right on the home page, tell your prospect what's in it for them. Sure, they have to know a little bit about you. But they want to know what it means in terms of benefit to them

So, "What you do" is actually "What you do to make the prospect's world a better place." Do you help them live longer? Make more money? Feel better? Look better?

In other words, like every other promo piece in your arsenal, you have to lead with benefits.

2.) What is available on your site

OK, they know what you do, and how it will make their life better.

Now, they need to know what is available on your site to help them make it happen.

You can do this with a prosaic explanation, much like a sales letter, or you can simply use a menu.

In the sales letter format, you'll describe your site content, including HTML links to each page as it's described. So, as they read, they can go directly to the information that interests them.

The menu approach is just what it sounds like; A list of options, each hyper-linked to the referenced page. Make sure your page titles are descriptive of their content ... always in terms of benefit to the prospect.

So, "about us," should be more like "who you're dealing with." Same meaning, but the latter is about the prospect in stead of just about "us."

3.) What value it is to them

When people first come to your site, you should assume they know nothing about you.

So, they need to be sold on the value of your products or services, and on the value of exploring your web site. Why should they hang around? Will they learn something new? Will they discover solutions to their problems? What problems?

Your web site has to sell itself. Don't assume they already know about you.

4.) How to get the answer to their question immediately

If you've heard the word "navigable" before, this is what they're talking about.

Your home page must make it easy for them to go directly to the solution to their problem.

Don't put a lot of content on the home page. This is not the place to dazzle them with information. Consider your home page to be like those directory signs in the lobby of a building. Make it easy to see where to go from here. Otherwise, they'll turn around and walk out. CLICK, Bye!

Be Consistent

Keep navigation tools in the same place on every page. Don't change subheads and titles in the menus. They have to be in the same place, with the same language, same colors, same type ... you get the idea.

This sounds really basic. And, it is. But go surf the web and look at how many sites ignore this very basic rule. It's like each page is from a different organization. You can hardly tell if you're still on the same site.

Establish a color theme, layout and navigation template, and stick with it on every, every page.

How will they find your site?

All this design stuff is well and good. But, if you don't have any traffic, it's all a lot of wasted effort.

You must promote your site relentlessly to drive traffic to it.

Let's start with the other marketing materials you already use.

> **IMPORTANT LESSON:** *Your web site address should appear on every piece of printed material that leaves your office.*

Your business cards, letterhead, brochures, post cards … every piece of paper you put into your prospects' hands should show your web site address.

Links

I've already mentioned some of the places where your can place links to your site.

Be careful about where you put those links. Some other sites will invite you to place a link on their site in exchange for you placing their link on your site. I think it's really important to be careful about who you will be associated with.

Unless adding their link to your site will add significant value to your visitors … make that your intended, targeted visitors … don't do it.

> **IMPORTANT LESSON:** *Any time you provide a hyperlink, set it up so it opens a new window. If you just transport them reader somewhere else, they may forget where they came from … and never come back.*

If you are going to provide links to other sites on your own, you don't want to lose your visitors when they click on one of them. It's easy to make the link open a new window rather than just leave your site. Then, they can close that window, or switch back to your site easily.

Meta Tags

Meta Tags are hidden, key words that the search engines use to identify your site.

Your Meta Tags should include all of the words people might enter into their browser's search box when looking for a business or practice like yours. A chiropractor might include low back pain, spine, Scoliosis, workers compensation, insurance, physical therapy …

You want to sit down and think what search criteria your prospects would enter into their browser if they were looking for a service or product like yours.

Your company name and product or service names will undoubtedly appear on your home page, so you don't have to put it in the meta tags. The search spiders will find them on the home page.

FREE HELP

Here's a web site you can go to, to help you generate meta tags for FREE: www.bizwebsolutions.com/metatags

Before you go there, take time to think of all the words your prospect might enter into their search box when looking for your kind of business or practice.

And, here's another that will analyze your tags for you, also for FREE: www.scrubtheweb.com/abs/meta-check.html

As I've said before: People will not work hard to read and understand your message. Whether your site is designed to sell, or just to deliver information, if it's difficult for the reader to navigate through the site and absorb the copy, they're not going to hang around for long.

And, as with any other promo piece, the graphic elements should serve the two purposes of 1.) Making the page attractive and inviting, and 2.) Walking the reader through your communiqué … <u>in the proper sequence</u>.

Graphic elements in your web pages are either distractors or directors. Any distractors that compete for the eye make the piece harder to read. One distractor that draws the eye to the starting point of your message should be the only one on the page. After that, graphic directors can guide the eye comfortably through the *Magic Formula* sequence.

Get Help

Don't try to develop your own web site unless your are highly qualified.

A poorly-designed site will turn visitors off. And that first visit may be the only chance you get.

There are so many things you can do with a web site, that one chapter in a manual like this can't begin to scratch the surface. Besides, I'm not qualified to write all the information you need.

At least I admit it. You should too. Get professional help to build a functional site. Work with them, using the design and copy writing skills you've learned here to create attractive pages that actually <u>sell</u>.

Chapter 20

Yellow Pages Advertising

This is the only ad you will ever design once, and be stuck with for a whole year. So, it requires special consideration.

It's important to give some though to a couple of key concepts before you even start to write and draw;

1.) Who would look for a supplier like you in the yellow pages?
2.) Criteria – When do they go to the yellow pages?
3.) What emotional appeal will work with these people?

Who

The yellow pages are sort of a last resort source.

People go to the yellow pages when they do not know of a supplier who can fulfill their needs. They just don't know where else to go. So, they're ready to turn the success of their project, business, health … to some total stranger. And they'll pick the one whose ad speaks directly to their needs.

You are a total stranger to these people. Sure, some may know you and just didn't think of you. But if they didn't think of you, you're really not much better off than a total stranger.

This is not an ad for people who already know you. This is not a media to build brand recognition. It is an instant-decision situation. If you look like the solution to their needs and fit their criteria better than the other suppliers, you'll get the call.

Odds are, they'll call a number of suppliers they find in the yellow pages. Don't dismiss these people as "shoppers." They will probably be making a buying decision, and they'll probably be making it very soon. The supplier who can fulfill their needs and treats them right will get the business.

They go to the yellow pages when they're ready to buy.

Think about it. When was the last time you went to the yellow pages to find something? For me, it was a Saturday afternoon. I had played golf that morning, and the Friday before. My back was killing me, and I needed a massage … badly. Of course, I called my regular guy first – not open on Saturday. So, being desperate for relief, I went to the "massage" classification yellow pages.

Criteria

Here were my criteria, in order of importance;

1.) Open Saturday
2.) Licensed Massage Therapist
3.) Close to my home

In other words, the license might be overlooked in a pinch(and I was in one), and "close to home" was way down the list.

Not one of the ads in my yellow pages gave the business' hours of operation. Why not? They probably change them occasionally, and didn't want to commit for twelve whole months when they designed the yellow pages ad.

> **LESSON:** *A business who publishes hours of operation in the yellow pages ... and sticks to them ... shows stability and dependability.*

So, I had no choice but to start calling. I started with licensed therapists closest to home. It took five calls to find one that was open on Saturday. They were 20 miles away, but I was in pain. They got me in late that afternoon, and money passed from my pocket to their cash register.

Notice that "price" was not one of my criteria. Too many businesses get hung up on price competition. For some things I buy, price is important. I buy gasoline from Sam's club because it's usually cheapest there. But, if I'm almost out of gas, my criteria change! People go to the yellow pages when they're "almost out of gas!!"

Unless you sell a commodity that people buy totally based on price, don't make the mistake of competing on price. It's just not high on the criteria list. That's not license to gouge – you still have to price fairly. But don't assume "lowest price in town" is what yellow pages prospects are looking for.

A note about follow up;

By the way, I left messages with two of the therapists that were closer to my home. Wouldn't you think that they would at least call during the week to say "Sorry we missed your call, we'd really appreciate a chance to so serve you in the future. We take appointments for Saturdays, but don't normally open" … SOMETHING to try to capture some return on the investment they made in the yellow pages ad?

> **LESSON:** *Any time you get a response to your ad or promo piece, follow up until the prospect either buys or dies. You spent all of that money to find prospects. When a live one calls you, you have to pursue them relentlessly until they buy(either from you or someone else), or tell you to get lost(or something stronger).*

And any time you acquire a new customer through the yellow pages, follow up and keep in touch to build a long-term relationship. After that huge investment to get them in the door the first time, it would be a crying shame to only serve them once.

Their regular supplier is still out there, and they'll probably go right back to them if you don't do something to bring them back again. If you've lured them away for this one purchase, you have a shot at replacing their regular supplier.

But it ain't gonna' happen if you don't go after it.

So, the prospect looking in the yellow pages doesn't know anyone who does whatever it is that you do, or sells whatever it is that you sell. But they're probably ready to buy today.

Only you know what you sell, and why people want or need it. And only you know what about you is different from all of your competitors in the yellow pages. If you're the only one open on Saturdays ... assuming you do or sell something people may need on Saturday ... tell the world!

Think about what's going on in the life of the yellow pages prospect. They're in the middle of a project and they need a part – and they have no idea who sells it. Or, the place they normally buy from doesn't carry that part, they're out of that part, or they're closed. They're in crisis. If you've got the largest parts inventory in town, including those hard-to-find items, say so!

Emotion

Remember the *Magic Formula*. Yes, you want to use it in the yellow pages, too. The first step ... your headline(or photo) ... must make an emotional connection with the prospect. And it has to play on the emotion they're already feeling at the time they see your ad. What emotion can you appeal to in the yellow pages? (As a reminder, there's a starter list of emotions in the back of the manual.)

Understand who will be looking for what you sell in the yellow pages, why they would be going to the yellow pages, and what emotional hot buttons you can push with your headline. I've already used the words "crisis" and "desperate." Those should give you a clue to the kind of emotions I like to appeal to.

My favorite emotions all fall under the category of "fear." You could also call them "pain" motivators. People go to the yellow pages when they're out of options, or when their regular supplier can't help them. They're in pain, they're in fear that their project may not come together without your help.

Hey Sailor, new in town?

When someone moves to a new city, they have a host of businesses they need to find.

They need a dry cleaner, a hairdresser, a grocery store, a driving range ... well, needs vary.

People find these new suppliers a couple of ways; First, they drive around and see what's nearby. The dry cleaner closest to my new home usually gets the first shot at my business.

But, if I don't see a business nearby, I go to the Yellow Pages. And, I think most people do.

So, if you want to draw these new movers, you have to let them know where you are. Yes, location is a prime motivator for the new mover. Don't try to get people to drive across town if your business is one of 50 similar businesses in town.

They're also interested in your specialty, if any. They'd like to know your hours – in fact, it irritates the Hell out of me when a business doesn't give their hours in the Yellow Pages. I'm looking for a new supplier of whatever, and can't tell whether they're open weekends.

First-time buyers

There is yet another type of yellow pages buyer: The person who has never bought what you sell, and therefore, has no idea where to go to find it. This person isn't desperate, but they are uninformed about the available suppliers.

They need to know that you're a stable, reliable, and trustworthy supplier. They need reassurance that it's safe to do business with you(still a fear motivator, right?).

Know which one you're addressing

Here's the important thing; Know which type of buyer you're looking for, and address their pain and fears specifically. Don't try to reach both the knowledgeable buyer looking for a new(possibly one-time) supplier, and the uninitiated buyer who is starting from square one. You have to know your market and your business, and make a decision which one your yellow pages ad should pursue. If in doubt, go for the uninitiated. You can never go wrong educating your prospect. Even if an experienced buyer reads your ad, you've demonstrated to them that you know what you're talking about.

A yellow pages makeover ...

Here is a typical yellow pages ad;

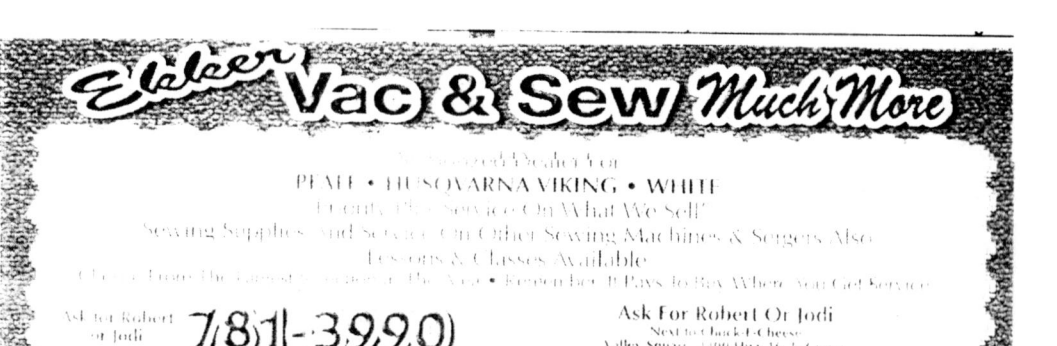

OK, it's hard to scan from a yellow background. Sorry the copy isn't better, but you can see what this ad is about.

> **IMPORTANT LESSON:** *The number one mistake business owners make in their yellow pages ad is to put their business name first. It's actually the LAST thing your prospect needs to know.*

Look through the section of the yellow pages that would be most appropriate for your business or practice. Read the headlines in the ads that are already there. What do most of them say?

Most yellow pages ads start with the name of the organization. That's actually the last piece of information the prospect needs.

First, they need a reason to stop and read your ad in stead of all the other ads they have to choose from. They need a benefit. Your name is not a benefit.

Want to know what's even less important to the prospect than your name? It's your photo. Look in the yellow pages again. How many ads carry the owner's picture? (Professionals, don't duck under the table now … this applies to you, too.)

Potential patients/clients don't give a flying hoot what you look like. They just want to know what about their life will be better after they avail themselves of your services. They need a benefit. Your photo is not a benefit.

Neither, by the way, are photos of your building, your vehicles, or your staff. Nobody cares, and you're paying by the inch to put this useless information in there! Don't make it your family album.

So, why do so many people make this common mistake in the yellow pages? **EGO!**

Now, don't feel bad if you're doing the same thing. Odds are, you didn't design your own ad, anyway. Am I right?

Now, I don't want to talk trash about yellow pages reps. Forgive them, for they know not what they do. OK, maybe they do know what they're doing. If so, shame on them.

They're selling you advertising. That's their job.

They're not as concerned about your business as they are about selling the ad. Odds are, they'll be gone by next selling season, so they have to make hay while the sun shines(as they say in the Midwest).

Consequently, the yellow pages sales rep will come to you with a "spec" (as in speculative) ad. They've already done all the work for you – all you have to do is sign on the dotted line. What could be easier? With a flick of the flanges, you will be exposed to thousands of prospects every day for the next year!

But wait. The ad looks good to you … but, will it look good to your prospects?

See, the sales rep is designing ads that will look good to YOU. Your name in lights! What could be easier to buy than that? Better yet, your photograph prominently displayed at the top of your ad. Your ego says: "BUY!"

And, by the way, did you notice that this year's ad is bigger than last year's? Oh yea, it's probably much larger. "That will get you preferred placement in your category," the rep explains. Ads are placed according to size, with the largest(read that: most expensive) ads appearing first, then working down incrementally to the people who just bought an itty-bitty ad.

But you sign, because your name looks real impressive on that big ad. And the photo just wouldn't look right all shrunk down to fit a smaller ad.

Don't fall for it!

NEVER, EVER let a yellow pages(or newspaper, or penny pincher, for that matter) sales rep design your advertising for you. They live on the ad sale, not on your business' success.

Ad reps are nice people. They're not out to screw you. They're interests are just not the same as yours. You design your own stuff, or pay a consultant or agency to do it for you. Heck, hire me! For a few hundred bucks I'll create a killer ad you can use in the yellow pages, the newspaper, the penny pincher ... you name it.

But don't buy a spec ad. Design your own ads or have it done by someone whose goal is to help you bring in more business, not get you to buy a bigger ad.

Enough lecture, let's look at what I did to the above sample ad;

> **Sew like a pro ...**
> Top brand equipment, "Priority Plus" service on all brands, hard-to-find supplies, professional instruction for all skill levels
> **Mention this ad and save 5% on any single item.**
>
> Authorized Dealer for
> - **Pfaff**
> - **Husqvarna Viking**
> - **White**
>
> *Ekker*
>
> Ekker Vac & Sew
> Valley Square - 4400 Hwy 16
> LaCrosse (Next to Chuck E Cheese)
> **Phone 781-3990**

Let's tear this apart;

First, remember *The Magic Formula*. Keep holy *The Magic Formula*. It will set you free.

Remember, step one is to grab the reader's attention.

In the case of this ad, the reader is looking for sewing machines/sales. That's the category this was in.

> (By the way, the next category was sewing machines/service & repair. The first category overflowed to the pages carrying the next, and you don't know which page you'll land on until the book arrives and you're committed for a year! So, if you offer both sales and service, say so ... just in case.)

Since the prospect is looking for sewing machines, I put one in the upper left-hand corner. This image is reversed ... the manufacturer pointed out that this looks like a left-handed version of their machine(they don't make a left-handed version!), so this graphic had to be redone. I had turned it around because this way, it opens into the ad, directing the eye into the space. Oh well.

Following the natural eye pattern of left to right, I gave the reader a benefit "Sew like a pro." This store sells quality stuff. I wanted to establish right away that this is not the store to call if you're looking for a cheap, "Brand X" machine. If you're serious about sewing, you have to notice this headline.

Then we proved the promise that you can sew like a pro. We offer top brand equipment, priority plus service(even on "Brand X" machines), hard-to-find supplies and professional instruction.

Even if you don't "sew like a pro" now, we can help you get their with the best equipment(or getting your equipment into top operating condition) and professional instruction that will take your skills to the next level.

Even in the yellow pages, you can include a proposition …

"Mention this ad and save 5% on any single item" is a strong offer for a 12-month run. But, I believe your proposition should be strong. Heck, if it was my store, I'd offer 20% off. I want to get them in the door for that first sale, then make a lifetime customer of them.

Make your proposition generous enough to get their attention, and to make them hold on to your ad. I even put hash marks around the ad, a signal to cut it out like a coupon.

"But wait a minute, Larry," you might say. "I don't want them to cut my ad out – how will they find me next time?"

Yellow pages ads are designed to attract first time buyers. Once they do business with you the first time, it's up to you to make sure they never forget your name or lose your contact information. Once they know you, they'll look in the white pages for your phone number. Or, they'll be prompted to respond to your direct mail pieces they see regularly now that they're <u>your customer</u>.

> **IMPORTANT LESSON:** *Yellow pages are for the first sale. Then, it's up to you to keep them coming back.*

That means your yellow pages language and proposition should all be directed at strangers who know nothing about you. You have to tell them what kind of buyer you're best prepared to serve(in this case, the serious sewer), and put down a proposition that makes them stop in their tracks and tear out your ad.

Your name and contact information comes last.

Like every other ad and promo piece we've discussed, the last piece of information they need is "Who do I get this from, and how to I contact them?" You make the sale first, then tell them where to go to get it.

Should you pay for color?

Your sales rep will make a big deal about color. They'll quote the study that says color attracts 78% more attention than black and white(or, black and yellow, as the case may be).

It's true that color attracts more attention. But no study has ever shown that color results in more sales. Just because it got you noticed, doesn't necessarily translate into getting you business.

> **IMPORTANT LESSON:** *A good black and white(or black and yellow) ad will outsell a mediocre color ad every time.*

If you just can't resist buying color … because the sales rep's kid needs braces and you feel obligated to help out, or whatever … use color for only one element. ONE, just ONE. ONE only. Got it?

Now, here's a little quiz to see if you've been paying attention;

Question: If color attracts 78 % more attention than black and white, and you only want to use the color on one element, which element should you use the color on?

Hint: The first step of *The Magic Formula* is "Attention."

Here's another hint: Your headline is 80% responsible for the success or failure of your ad.

YES! Put your attention-grabbing, benefit-laden headline in color. One element, one different color.

I know, all those colors are available. It seems like a shame to pay for color and use so little. You could make the whole ad color! Well, open the yellow book again and look at the full color ads others have put in. They look like someone swallowed four colors of paint and vomited on the page.

And if you notice, most everyone is buying color now. They've made it relatively inexpensive, so it's an easy upsell for the reps.

But face it, the print quality on the newsprint paper stock isn't the greatest. All those colors kind of bleed together like rainbow sherbet.

Your clean, simple ad is going to stand out on the page loaded with pigment.

If anything, pay for the white background, and print all in black. A black-type ad on a white background will stand out more than any color combination your competitors will come up with. It's especially true if all of your competitors are using color. The black and white will stand out like a ~~sore~~ green($) thumb!

The yellow pages are no different that any other ad or promo piece. The selling sequence is the same, and you must stick to *The Magic Formula*.

Don't Over-spend

One of the most common, and most disastrous mistakes I see ... all too often ... is the consulting client who has committed themselves to more Yellow Pages space than they need. They're stuck with it for the whole year.

Many paid for color, on top of the outrageous cost of a much larger ad than they needed.

I recently consulted with driving range in North Las Vegas. They had bought the largest ad in their category in the Las Vegas yellow pages, and paid for color to boot. There was only one problem with that: They really had no competition. Oh, there are other ranges in the area, but none in their area. Why pay for a big, color ad when you really have no competition?

Plus, this business was way outside Las Vegas. The Las Vegas Yellow Pages covers the whole region. Unfortunately, there were no regional directories for North Las Vegas. If there had been, I would have advised them to drop the big book, and just list in the regional directory. Then, they could use the hundreds of dollars they save every month for other advertising and promotion.

At least my timing was good with the consulting visit. The yellow pages rep had just dropped off a proposal for an even larger(and, you guessed it: Color) ad for the next year. Needless to say, I recommended against increasing the ad.

So, we discussed who would use the yellow pages to find them. We agreed that it would be the golfer who doesn't know they're there. If they already knew about them, they wouldn't have to look in the yellow pages. They'd just get in the car and drive down. This is not a business that people deal with on the phone. They drive down.

We also agreed that the prime criteria for those golfers is a place that's convenient. They don't want to have to drive for an hour to get to a golf practice facility. The other ranges in the book were clear across town. This is the ad I recommended for the next year;

JUPITER GOLF CENTER

North Las Vegas

Golf Range • Kids' Fun Center

www.JupiterGolf.com

70 W. Craig Road   341-1590

This ad says what the yellow pages prospect needs to know. All the other ranges in town talked about their facilities first. The facilities are important, but convenience comes first.

By the way, once you've hit balls at this range, you'll be glad they're in your neighborhood. They were named best new range in the US by one national magazine, and top ten in the US by another. The facility speaks for itself once the prospect gets there.

This ad will cost half of what they paid in the previous year. They can invest the savings in direct mail – talking one-to-one with their database-full of prime prospects.

Always remember, the yellow pages will reach new customers … first time buyers. Your ad should be designed entirely around drawing total strangers to your door.

You'll maintain relationships and repeat business with other media.

Take time to think about what the prospect is looking for in the yellow pages. Is it the most convenient location? The lowest price? The highest quality? Match up what they're looking for with what you have to offer, and make that the first thing they see in your ad. Then buy the minimum ad size you need to tell them enough to get them to give you a try. Don't buy any more than you need.

Always know who your ad is talking to. Here, it's strangers. Address them and entice them as such.

Chapter 21

Direct Mail 101

Direct mail is, in my humble opinion, the most efficient, and if done well, effective way to promote just about any business or professional practice.

That "if done well" is the caveat. If you've ever had a direct mail promotion bomb, you may think the problem was with the medium. (Of course, you don't want to blame yourself!)

There is no other medium that practically guarantees that your prospect will see your promotional piece. If you run ads somewhere, you have to hope they read the issue you're in, read the page you're on, and notice your ad while they're there. If you run broadcast spots, you have to hope they're tuned in to your channel at the exact minute your spot runs. And you have to hope they don't choose that moment to do a channel surf or go get a sandwich. And online, you're competing with literally millions of distractions.

But good old direct mail puts your marketing piece right into their hands.

Getting them to open it and read it is the challenge. If your design and copy don't grab their attention, make them put the rest of the stack of mail down, and open your piece right then and there ... it's in the trash.

Or, not much better, in the "maybe I'll read it later if I find the time" pile. You know what happens to that pile eventually.

The Envelope

Your envelope has several jobs; 1.) To protect the contents and keep them in one place while in transit, 2.) To carry the recipient's address and necessary postage, and 3.) To motivate the recipient to look inside.

Don't just send a plain envelope. Put some "teaser" copy on the outside to draw them in.

Teaser copy goes near your return address. When people look at each piece in their stack of mail, they look first at their own name. Then they go to the upper, left-hand corner to see who it's from. As they make that scan from their own address to yours, you have the opportunity to grab them with a teaser headline.

This teaser has to promise a benefit to the recipient.

A "benefit," you will recall, is something that will be better about his or her life after they take advantage of your offering. What will change after they attend your event? Will they be healthier? More profitable? Better parents? Heck, it might just be how much they'll enjoy being the proud owner of your product.

There has to be something in it for them if you want to get their attention.

The Sales Letter

Why not just a brochure? Think of it this way; What if a sales person walked into your office, quietly placed a brochure on your desk, then left without saying a word? Since they went to the effort of delivering the brochure in person, wouldn't you expect them to tell you a little bit about what's inside, and why you should take time out of your day to read it?

The cover letter is your sales person. It tells your recipient what's in it for them – why they need to drop whatever they're doing and read the brochure.

The letter picks up where the teaser copy left off. It starts with the benefit the envelope copy promised, then continues to pile on as many benefits as you can think of. "You'll make new friends, learn how to improve your health, pick up new business-building skills, make contacts that can help you get to the next level in your career."

Give them as many reasons as you can ... all in terms of "what's in it for them."

The Brochure

The brochure gives the facts and details. When, where, what time. All that stuff.

This is the pretty, full-color piece in the envelope. But pitty the poor recipient who wasn't expecting it today.

Keep it clear and simple. You're asking them to drop what they're doing and read this thing. Don't make it a mystery or a graphic puzzle.

And give them the information in a reasonable sequence. Start with photos of people just like your prospect enjoying the benefit your product or service provides. We're back to *The Magic Formula*, only now the brochure picks up where the sales letter left off.

Inside, you want to walk them through all of the information they need about you, your products and services ... in benefit language. Tell them why it's important to THEM.

Finish the brochure with everything they need to know if they're ready to buy.

The Response Coupon

Now, it's time for the recipient to talk to you. Give them lots of options, and make them all fast, easy and free. Give them a toll-free phone number, a toll-free fax number, online registration, a paper form with a postage-paid envelope.

The form they fill out, whether on paper or online, should be written as them talking to you.

Repeat your key benefit as you would like to hear them repeat it back to you.

"Yes, I want to experience the fire walk hand-in-hand with my team members."

The Dance

You can see that each piece is designed to take your prospect by the hand, and walk them to the next step in the dance. The envelope is designed to draw them inside. The sales letter should get them all excited, and make them want to jump into the brochure to get the particulars. Then, the response form becomes their voice screaming out; "Yes, I want to be part of this wonderful event. Sign me up immediately!"

Grab their attention right up front, right on the envelope. Tease them to open it, then take the next step in the dance ... and the next. Lead then inexorably toward an enthusiastic response, and your registrations will come in early and enthusiastic.

A FREE direct mail education delivered to your door ...

If that was the headine in an ad for a product, wouldn't you give it a try?

Imagine, daily lessons from the top copy writers and designers in the business, delivered to your door ... FREE ... every day.

You're already receiving this amazing offer. Are you taking advantage of it?

If you're not an avid reader of your incoming mail, I want you to start immediately. There's a complete education to be had at zero cost.

Every day, a handful of new lessons in direct mail effectiveness are delivered to your door. Read them, analyze them. Swipe ideas from them. I'm not saying you should plagiarize. I'm saying you should look for working concepts you can apply to your own direct mail package, and especially, to your sales letters.

Marketers with huge budgets and buildings full of well-paid designers and writers have tested for years to find what works best for their promotions. When you receive a mailing from someone who's been around for a while, you've got to know they've put a lot of money and research into fine-tuning it for maximum response.

Take a hard look at every component:

What did they do to motivate you to open the envelope? Is it colorful? Is there teaser copy on the outside that promises a reward for going inside? Are there little windows that invite you to peek inside?

When you opened the flap, what did you see first? Probably a sales letter with a compelling headline, something that spoke directly to your emotions. Maybe it made a promise, or broached a proposition. Is the letter personalized? Does each line make want to stick around to read the next? Could you skim the letter and get the whole message? Who signed it? Is it signed in blue ink? Is there a PS? Margin notes handwritten in blue? Did they circle, underline or highlight key points in the text?

What's next? Probably a full-color piece that gives all of the details you need to know about the product or service they're offering. One by one, it backs the benefits the sales letter promised with features, facts and statistics.

Is there a "secondary" proposition? If you're not ready to order, is there a smaller step you can take so they know you still might want to dance?

Lift Letter

If you see a lift letter, you know this is a mailer that's done some serious testing. You don't throw extra pieces of paper into a mailing just to make the envelope thicker(and heavier, thereby more expensive to mail). It's there because it lifts response. It's probably signed by someone other than the person who wrote the cover letter ... kind of like when a second salesperson comes in to help out when the first sales person is having a hard time closing the sale.

Do they make it easy and safe to respond? How many ways can you respond? Is one of them a medium you're used to using and comfortable with?

You don't have to go back to college, and you don't have to buy a library full of books(but aren't you glad you bought this one?) to learn what works in direct mail. You only have to study the free lessons that are delivered to your door every day.

Additional Resource

Direct Mail
It's still the best
By Larry Mersereau

Order online www.MagicFormula.com

Direct Mail Checklist

Purpose

    Maintain Contact   Specific Offer   Lead Generation

Offering

  Product/Service   Event   Lead Generation

List

  Outside List   Customers   Prospects/Responders

Format

  Letter Only   Self-Mailer   Postcard

  Package Components

      Envelope Size _____   Cover Letter

      Brochure

      Involvement Device

          Stamp   Token

          Acceptance/Rejection   Address Correction

          Other _____

      Order Form/Registration/Application

        Lift Letter   Business Reply

                                        Card

                                        Envelope

Budget

List Rental/DP	$ _____	In-house	Outsourced
Design/Creative	$ _____	In-house	Outsourced
Production	$ _____	In-house	Outsourced
Printing	$ _____	In-house	Outsourced
Lettershop	$ _____	In-house	Outsourced
Postage	$ _____	In-house	Outsourced

Measurement

  Response _____   New Sales _____   Repeat/Renewal Sales _____

Chapter 22

Testing

What if you hired a salesman, put him out on the road for a year, and couldn't track a single sale to his efforts? What would you do? Unless he's your son in law, you'd fire him! Heck, even if he is your son in law, you should fire him.

Unfortunately, that's exactly what too many businesses fail to do with advertising and promotion. They keep putting it out there month after month, but can't really tell if it's doing anything.

And this is no small item. For many businesses, the advertising and promotion budget chews ups 10% or more of their revenue. How can they put out that kind of money, and not demand a measurable return on investment?

Many of them stop advertising altogether, throwing their hands up in the air and saying: "I tried advertising, and it doesn't work." If you've ever been tempted to stop advertising altogether, this chapter will set you free.

Promote yourself relentlessly ...

You know, deep down inside, that you absolutely must advertise to keep your business in your prospect's mind. If you don't promote yourself relentlessly, you might as well plan on being passed over in favor of someone who does.

In the town where I live, there's a sewing machine and fabric store that's been in business for years. Now, if you wonder why I would notice a sewing machine and fabric store, let me tell you. In mid-2002, I spoke a dealer conference for the nation's leading sewing machine manufacturer. I don't sew, but as soon as I confirmed that booking, I started noticing sewing machine ads. Your mind helps you sort out the advertising that doesn't apply to you, and helps you zero in on the stuff that does. Suddenly, sewing machine stores applied.

Back to the story: The old sewing machine and fabric store rarely advertised – maybe Christmas-time and Mothers Day. Recently, a new store opened just a few miles from their location.

The new store is advertising relentlessly. They didn't do an especially good job of design and copy writing, but any advertising … even badly done advertising … is at least something.

Suddenly, the old store is on the defensive. They're running ads every week now. But their ads are in response to the new competitor's. See, the owner of the new store uses a tag line that incorporates the key words from the old store's name: "sew much more." So, now the owner of the old store feels like the new store is infringing on their trade name. (Before you ask; No, it's not registered to either store owner as a trademark.)

So now they have this pissing match going on in the press. The new store just runs their normal advertising. But the owner of the old store is not happy at all, and keeps running ads that say: "Don't be fooled, we haven't moved. We're still in business in the same location we've been in for 20 years …" You get the idea.

The point of the story is this; Had the old store been advertising regularly, even though there was not a lot of competition out there, their name, their location, their identity … would have been so ingrained in the minds of the sewing public, that the new competitor would have been insane to use a play on their name in a tag line.

But, no! Old competitor had decided at some point in his business experience that "advertising doesn't work. I tried it, it doesn't work." Or, maybe they get so complacent when business is good that they just don't bother. Don't let this happen to you.

Recommended Reading

My Life in Advertising
&
Scientific Advertising

Two Works by Claude C. Hopkins

"Nobody should be allowed to have anything to do with advertising until he has read this book (Scientific Advertising) seven times. It changed the course of my life"
–David Ogilvy

My Life in Advertising
&
Scientific Advertising
NTC Business Books ISBN 0-8442-3101-0

The "Science" of advertising ...

Like any other major business expenditure, advertising and promotion should be planned, executed, analyzed and adjusted.

"Science" is an intimidating word, especially to the small business owner who already has enough complexity in his or her life. This doesn't have to be terribly difficult, but it does have to be done if you want to get maximum return on your investment in marketing.

In fact, if it gets too complicated, you just won't do it. So, let's try to keep it simple.

Thou shalt track!

The first mistake most organizations make it not tracking results. They run an ad, send out a mailing, or launch a web site promotion, then do nothing to measure response.

It's important to keep careful records of all responses that come into your organization. You want to know which of your promotional activities and pieces generated each prospect response.

There are several ways to track your responses. Each requires some level of commitment from your sales or customer service staff. They will have to keep track of results, so they have to care. That means you have to motivate them in some way to manage this important information for you. You may have to reward them, recognize them … hey, there are lots of books out there on motivation. If you have a hard time getting your staff behind initiatives like this one, go buy a book before you start. You can put the world's most sophisticated tracking mechanism in place, but if your people are with you, it ain't gonna' happen.

How it's done …

1.) Ask them!

Simply ask each new contact where they heard about you. This method requires maximum staff commitment. If they forget to ask, or forget to record the response, you have nothing.

2.) Use dedicated lines

If you can set up one or more specific incoming line for testing, it will be easy to see how many calls are generated by a specific ad or promotion. If you want to get technologically sophisticated, you can even have responses tallied electronically.

To use a dedicated number, you publish that number in only one place at a time. It's not in the phone book, it's not on your business cards or brochures. It's only in the ad or promo piece that's in circulation right now.

And it's only in one of those items – if you've got a print ad running at the same time a mailing is being delivered, use the dedicated number in only one of them. Even if they're promoting the same offer, you want to separate mail from advertising responses. Of course, you want to track both. But you must track them separately to know which one is working.

The drawback with this method is that, during peak times, you may not have enough open phone lines to handle response. If your prospects are hot to buy, and they get either a busy signal or the dreaded "please press one if you're using a touch-tone phone," they're not likely to hang around to wait for service.

Imagine, they're salivating for your product or service, and you lose them because they can't get through! All of that advertising money and effort are wasted. Worse yet, you have no idea how much response you would have gotten had they been able to get through.

3.) Specific Proposition

If you are promoting yourself through more than one medium(and I hope you are), you can run different offers in each. Tracking is then simply a matter of counting how many responses each proposition brought in.

> **IMPORTANT LESSON:** *If you advertise in the Yellow Pages, it's important to track response to your ad. A low-cost, low-risk-to-the-prospect proposition that runs <u>only in the Yellow Pages</u> ad is the easiest way to track response.*

Most businesses and practices do nothing to effectively track Yellow Pages advertising. They won't let you put in a separate phone number, because they don't want you to track response. "Trust us, it's working," is their mantra. Don't you believe it!

You have to <u>know</u> it's working, and the only way you can is to put something in your ad that makes it easy to tell when a caller is responding to that ad.

There's a whole section in this manual on Yellow Pages advertising. It's right for some people, and wrong as rain for others. The only way you can be sure, is to test. If you're just pumping money into Yellow Pages advertising without confirming results, you're flushing money down the toilet … trust me.

It's extremely important to test, and to track the results of each test.

Test one element at a time

The second mistake many organizations make when disappointed with results is to totally redesign and rewrite the piece. The key to effective testing is to test only one element of any given communiqué at a time.

If you've been in business for any length of time, you have already done some advertising and promotion. If you have tracked response, you already know which of your ads or promo pieces has been the most effective. That piece is your "control."

The control is the piece you will test against. If it's been fairly effective, you don't want to scrap it altogether for a new look and feel. This is like taking golf lessons. You don't want to try to learn a completely new swing – you want to work with what you already have and make it better. You want to tweak it for incremental improvements rather than starting all over … possibly playing much worse until the new swing starts to work(if it ever does!).

So start with the ad or piece you know is your best, and test to beat the results you already know you can count on if you run that one again.

If possible, test your new element on a percentage of your market. That's easy with direct mail, because you can mail your control to half of your list and your test to the other half. If the test draws better response than the control, it becomes the new control. If not, you'll continue to test against the original control. Direct mail is a separate ball game, so I won't go into detail here. But you get the idea.

In print media, it's a little more difficult to split test. If you advertise in several publications, you may want to choose one that hits a good cross section of your market, and run the test in that publication while sticking to the control in the other(s).

This is not completely accurate testing, because different publications have different audiences and circulation. But at least it's better than just scrapping the ad you already know works. You may have to test the new ad a couple of times. Run the test ad in publication "A" and the control in publication "B." Then, switch to the control in "A" and the test in "B."

That would give both publications more of a fair evaluation.

Or, you could run your control and your test in the same publication on the same day, assuring exposure to the same audience. Tracking is a little more difficult for this one, because you have to find out more than where they saw your ad. You have to be able to tell which one they're responding to. You'll have to make your proposition slightly different to know which they're responding to.

If you have two ads with different propositions in the same publication, make sure neither is a better deal than the other.

For example: One ad could offer "two for the price of one," while the other offers "50% off." The value is basically the same. But your profit on the two for one is higher, and the perceived value of the two for one is going to be higher. (I think you'll find "two for one" will outsell "50% off," but you have to test with your product or service and market to be sure.)

Your ads shouldn't compete with each other, just test against each other.

There are lots of complexities you can get hung up on here. If you've got two ads in the same publication, was it the fact that they saw you twice that made them respond? Was one of the tests on a day the publication gets fewer readers? Did the front page story affect sales of the paper, thereby reducing the audience. Am I driving you crazy yet?

It's about improvement.

Don't get hung up on variables. We're not trying to be that sophisticated here. Yes, those variables can affect your response. But, if you haven't been doing any scientific testing at all before now … and most organizations have not … anything is going to be an improvement.

You're working to make your advertising and promotion better and better. Just starting to track results and test key elements is going to make a positive difference that will pay for this manual many times over.

If you don't test and track, you will never know what's working and what's not.

You'll either keep shelling out cash for advertising and promotion that you can't justify, or you'll just throw your hands up and say "I've tried it and it doesn't work." Either way, you lose.

It's your money. Invest it wisely and advertising and promotion will give you a measurable return.

Testing by the book

What you should be doing in stead, is testing these elements <u>one at a time</u>;

> **Headline/Photo**
> **Proposition**
> **Price**
> **Media or List**
> **Copy**

There are other things you can play with, but these are the most important. I didn't include type faces and graphics because I'm assuming you've read earlier chapters in this manual and that you're already using a sensible layout and typography. If you've got more than two type faces in a print media ad, don't start testing yet. It won't work to test ads that nobody reads anyway. A cluttered, illegible ad isn't going to draw response no matter how good the proposition is … because nobody's going to read it!

Headline

The headline is listed first, because it is the copy element that is most likely to affect response.

It's been estimated that your headline is up to 80% responsible for the success of your ad. How can one element be so important? It's the first thing the reader sees. It's the information they base their decision on whether to read the rest of the ad or not. If it doesn't connect with them emotionally, they're gone without seeing the rest of the copy.

The same rule applies to mailers, flyers, brochures and sales letters. Web pages, too. Web pages especially.

If the first thing they see or read doesn't stop them in their tracks, it doesn't matter what the rest of the piece has to say, because they aren't going to read it anyway.

When testing your headline copy, stop and ask yourself the following questions;

1.) Is this about them … or about me?
2.) Have I exploited an emotion?
3.) Does it address my clearly defined prospect specifically?
4.) Does it beg them to stop and read more?

Of course, if you are using a photo, it becomes your headline. It has to make the emotional connection with the reader. The same questions apply.

Your headline is so important, there's a whole chapter on headlines elsewhere in this manual.

Proposition

Proposition is right behind headline for testing validity.

A great headline alone won't draw response. It may get attention, and may get people to stop and read more. But if there is no compelling proposition … or if your proposition is not strong enough to motivate your prospect to act … you still have no response to measure.

So, if you're testing headlines and getting nowhere, pick the best and keep it as your control. Then start testing propositions.

Propositions to Test

There is not limit to what you can use for a proposition. In case you don't have a wild imagination, let me give you some typical propositions to work with. All have been used with some success … by someone. Not all will apply to your unique situation, so try the ones that seem to make sense for you. Test several to see which draws the best response, then ride that pony 'til it runs out of wind!

1.) Discount

I listed this first, because I want to get it out of the way. I hate discounts. Let me say it again, a little louder;

I HATE DISCOUNTS

Lowering your price by 50% does several things;

First, it tells the prospect that you were asking more than you needed to in your original price. If you can still make money at half price, their thinking goes, you must have been gouging me at full price.

Second, it trains your customers to wait for the discount. Too many department stores try to charge premium prices when the new merchandise arrives, then deep-discount them after a while to clear them off the shelves. Most of the public waits for the sale. Sure, a few buy at the premium price, but most are trained to wait for the sale ... because they know it's coming.

Third, it puts your competition in position to match or beat your discount. Then you match or beat theirs, then they ... you know what's coming. Nobody's making any money.

Fourth, and worst: It makes you a discounter. It devalues you.

Charge fair prices, give your customers/patients/clients more value than they paid for, and they'll gladly pay your price. I'd rather pay a fair price for a suit, get the help of a qualified tailor to make it fit right, free alterations for the life of the suit ... VALUE, than get the same suit for "half price" and be left on my own to make it fit in the first place, and after each of my subsequent(inevitable) diets.

2.) Rebate

As I write this, I'm in the "game" of chasing a rebate. Anyone who has had to play this game is reluctant to trust rebates.

I bought an MP3 player to play music at my workshops, and to be able to listen to music on airplanes.

I made one big mistake, one that I promised myself years ago I wouldn't make again. I've done it several times since the original promise to myself, and each time renewing the promise never to do it again. The mistake? I went to "Worst Bye Superstore"(a factitious name cleverly designed to protect the guilty party's identity).

I went in with a budget in mind, but not real knowledgeable about MP3 players. I'm not on the leading edge of technology. In fact, I've been lacerated frequently by the leading edge.

You can buy an MP3 player for $29.95. It won't hold much, and won't have any power for playback, but you can own it for pocket change. Of course, as storage capacity and sound quality improve, the prices go up.

I bought the $229.95 model ... because it was on sale, sort of. You had to pay full price, but you got to send in for a $50.00 rebate. My budget going in was $150.00. I'm still over budget, but getting a top of the line MP3 player. When you're getting a bargain, and getting top of the line, it's OK to go over budget, right?(My wife, the super-shopper, taught me that one.)

Doesn't sound like a game so far, does it? Let the game begin ...

Six weeks after the purchase, I went to the web site: wheresmyrebate.com. That's not made up, it's a real web site. You can go there to track the progress of your rebate from this particular vendor.

The status of my rebate was; "Rejected."

I called the store. Let me rephrase that: I TRIED to call the store I bought the MP3 player from. I landed in voice-mail Hell. I tried to connect to customer service, and got nowhere. So, I went ahead and connected to sales in the stereos department. MP3 players are actually in the computers department, and no, she couldn't connect me. So, I had to go back through voice mail Hell to talk to someone in computers. Can you guess what he told me? "You have to call the manufacturer. The phone number is on the rebate tag."

So, I called the manufacturer. Voice mail Hell again. Finally got a near-human, and explained my situation. She was able to pull me up on the computer, and found that I had sent the wrong UPC. I sent the one on the shrink wrap. You have to send in the one on the box ... they're not the same. I asked her how I could have known that ... and she hung up on me.

That's right, she hung up on me.

So, I resubmitted everything, and included the UPC on the box.

Four weeks later, I went to wheresmyrebate.com, and put in the code that had been assigned to my case the first time around. Someone else's name came up ... their rebate was in the mail. But, where's my rebate, dot com?

So, I started the telephone approach again …

I can't go on with this story. The veins are starting to pop out on my neck.

But, you get the picture. I had to do all of the work, and that's the flaw with rebates;

> **IMPORTANT LESSON:** *If the buyer has to do all of the work, they're much less motivated to buy at any price.*

And it's not just rebates. Any offer that requires the buyer to jump through hoops is a.) less likely to be successful, and b.) engenders distrust that will be remembered long after the sale(or no-sale).

OK, I still send in the form for the $5 rebate on the item I was going to buy anyway. I just bought an optical mouse(close to leading edge of technology!), but not at Worst Bye … because I'll never set foot in that store again. But, I found out at the checkout counter that there was a $10.00 rebate. Hey, that's pennies from Heaven – of course I'll send that in. But I would not have changed brands for the ten bucks. And I certainly would not have gone out of my way to go to Worst Bye for ten bucks(especially if I knew I'd have to jump through hoops to collect it), even if they had it and the other store didn't.

By the way … I bought the mouse a month ago, and still haven't seen the $10.00. Who knows if it's actually coming.

I don't trust rebates, and I think a lot of buyers think like me. I don't want to jump through hoops, follow up online and by phone … I don't want to do all of the work. Either give me a good price up front, or shut up already.

3.) Free Trial

OK, here's one I like. It's kind of like a product demonstration, but he prospect gets to do it themselves, in their own home or office, on their own time. They get to really find out of the product is going to work for them or not.

The Free Trial gives the buyer a chance to use your product for a prescribed length of time before they actually buy. You ship the product, let them beat it up, try to break it, try to make it fail … you know what they do with it!

Your Free Trial version may not include all of the features of your product, but enough to demonstrate its value. Many software packages are sold through Free Trials. You get a certain number of trial transactions, or less than complete functionality. You get enough to really see what it's all about, and whether it will work for you. But you don't get enough to just use the trial version without buying eventually.

The hallmark of the Free Trial is that there is NO RISK to the buyer. People go through life terrified that they will make a wrong buying decision. This gives them a chance to try it in their own world before they buy it. If they don't like it, or it doesn't do what they need or what they thought it would do, they pass.

No money lost. Zero risk.

4.) Free Gift

There are a couple of ways you can use Free Gift propositions;

> a.) You can offer a Free Gift just for responding to your ad or mailing.

You would use this for lead generation – a promotion designed to collect names of qualified, interested prospects.

> **IMPORTANT LESSON:** *The free gift should be of value to a specific prospect but inexpensive for you to fulfill, and should be related to the ultimate product or service you are selling.*

"Of value to the prospect" means it has to be something they would want badly enough to pick up the phone and call. It's very possible that they would buy it if the opportunity presented itself, but when it's free, they just can't pass it up.

"Inexpensive for you to fulfill" means it doesn't cost you much. "Free Special Report," or "Free Booklet" are great lead generation offers. You write a document loaded with valuable information. Print it inexpensively and offer it as a gift.

The information you offer should only be valuable to a specific kind of person; *your clearly defined target customer.* That's who you want to respond. You don't want to send out a lot of booklets to non-prospects. "Ten Golf Practice Tips that will Lower Your Handicap" would not draw responses from non-golfers. In fact, it would only draw response from golfers that are serious enough about the game to actually work at it a little bit.

"Related to the ultimate product or service" should be self-explanatory. The "Ten Golf Practice Tips that will Lower Your Handicap" was a free gift idea I came up with for a golf practice facility. Only people who are willing to practice would ask for this special report. The next step is to pull them to our practice facility after they get the piece.

(This is a 2-step promotion. Step one: get them to respond. Step two: communicate one-to-one and draw them in. One-to-one communication is highly personalized, where as the first step just asks the serious golfers in the universe that reads the publication to raise their hands. There's more on 2-step promotions in another chapter in this manual.)

5.) Free Bonus Gift

The other way you can use the Free Gift, is as an added bonus with a purchase.

This adds value to the purchase, and makes it easier for the prospect to make a buying decision. If you've ever seen the old Ginsu Knives commercial, you've seen the Free Bonus Gift proposition. As they added more knives to the deal, the value went up. By the end of the commercial, you were buying a whole kitchen full of knives for $29.95. You'd have to be a fool not to call!

And that's the idea. You want to motivate the buyer to act now. Sure, it's a bribe … and that's OK. If it's of value to them, but doesn't cost you all of your profits to throw it in, everybody's happy.

To make the Free Bonus Gift even more powerful, tell the prospect "Even if you return the product, the Free Bonus Gift is still yours to keep. Our way of saying 'thank you' for giving our product a try." (I'm assuming you've guaranteed the main product, and that it can be returned.)

This is a better-than-risk-free proposition, because there is not only zero risk, they're going to come out ahead even if they return the product.

> Variants to add to the Free Bonus Gift:
> Deadline: You must respond before …
> Limited Availability: The first 40 to respond …

6.) Deferred Billing

This is a lot like the Free Trial, except that they are more committed, and you're shipping a full-function version of the product.

This say's "We'll wait 30 days(or whatever) to bill your credit card. If you're not satisfied, call us and tell us you're returning the product. The charge will never show up on your credit card."

The purchase is assumed unless you hear otherwise. But, if the product doesn't do what you said it would, it's coming back. But this way, the buyer doesn't have to trust you to refund their money – you didn't have it to begin with.

And that's an important point: You(the seller) are taking all of the risk.

7.) Terms

How many times have you seen "12 easy payments of ..."?

They're offering payment terms that make the purchase easier on the budget. This is especially valuable for expensive items that will have a long useful life.

Automobiles are the classic example. How many people can plop down $40,000 cash for a car? Yet, how many $40,000 cars do you see on the road? You know most of those people could never afford their cars unless the manufacturer offered great terms.

As I write this, you can take five years to pay for many new cars ... with zero interest. Five years!

Of course, you pay more for the car if they're going to carry you for five years. But you don't care, because you're looking at the monthly outlay more than the total price. You can't afford $40,000 today, but you can afford $666 a month for five years.

8.) Cash Discount

The flip side of offering terms, is offering a discount or rebate for paying in cash.

If you are one of the people who can plop down $40,000 cash for your car, you may get a rebate of several thousand dollars that the "terms" buyers don't get. You buy the same car for $35,000 or less.

Both "Terms" and "Cash Discount" are cash flow propositions. If you can wait for your money, or charge enough more to be able to borrow money while you wait, offering terms can be a strong incentive to your prospects. If you need cash flow, and can settle for lower profit on the sale, offer a lower price to the buyers who can fill your cash drawer for you.

9.) Quantity Discount

OK, I don't hate ALL discounts. If you call me today, and tell me you want to buy 100 copies of this manual ... I might be willing to give them to you at a lower price than you paid for this copy.

I only have to ship once. I only have to invoice once. I only have to pack the things up once(in fact, my printer is going to do that, anyway!). My cost per copy actually goes down if you buy 100, so why shouldn't I reduce the price?

10.) Prepaid Discount

As much as I hate the word "discount," I must admit there are situations where they are warranted.

If you perform a service that your patient or client might use several times in the coming year, wouldn't it be nice to have them prepay 5, 10, 15 units in advance?

I get a massage once a month or so. I know it would help her cash flow if I gave her a check today for the next 5 massages. Would it be worth her while to offer me a 20% discount on all five?

That's another cash flow issue. She has to decide.

11.) Auto-Renewal Option

Do you provide a product or service that should be used on a regular basis?

Let's say you clean swimming pools. You know that should be done once a week. You can wait for your customers to call you once a week, or you can set up a weekly day and time that you automatically come back. Certainly, you would rather have 9:00 AM Wednesday booked for the whole Summer, than wait for someone to call.

Rather than just give a discount, you might want to offer every fourth week free. Or, make it every fifth or sixth week … whatever makes economic sense for you, yet still motivates the customer to commit.

> **IMPORTANT LESSON:** *Automatic renewal should be done with a credit card authorization only. You don't want to give a price break, and have to chase down checks every week.*

If you sell a product people use regularly, like say: vitamins. You can calculate how long a unit lasts, and set them up for automatic shipment of a replacement unit so they never run out. They never have to remember to order, either.

Ideally, you want to automatically charge their credit card each month. You have to get their permission in advance. But once you have it, you automatically ship, charge their card, and the money magically appears in your bank account. Is this a great country, or what?

More importantly for you, they would have to put forth some effort to cancel. I've told you people are lazy, and don't want to work hard to buy from you. They're just as lazy about cancelling an auto-fulfillment proposition.

If you can get your customers on an automatic re-order/appointment/fulfillment program, they're like an annuity you can budget around every month. The predictable cash flow at your end is well worth giving the customer one free for five, or whatever.

12.) Seasonal Sale

December sucks for me. Nobody holds meetings between the holidays. Retailers who might need my consulting services are up to their elbows in Holiday sales. Corporations are short-handed because everyone is using up left-over vacation before the year ends, so they don't want me around. Should I go on? Can you hear the violins in the background?

The other side of the equation is that December is an expensive month for me. Gifts to buy, year-end expenses, tax deposits, charitable giving … what's a fella' to do in a low cash-flow/high expense month?

Point is, if you hire me in December, I'll give you a deal like won't believe. ANY work in December is better than sitting home, listening to Christmas carols(my wife loves them).

Now, ask me to come see you in January, just a few days later, and it's full fee. Everything breaks loose in January. New year, new budget for corporations. They were broke in December, now they've got twelve months worth of budget at their fingertips.

Some months are busier than others. You are fully justified in offering lower prices … or bonuses … or any kind of deal you have to to bring in business in a normally slow month.

In the speaking business, there's a lot of talk about "fee integrity." The idea is, if you publish a fee, you should always charge that fee. But I've found that there are audiences that need me and can't afford my normal fee. If they're flexible, and I can schedule them at an other-wise slow time, I can bend a little.

Ultimately, I'm in business to help the people I can help. I would guess that you're in business for the same reason. Yeah, We've got to eat(and I like to eat well). Where's the integrity in being so inflexible that you flatly say "no" to the people who really need your help, but can't afford your normal price? If they can meet in December, they'll find me in a particularly charitable mood – and I can be very flexible with my fee.

You have slow months, maybe even slow days. Hey, the reason I tried Sport Clips the first time, was because the woman I had be going to decided to close her shop on Mondays. It was typically a slow day, so she decided the customers would have to be flexible and schedule another day. Monday is often my day to run errands. I often speak on weekends … because that's when a lot of people hold conventions … so Monday is my day to take care of personal business.

If Monday is a slow day, why not offer an incentive to get people to come in on Monday? Free champagne on Mondays? Free shampoo with a haircut? I don't know. But a seasonal proposition might fill the book on Monday, and take some of the pressure off of Friday in the process.

13.) Package Pricing

This is a great way to build up your average unit of sale.

By that, I mean, your typical sale might be one product at an average price of $50.

By putting together a package of three or four complimentary products … all products the buyer of any one of them would want …you may entice your customer to spend more than that $50.

Next time you're in a department store, take a look at the cosmetic counter. You can buy any one of a thousand different products. But there are always packages available. They offer a complete set of facial products – everything you need to be beautiful. The price for the whole package is much less than the total of the individual items' prices. In fact, it's not a whole lot more than you would pay for just one or two of the six items in the package.

But wait, there's more. Not only is the package a bargain price, you get a lovely carrying case to go with it – the Free Bonus Gift.

Now you're spending $68 in stead of the $46 for the two items you needed. The store just increased their average unit of sale.

Now, you have to know your markup. The package still has to be profitable to sell, of course.

And, it has to be an attractive enough price to be a small leap from buying just one or two items.

14.) Repeat Buyer/Club Discount

I'm really looking hypocritical on the "I hate discounts" statement, aren't I? I still hate discounts all by themselves. If there's a good reason … like motivating a first-time buyer to come back again … they work for me.

I recently booked a speaking engagement for a client that couldn't afford my normal fee. But, they were willing to commit to two annual conventions at the reduced fee. I came down about 20%, but got definite dates in 2003 and in 2004. I'm happy. They're happy. Who could ask for more?

On a smaller scale, I recently tried a new barber. My current hair style is pretty easy to cut, so I don't have to be real picky about my stylist. So, I tried a place called "Sport Clips." You may have one in your city. The cutters aren't award-winning stylists … but the price is a fraction of what you'd pay for an award-winning stylist.

But, here's the deal: After my first haircut, they handed me a card with four progressive coupons on it. The first was good for $5 off my next haircut. The second was good for $4 off, the third for $3 off, and the fourth for $2 off. I've used the $5 off, and I'll probably use the next one, too. But I won't go out of my way to save $3 or $2.

(If I were in their shoes, I would have reversed the offer. The first coupon would have been good for $2 off, the second for $3, and on up. Then, the more I come back, the better the deal gets.)

Your nagging question on this one must be: "Aren't I diluting my profits by offering a discount to the people who would have come back anyway?" The answer: "In some cases, yes."

But the additional business that would not have come in without the proposition more than makes up for the small loss on already loyal customers. You're adding to your list of loyal customers – making a little less on each one is worth the increase in overall profits.

And, you can always limit your offer. Make the coupons an one-time event with a time limit, just to get people acquainted.

> **IMPORTANT LESSON:** *The more limitations you put on your proposition, the less attractive it becomes.*

Don't put so many limitations on the offer that it becomes hard work for the prospect to take advantage of it. They're not going to work hard to give you their business. You have to make it easy and painless.

The haircut promotion got me to come back, and that's the idea. They had to buy a lot of advertising and signage to catch my attention in the first place. Now, it just costs them a few bucks to bring me back. I don't know if I'll get coupons again or not, but now I know my cutter, she knows how I like my hair cut … I'll probably keep going back even without the coupons.

This strategy is designed to increase the frequency of sales. You want people to come back, over and over again. It's a lot easier and less expensive to give people a deal for coming back than it is to go out and find brand new customers.

15.) Add-On

This proposition offers additional products along with the original, at a special add-on price. It will be good only with a purchase of the primary product, so it's "now or never."

You can also use this to sell more than one of the primary product. Sharper Image does this with their Ionic Breeze air cleaner. If you buy one a the regular price, you can buy a second one for half price. That makes the original purchase more attractive, plus adds the profit(slight as it may be) of the second unit. And, it increases their average unit of sale. Always a good thing!

16.) Up-sell

You've sold them on your product ... they're ready to order. Then you say: "For just $15 more, you can have our deluxe version." Normally, the deluxe unit is $35 more. Hmm. They have to ponder that, don't they.

It's another chance to increase your average unit of sale.

17.) Bounce-Back Offer

This won't be part of your advertising or initial contact promotion. It goes with your delivery of a product or service.

For example, if you ship your products, the bounce-back offer would go in the box. They receive your product, they're all excited(every time FedEx delivers a package, it feels like a holiday!). Your relationship with your customer will never be stronger than it is right now. You delivered the quality you promised, on time and in good condition. They love you!

And there's more – As they open the package, they find a special offer "for valued customers only. This is the only place you will see this offer, and you must act fast ..." It's a "bounce back" offer, designed to bounce them right back to your web site or fulfillment department while you're in the honeymoon stage of the relationship.

"Back End"

The last four propositions above are what direct response marketers call "back end" opportunities.

These are opportunities to increase the amount of business we get from anyone who is buying from us. Once you've made the investment in advertising and promotion to bring in new customers, you want to maximize your relationship with them when they respond.

These all offer the buyer an opportunity to buy additional products or refills that they would probably buy eventually anyway, at an attractive price. The attractive price will not be available later, so they have to make a decision now.

The reason you do this is either to increase your average unit of sale, or to increase the frequency with which people buy.

Average Unit Of Sale

Look at your financial statements from last year. Divide the total sales revenue for the year by the total number of transactions. That number is your average unit of sale(this stuff is simple, isn't it?). Let's say yours was $9.95 on 20,000 transactions. Now, divide your gross profits by the same number of transactions. That's your profit per transaction. Let's say it's $1.00.

What if you could up that average transaction to $14.95? Now, the profit on that $14.95 may only be slightly more than you were making on the $9.95, because you gave a great deal to pull in that extra $5.00. Let's say you only made an additional .25¢ on each sale.

But now, you have the same number of transactions: 20,000. That's the same number of calls, the same number of invoices, the same number of boxes to ship or paper bags to fill. But, in stead of a profit of $20,000, you've raised it to $25,000. Hmm. Cool, huh?

Granted, your sales people are going to have to push the back end proposition. You may have to incentivize them. Even if you have to spend a dime of that added profit on the sales people, you'll still clear $22,000 in stead of the old $20,000.

Increased Frequency

The other way back end sales can grow your business, is by getting people to come back more often.

Unless you sell only one product … that never needs to be replaced … you should be working on repeat business with every customer.

I fly a lot. I fly first class a lot. I don't charge my clients first class air fare, and I don't pay for it myself. You know how I get to fly first class: I use the same airline every time I travel, and they upgrade me for free as a reward for my loyalty. I can choose from dozens of airlines, but I come back to the same one over and over …

because they reward me for it.

The airlines' "frequent flyer" programs are a classic example of back end opportunities to increase frequency of sale.

It starts the first time you deal with them. When you make your very first reservation, they ask if you'd like to "earn valuable mileage credit you can exchange for free travel, upgrades and products." Of course you would! Then, you get on the plane, and they offer "a special welcome" to their frequent flyer program members, reminding you that you're earning "valuable mileage credit for today's flight."

You get a nice membership card, and booklet explaining the benefits of membership. There's a chart showing how easy it is to earn free travel.

Next time you fly, that airline and another you've never flown on both serve your destination city. Which one do you fly on? It's a no-brainer! You're now a frequent flyer with Air XYZ.

But you don't travel very often? Just wait ... you will receive offers in the mail, encouraging you to travel more.

You'll get the opportunity to earn bonus miles by switching your long distance service. Why? Because, as you earn more miles, you start to get closer to earning a free ticket. You're thinking, "if I take one or two more trips, I'll earn enough miles for a free ticket."

They're relentless.

But here's an important point: They are not doing you a disservice. They are offering you an opportunity.

Many businesses and professional practices are hesitant to offer back end opportunities, because they think they're being pushy, maybe even unethical. Nothing could be further from the truth.

You are doing your customer/client/patient a favor by making additional products and services ... or visits, whatever ... that they would probably use anyway, available to them at a value price or with some free benefit.

They can buy those additional items from you, or from one of your competitors. You want them to buy they from you, so you're willing to reward their loyalty.

They don't want to have to look around for another supplier. They may not even know you offer these extra products and services if you don't tell them about them. You would be doing them a disservice to keep your mouth shut, and deny them of these important extras, and the extra value that comes with them!

I highly recommend that you always have a back end opportunity in place. You may want to increase your average unit of sale, or you may want that first-time buyer to come back again and again. Either way, you and your sales or customer service people should be ready to present the back end opportunity before the customer/client/patient ever contacts you.

Price

Testing price is not like doing the Limbo. It's not: How low can you go?

Testing price is about balancing response and profitability.

You can send response through the roof by giving your product away. But is that a successful promotion? I don't think so. You want to arrive at the price that draws the ideal mix between response and profits.

Notice that I put proposition before price in the testing sequence. Once you've arrived at a proposition that your target customer responds to, you can start tinkering with price to improve your profitability.

Say you've got a control that sells 100 units at $19.95 every time you run it. So, the control is regularly bringing in $1,995 at a pop.

What if you changed your price to $29.95? Let's say response dropped off to 50.

Is that a bad thing? Now the ad is bringing in $1,497.50. If you're only looking at units and price, that's not good. But if your cost per unit is $5, you're bringing in a net of $1,495 with the control, and $1,247.50 with the test. But there's more to look at. Your customer service or sales staff is fielding half as many responses. Your variable expenses are cut in half.

What if you changed the price to $9.95, and response doubled?

Now you're bringing in $1,990. Your staff is working twice as hard. Your variable expenses are doubled, too. Hey, you're busy. You're popular. Is that a good thing?

Point is: you have to run the numbers on your own business. Testing is a scientific approach to advertising and promotion. More response is not necessarily your goal. "More profits" is much more attractive to me! Early in the life of an organization, just making the phones ring seems like a good thing. But after a while, you realize that getting calls from qualified, interested prospects is a lot more important. Then, you reach a point where making more(and more profitable) sales to those qualified, interested prospects is what matters most.

One sale does not a customer make ...

Here's another thing to consider when testing price. In many cases, the first sale to any customer is marginally profitable. You had to spend a lot of money and effort to get that individual to respond to you the first time. In fact, if you look at your whole advertising budget vs the number of new customers it brought in(your "cost of acquisition"), you may well find that you are losing money on each first sale.

Many businesses are totally comfortable with that. They know that first sale is just like a first date. The courting process is just getting into full gear.

Once you've made that first sale, it's imperative that you have a plan and mechanism in place to initiate the second sale, and the third. The cost of acquiring a customer is too high to settle for one sale. If you want to run a profitable business, you can't build it on first-time buyers.

Lifetime Value of a Customer

Smart organizations realize that, over the life of the relationship with any individual customer, that first sale becomes a drop in the bucket. If you are drawing the kind of customer that you can serve in many ways, you should be establishing long-term relationships that result in many future transactions after the first.

Once the customer has been acquired, you can now establish a one-to-one dialogue that consistently addresses their individual needs. If they had a pleasant experience with the first product/service and the way the transaction was handled, they will be predisposed to buy from you again with minimal persuasion. They know you, they trust you, and they have had a positive experience doing business with you. It's easy to buy from you ... meaning it's easy for you to sell to them IF you go after it.

This is called the "back end." It encompasses all the sales after the first one. These are much more profitable than the first one, and should come to you many times over the life of your relationship.

Don't make the mistake of getting greedy with price and propositions in general media or mailings. You're trying to get the right kind of person to respond so that you can concentrate on one-to-one relationships with them for the long term.

Media or List

Here's what I see at most of my first-time consulting visits;

They're advertising in the local newspaper. And in the penny-pincher. And on placemats at two local restaurants. And on the radio. And by direct mail. And on and on.

When I ask which one works best, I get a blank look. They have no idea, because they've never tested.

They hired me to tell them. Hey, a consultant should know these things, right? Well, every business or practice, product or service, and market ... is unique. Only scientific testing will tell you for sure.

Remember, test one item at a time

When you decide to put your media to the test, it's important that you don't test other variables at the same time. If you're fiddling with your proposition, your headline, and your media all at once, you can't tell which one made the difference.

So, the key is to isolate your response from each medium. Earlier in this chapter, I talked about tracking. You may have to use a combination of tactics if you have newspaper and radio going at the same time. When you've got the same promotion going in more than one medium, it's extremely important to track which one generates each response.

But don't just try everything that sounds like a good idea. Depending on what kind of business or practice you run, there are certain media that simply make sense.

I suggest you get your headline and proposition working in a low-cost medium. Once you know you have a winning combination, you can try the exact same thing in other media. If it doesn't draw good response, you know the problem is with the medium, not the message.

There's a chapter on media selection in the manual too. Yeah, just about everything is covered here!

Copy

Don't mess with your copy every time you put out a promotion.

You should write your copy the first time, then go through and fine-tune it with the words and phrases in the appendix.

Assuming your copy follows *The Magic Formula* sequence, changing a few more words here and there probably aren't going to make a huge difference.

Long Copy or Short?

One thing you should test is the results you can get by making your copy longer or shorter.

Of course, if you're advertising in print media, adding copy adds to the cost of your ad. By the same token, shortening your copy can either make for a cleaner ad, or for a smaller(less expensive) ad.

> **IMPORTANT LESSON:** *You must give your prospect all the information they need to make an intelligent decision on the action you're asking them to take.*

You've seen that "Important Lesson" before, I know. But it's so, so important.

But, you can give too much information. So, if you're using long copy, you might want to test a condensed version. You may be giving so much information that it's getting boring. Or, maybe you're getting too repetitive. Heaven forbid that you might be prattling.

If you're ever in doubt about whether your copy can be shorter, go back and see if you can say the same thing with fewer words.

Writing small space and classified ads is great brain exercise for a copy writer. The economy of words you have to practice there can help you write better sales letters, too.

If people are reading your long letter, and saying to themselves; "Get to the point!", they're not going to stick around long enough to get the whole message.

Write your letter or piece the first time. Then, go back and edit with the words and phrases in the Appendix. Then, try to say the same thing with 20% fewer words.

Just because you can write a sixteen page letter doesn't necessarily mean you should.

Test Constantly

Never settle for the results you're getting.

Test to make your piece better, or to find media that better reaches your target customer.

But don't get crazy. Test one thing at a time. And track your results carefully. Testing without tracking is just like throwing spaghetti at the wall to see if anything sticks.

Chapter 23

The Last Word

Did you notice a trend in the preceding chapters?

Hopefully, you've realized by now, that *The Magic Formula for Persuasion* is the key to effective marketing communications of all kinds. Selling is a sequential process, and *The Magic Formula* is the sequence.

Your ads and promo pieces are nothing more(or less) than sales people in print or on the air. They must start just like a live sales person would. They have to break through all of the distractions in the prospect's world, and grab their undivided attention. That's no small task!

In fact, it's been estimated that your headline is 80% responsible for the success or failure of any piece. The headline may be a photo, or it may be words. It may be the voice-over's first line, or it may be a video vignette.

Whatever your prospect sees or hears first must grab them, and make them want more. If it doesn't, they're gone. We live in an attention deficit world. If you can't break through and make the prospect want to know more within about 6 or 7 seconds, they're on to the next distraction.

You may have noticed that there are a couple of items listed on the cover that were not specifically addressed in the book. The same formula applies, regardless of the medium or piece.

Once you have their attention, you have to make a promise that stops them in their tracks. They have to be thinking "You can really do that for me?". Your product or service has to do something that makes their world better in some way. Maybe it protects them from potential harm. Maybe it makes them look or feel better(or both!). Maybe it will help them get ahead, or find their mate.

You have to promise some kind of benefit.

Then, you have to back your promise. People are skeptical, and need proof if you're going to keep them reading. So give statistics, quote testimonials or show photos of the product in action.

If you think they will doubt you in any way(Trust me, they will!), you should offer a guarantee. You have to take away all of the risk if you want them to give you a chance.

People are paralyzed by the fear of making a bad decision. If they buy your product or service, and it doesn't do what they thought it would, they'll feel like they've failed. They'll be embarrassed in front of their peers. They'll be afraid to face their spouse. With all of that fear in their hearts, it's much easier and safer to just not buy anything. And that's what many people do.

They don't buy anything until there is absolutely zero risk.

So, you have to be the one that takes all of the risk. Scary? It shouldn't be. If your product or service does all that you promise it will, you should have very few(if any) returns. In fact, it's a good test: If you get lots of returns, you are overpromising and/or underdelivering. Something has to change.

OK, you've grabbed their attention, promised an irresistible benefit, and they're comfortable that you really can deliver. Now what?

Too many advertisers drop the ball about now. They hope they've made their case, and that the prospect will somehow find their way to the store or the phone to buy some day. They have a hot prospect salivating for their benefit, and they're about to leave them unsatiated.

Now is the time to get them to make a commitment. They must be motivated to make a move, and it has to happen right now. If they don't do it now, your ad or piece gets put aside ... and soon forgotten. Don't let this happen to you!

Now is where you make a proposition. You offer an extra reward for fast action.

Don't assume this isn't necessary. They won't beat a path to your door on their own. You have to take control, and get them to act right now when their interest is piqued.

The proposition doesn't have to be a lower price. In fact, I don't like to use that one <u>ever</u> if I can avoid it. Try to offer concessions that don't cut into your profit at worst, and may add to your profit at best. Add value to the deal, but don't do it by giving away all of your profits.

The action you ask them to take has to be easy and fast. Give them a toll-free number, a toll-free fax number, a postage-paid business reply envelope, a secure web page. Give them every possible option. Some people don't like ordering online. Some don't have a fax machine. I wouldn't even assume every prospect has a phone.

If it's a hassle for them to respond, your odds of success go down. If they have to pay for the phone call, or go find a stamp ... anything that slows down the process loses people in the process.

Graphic design has to lead the eye.

Now that you've put together this terrific "sales presentation on paper," you have to design it to be attractive, and to make sure the prospect gets the whole story ... and in the proper sequence. If they're allowed to bounce around willy-nilly through your message, picking up bits and pieces out of the sacred sequence, they don't get it. They read the proposition before the benefit, or they skip from benefit to action, missing the proof step.

The designer has to be in sync with the copy writer, or this won't work.

If you're a do-it-yourselfer, you do the design and the writing. That's OK. Just don't get cute with the design and type.

Present the copy in a kind of type hierarchy; Big, bold headline. Bold, but smaller subhead. Then lead them into the first paragraph with a drop cap, or a few words in bold to lead the reader in. Maybe some bullets or a chart in your proof step. Key words, like **guaranteed**, can be in bold type for emphasis.

But stick to a couple of tried and true type faces. Don't get fancy, and in the process, make your piece difficult to read. Classics like Times Roman and Helvetica may seem boring. What they really are, is what people are used to reading. Your prospect is comfortable with them. They're easy to read. What more do you want from a type face?

Know your prospect ...

If you're going to write emotionally-charged copy, you have to know what gets your target prospect emotionally charged. You have to know what kind of photo would draw their eye. What kind of action will make them stay in the Barcalounger to watch your TV spot in stead of getting up to make a sandwich?

And, just as important: You have to know what they read, what programs they watch, and what radio stations they listen to.

All this design and copy stuff is a total waste of effort if the prospect never sees the piece. The best ad in the world, placed in a publication the target customer doesn't read, is not going to sell anything. Sound basic? Yeah! But, it's amazing how many misplaced ads I see.

Customer Service is nearly dead in America

I am sick and tired of handing my hard-earned money over to people who don't appreciate it.

And I hate doing business with people who are fast to collect my cash, but slow to deliver my product. I buy from infomercials. It's amazing how many expect me to wait 6 or 8 weeks for my product. I'll have forgotten I ordered it by then!

I bought a product called the de-weeder last year. The wait was several weeks. Why? They wanted to accumulate a bunch of orders before they produced the product. Then, they could build a batch and ship them all at once. This is a policy that totally favors the seller, at the expense of the buyer.

Anything that benefits you at the buyers' expense (literally or figuratively) is bad. It's bad business, and the buyer will know it. Some may still buy. I still bought a de-weeder(by the way, the product sucked). But I'm sure a lot of people, faced with a several-week wait for the product they're excited about enough to pick up the phone and order, simply said; "never mind." I wish I had!

The point is, once you've spent the money and effort to bring in a real live buyer, you must realize that he or she is the most important person in your business or practice. They are handing over the money that will ultimately make your house payment and put food on your table. They pay your country club dues and make it possible for you to eat in fine restaurants.

Everything about your product, your company, your employees, your procedures, your packaging, your shipping method ... EVERYTHING should be designed with the customer in mind.

The first edition of this book was printed in what they call a "comb" binding. A lot of books arrived in bad physical condition. It was too easy to tear pages as you turn them. Often, the cover would get torn, either in transit or when the customer first lifted the book out of the package.

That's unacceptable! The book you're reading now was more expensive to print than the first edition copies. I don't make as much profit on the new bindings. But you get a book that stands up to lots of use.

And I want this book to get lots of use. This isn't a read-once-then-place-in-the-bookshelf book. It's a reference you should use every time your design and write an ad or promo piece. It has to be functional.

And, I want everything about the book to be a pleasant experience for you. I'm confident the content will help you. But, I also want it to be easy to read. And, I want the book to last under repeated use.

> **Important Lesson:** *Everything should be designed with the single focus of making the customer's total experience with your organization a pleasant one.*

How is your phone answered? Is your customer greeted with: "Please press one if you're using a touch-tone phone"? Or, is there a human being who sincerely cares about the customer waiting anxiously for their call?

Next time you're on the golf course, have one of your buddies call the office. Listen in while they ask a question about your product, or the proposition you have advertised in the morning paper. Does the person who answers sound like they're glad the person called? Or, do they sound disgusted that they interrupted the heretofore peaceful afternoon? Do they know about the current proposition? Are they prepared to make the final close on the sale?

If not, you just burned a whole bunch of cash on advertising. If people are excited enough about your product to call, come in, visit your web site ... they should be greeted like benevolent kings and queens visiting their loving subjects.

Everyone in your organization has to understand that the money in their pocket, the car in their driveway, the clothes on their back ... everything they own came from these people who are interrupting their day! And the people who don't get it have got to go. You can't afford them.

Returns and Complaints

You will get returns, and you will get complaints. There is no perfect product. There are some very demanding consumers out there.

When someone wants to return a product they are not satisfied with, accept it graciously and refund their money immediately. If you're unhappy with this book, I don't want you to be stuck with it. It's not worth $47 to me to have an unhappy customer out there. You call me right now if you're dissatisfied, and I'll refund your money immediately. If you paid with a credit card, you'll have the credit the same day. If you paid by check, I'll mail the refund immediately. I know I can't please everyone. I know that not everyone can grasp what I'm saying here. Some people may have expected more illustrations, or more pages, or larger print ... maybe smaller print.

If I treat them badly when they're unhappy with one product, they'll remember me forever ... and they'll swear never to buy from me again. And, they'll tell their friends not to buy from me. I don't need that over forty-seven lousy bucks!

I want the refund to be so fast and so cheerful that they remember me and speak highly of me. They may want a copy of my next book, or a set of my audio tapes some day. A pleasant experience with a returned product is still pleasant experience. Remember, everything about your organization should be build around giving the customer a pleasant experience. And that's true whether it's particularly pleasant for YOU or not.

Look at the experiences you have with the organizations you buy things from.

When you walk into an office supply store and hand over your hard-earned cash in exchange for their products, does the person who takes the money have a clue what it means to them? Are you the center of their world? Or, arc they continuing the side conversation with a co-worker as they process your sale and push the credit card slip in front of you for a signature? Do they even say "Thank You" at any point?

No wonder people order office supplies online! It's more pleasant than dealing with the "humans" at the store. It's more pleasant to interact with a keyboard and a screen than with a live person. The only person I see from Office Depot anymore is the delivery driver. So far, he's been pretty pleasant.

The Back End

A one-time sale does not a profitable customer make ...

Think how much is costs you to get someone to buy from you for the very first time. You had to pay for advertising that reached thousands of people. Of those thousands, a relative few actually responded and bought something from you. If you calculate the *cost of acquisition* for each of your customers, you'll find that the one-time sale is rarely profitable on its own merit.

That means you have to be thinking of ways to get the people who do respond to buy more, or to buy more often. You've spent all of that money and effort to get them in the door, you want to have a plan in place to make them your friends for life.

Every time someone buys from you, you should be prepared to increase the size of the order.

You can do that by offering a second item at an extremely attractive price. Or, you could create a "package" including several products, attractively priced if bought as a bundle.

One of the most effective ways to build your business (and your profits) is to increase the average tranaction. Look at your books. How many sales did you make last year? What was the total revenue? Divide the revenue by number of sales, and you'll get an average transaction amount.

Now, what can you do this year to increase that average transaction amount?

If you ever order something from an infomercial, you will be offered an upsell. In fact, there is often little or no profit in the first sale they make. They bank on upselling a large percentage of the callers, and/or selling them something else down the line. They will also sell the address as a "responsive" to mailing list brokers.

The first response from a prospect is the beginning of a long romance. At least, it should be. Once you've spent all of that money to get them to respond in the first place, it would be a shame to drop the ball and not make the most of the relationship.

Is this manipulative? Is it a "bait-and-switch" to offer a product with the full intention of selling them something more? Not necessarily.

> **EXAMPLE:** *You bought this book. I assume you own a business or professional practice, or you are responsible for doing the marketing and promotion for one. My next book will be about effective direct mail. I think you need that book, too. I can't force you to buy it, but I can make it attractive, either by selling it with this book as a package, or by making a special offer to people who bought this book, but not the other in the first transaction. You get more information that will help you grow your business, and I sell another book. Is that bad? NO! It's good for both of us. That's how business should be!*

The second sale to a new customer is relatively easy, and definitely less expensive to consummate. You have their name and address. You know something about their individual likes and tastes(What did they buy the first time? What kind of copy did they respond to? What publication did the ad run in?).

Even more important: They know you now. You've delivered a quality product that they are happy with. How hard can it be to get them to buy from you again? Piece of cake ... IF you go after it while the honeymoon is still on.

Don't wait a year to contact them again with another offer. Within a week or two of receiving their first purchase, they should be contacted with another offer of a complimentary product – something that anyone who bought the first product would surely want.

Let the dance begin ...

Advertise where your likely prospects will see it. Speak directly to them and address their hot buttons. Make your sales presentation in the proper sequence, moving the reader inexorably from "preoccupied with other things" to "ready to buy." Be sure your graphic design starts their eye at the beginning of that sequence, and walks them step-by-step through the whole sales presentation. Motivate them to buy with irresistible propositions. Then, having gone through all of that, give them a pleasant experience when they do come to you, open wallet in hand.

How tough is that to understand? Now, go get 'em!

Appendices

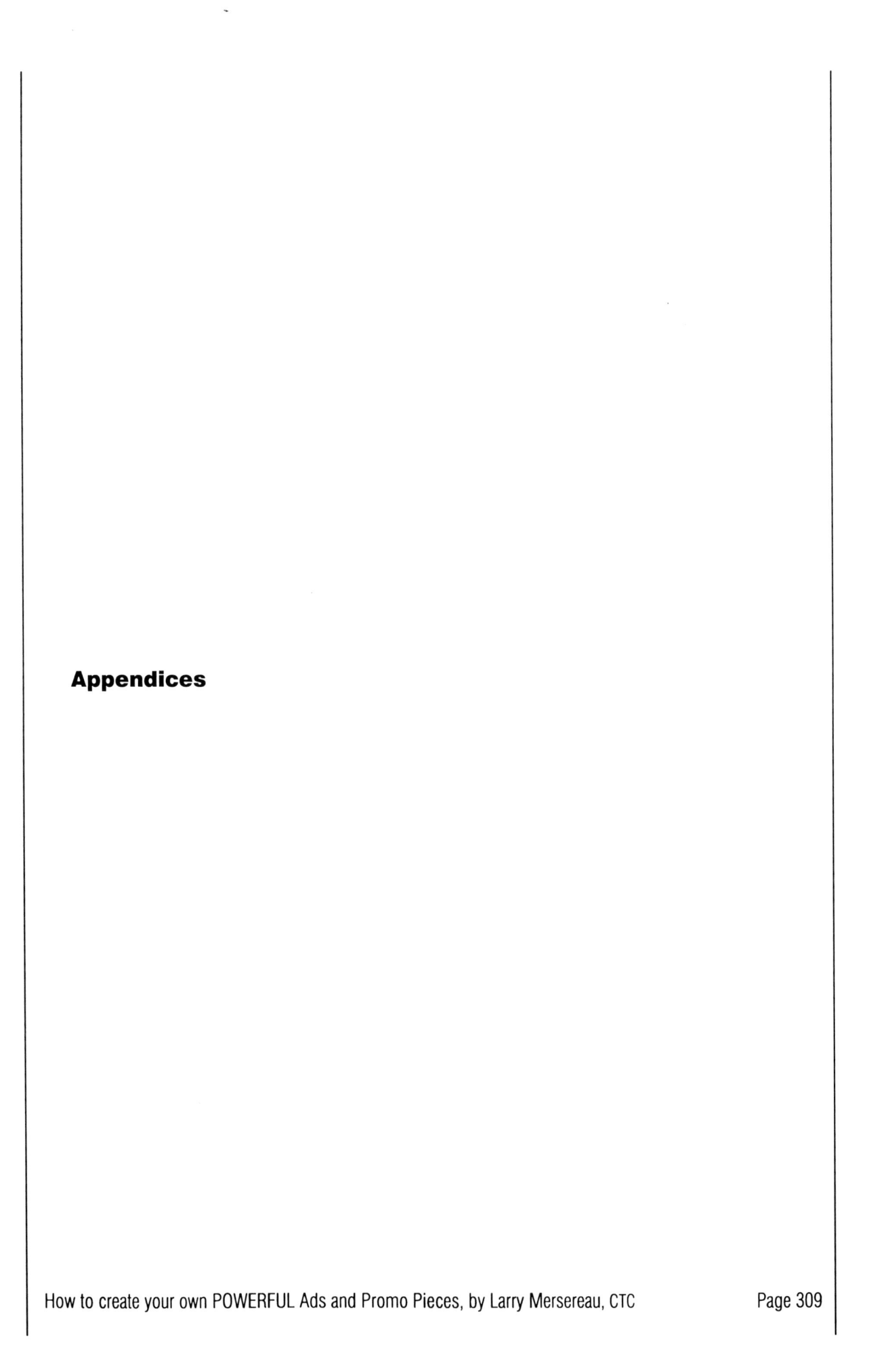

EMOTIONAL APPEALS

GREED/DESIRE	GUILT	FEAR
Safety	Pleasure/Comfort	Popularity
Love/Sex	Envy	Escape/Release
Profit/Wealth/Prosperity	Education	Discovery/Something New
Exclusivity/Being First	Pride/Ego	Pity/Sympathy

WORDS THAT SELL

You	Save	Sale
Money	Results	Discover
Hot	Opportunity	Value
FREE	Luxury	Guaranteed
Imagine	Announcing	Bold
Current	Discover	Profit(able)
Amazing	No-Brainer	Safe
Proven	Easy	Rewarding
High Tech	NEW	Breakthrough
Dynamite	Health	Incredible
Affordable	Unlock	Enlightening
Crucial	Timely	Only
Innovative	Lively	NOW
Stimulating	Shrewd	Love
Bonanza	Exciting	Real-world
Prosperity	Insight	Revolutionary

How to create your own POWERFUL Ads and Promo Pieces, by Larry Mersereau, CTC

"The Phrase That Pays"

You will enjoy/love _____, because _____

HOW TO ...

Your opportunity to ...

Last Minute

Right Now

How would you like ...

__#__ reasons why ...

Advice to ...

Return On Investment

Secrets of ...

Do You ...

An urgent message for ...

Good News!

Glad you asked about ...

Yes, you can ...

See for yourself why/how ...

How will you use this valuable ... ?

Here's what _____ had to say about ...

Can you make the phrase an alliteration?

(Seven Secrets of Sales Superstars)

The truth about ...

Don't miss (out on) this ...

At last!

Sure-Fire

No Obligation

You're invited ...

What would you do with ...

How much ...

Low-Risk

__#__ secrets of ...

Are you ...

Here are the key benefits of ...

Here it is, ...

Wouldn't it be nice if ...

Cutting Edge

The Marketing Master's Complete Library

Want to be a marketing and advertising expert? Read each of these <u>twice</u> within the next year, and you'll promote circles around 75% of the advertising agencies and 99% of the competitors in your market!

2239 Tested Secrets for Direct Marketing Success
    by Denny Hatch & Don Jackson
    NTC Business Books ©1998 ISBN #0-8442-3007-3

Direct Mail that SELLS
    by Larry Mersereau (www.MagicFormula.com)
    PromoPower Publications ©2003 ISBN #0-9742286-1-3

My Life In Advertising + Scientific Advertising
    by Claude C. Hopkins
    (A classic, read this book before any others!)
    NTC Business Books ©1986 ISBN #0-8442-3101-0

Ogilvy On Advertising
    by David Ogilvy
    (Another classic - read it early in your growth curve!)
    First Vantage Books ©1985 ISBN #0-394-72903-X

Pantone® Guide To Communicating With Color
    by Leatrice Eiseman
    Grafix Press, Ltd ©2000 ISBN #0-9666383-2-8

Secret Formulas Of The Wizard Of Ads
    by Roy H. Williams
    Bard Press ©1999   ISBN #1-885167-39-3

The Non-Designer's Design Book
    by Robin Williams
    Peachpit Press ©1994   ISBN #1-56609-159-4

Words That SELL
    by Richard Bayan
    Contemporary Books ©1884 ISBN #0-8092-4799-2

About the Author ...

Advertising's Ante-Agency: Larry Mersereau, CTC

You can trust the information you're picking up in this manual. It comes from a freelance writer, consultant and professional speaker who has helped thousands of business owners, professionals, sales and marketing executives worldwide build their sales ... and *PROFITS*.

You'll enjoy the benefit of his cross-pollenation of ideas gleaned from his work with a broad range of businesses and industries.

In his work as a professional speaker, he has addressed over 579 audiences in diverse industries, both as a keynoter and as a workshop presenter. His programs are highly interactive, meaning he learns as much from the audience has they learn from him. Many of the examples and ideas in this manual came strait from presentations of his now-famous workshop: **Marketing Makoever**.

He has worked with some 234 consulting and copy writing clients, and has created a catalog-full of Books, Tapes, and Special Reports on Marketing, Advertising and Personal Development.

Since 1972, he's been involved in a dozen businesses. He's worked for big companies, and for little ones. He's started a number of his own entrepreneurial ventures; some are success stories, some are ... *learning experiences*. He is dedicated to helping you sidestep the pitfalls of ineffective and inefficient marketing, and cut strait to workable strategies and tactics.

Educated at Drake University, he remains a student of marketing and psychology, and carries the mission of finding – and bringing you – the most effective marketing and business promotion techniques available.

If you are part of an association, dealer or distributor network, or professional organization that could benefit from one of Larry's business development presentations, please visit his web site for more information and topic descriptions.

Visit Larry's web site - www.MagicFormula.com

PromoPower
PRESENTATIONS • CONSULTING

Additional Resources

The $50,000 Business Makeover Marathon
Harness the power of 11 of the world's leading business experts
on Audiotape, as they teach you over $50,000 of ready-to-use secrets
and strategies <u>Guaranteed</u> to supercharge your sales and marketing

Includes Larry Mersereau's
How To Write Sales Letters That Sizzle and POP!

Direct Mail that SELLS by Larry Mersereau
Enough with the cold calls already!
Send out your salesperson in print.

Shoestring Marketing by Larry Mersereau
Marketing 101 for Small Business

Juggling Priorities by Larry Mersereau
Videotape learning program shows you how to achieve
Career Prosperity Balanced with Personal Fulfillment

You can order these and more
business and personal development resources at
www.MagicFormula.com